I0092227

ADVANCE PRAISE FOR

Critical Animal Studies and Activism

"Critical Animal Studies and Activism is a vital and timely book that is essential reading for scholars and activists wanting to fully understand the growing intersectional movement for human, animal, and Earth liberation. In these dark times, a radical understanding of Critical Animal Studies is needed more than ever."

—Dr. Will Boisseau, Member, Board of Directors, Institute for Critical Animal Studies

"Critical Animal Studies and Activism is an insightful and provocative book for anyone seriously interested in global radical change."

—Dr. Jason Del Gandio, Temple University

"Critical Animal Studies and Activism offers readers insight into what will be one of the defining issues of the 21st century: how will we challenge speciesism—globally, locally, individually and collectively? The editors and contributors educate, elucidate, and provoke, offering a road map through the critical questions and conflicts that have shaped the field. But most of all, they offer us the hope that praxis will make total liberation possible."

—Dr. Nancy A. Heitzeg, Professor of Sociology and Critical Studies of Race and Ethnicity, St Catherine University

"A powerful brilliant intersectional work that moves critical animal studies forward. This book is one of the most outstanding critical and radical books within the field of animal rights."

—Alisha Page, Board Member, Save the Kids

"Having followed the work of Anthony J. Nocella II and Richard J. White for many years, I am not surprised to see yet another excellent book challenging readers to dig still a little deeper in the search for truth. Among other contributions, Critical Animal Studies and Activism brings animal liberation together with other centers of activism, thus giving concepts like 'intersectionality' a fresh and important new place in our understanding of oppression and liberation."

—Dr. John C. Alessio, Professor Emeritus in Sociology, former University Dean, and author of Social Problems and Inequality

"Penned in the chaos of pandemic, this transformative book spans theory and activism, total liberation and bridge building, intersectionality and ecofeminism, anarchism and bearing witness, daring to offer hope through anti-capitalist solutions to the global domination and oppression of non-human animals."

—Elisa Stone, Master Vegan Lifestyle Coach and Educator, Main Street Vegan Academy and Professor of English, Salt Lake Community College

"A powerful book where eleven voices converge, from different points of the globe, proposing current and critical discussions on the practices of activism, the strategy of intersectionality, and total liberation action. A must-read, this book will leave a legacy of struggle for future generations. The struggle to achieve that animals finally stop being consumable and usable bodies just because they are vulnerable to human beings."

—Alexandra Navarro, Director, Latin American Institute for Critical Animal Studies

"This is an outstanding critical theory book that truly holds to the values and definition of total liberation and intersectionality. The editors grounded in anarchism created a brilliant text that moves social justice and animal rights forward in a more inclusive manner."

—Arash Daneshzadeh, Editor, Transformative Justice Journal

"Critical Animal Studies and Activism is a fierce call to action of humans to radically understand, act and liberate non-human animals and our Tierra Madre. To deeply ground our work of liberation and racial justice through intersectional empathy and ways of knowing. To extend our compassion and passion to non-human animals in a collective effort of a more just planet for all."

—Chelsie Joy Acosta, Coordinator, National Week of Action Against School Pushout, Save the Kids

"This impactful, applicable, and wide-ranging collection shows that veganism is not simply a white, privileged, consumption-driven movement but grounded in radical systemic critique. Veganism, activism and total liberation go hand-in-hand and contributors to this book highlight not only that the time and place for action is here and now, but how to go about activism effectively and inclusively."

—Nathan Poirier, Co-Director, Students for Critical Animal Studies

"Poignant, powerful, and most certainly praiseworthy of reading! Critical Animal Studies and Activism is a timely and purposeful read that will strengthen and encourage vegan activists to continue the disciplined lifestyle towards animal liberation, while simultaneously challenge those of us who are not. Critical Animal Studies and Activism is a call for everyone to finally stop being idle and join the fight for total liberation of all species, animals and homo sapiens!"

—Gina C. Alfred, Member, Executive Board of Justice, Equity, Diversity, and Inclusion, Salt Lake Community College

"Critical Animal Studies and Activism is an empowering journey through the history of animal rights and the solutions towards animal liberation."

—Marisol Adriana Burgueno, Co-Editor, Poetry Behind the Walls

"Delving into the latest CAS scholarship, this book is sure to enlighten those interested in adopting CAS principles into their daily practice. As a beacon of invaluable knowledge, the insights garnered from diverse radical communities are sure to promote inter-species liberation."

Dr. Amber E. George, Editor, Journal for Critical Animal Studies

"In times of extreme crises such as climate change, four years of the Trump Administrations, and COVID, Critical Animal Studies and Activism provides readers an insightful lens to analyze and organize these turbulent times. More importantly, it transcends traditional academic boundaries of safety and precaution to develop a praxis to improve the current human and nonhuman condition."

—Dr. Erik Juergensmeyer, Editor, Green Theory and Praxis Journal

Critical Animal Studies and Activism

RADICAL ANIMAL STUDIES
AND TOTAL LIBERATION

Anthony J. Nocella II
Series Editor

Vol. 9

Critical Animal Studies and Activism

International Perspectives on Total Liberation and Intersectionality

Edited by
Anthony J. Nocella II and Richard J. White

PETER LANG
Lausanne • Berlin • Bruxelles • Chennai • New York • Oxford

Library of Congress Cataloging-in-Publication Data

Names: Nocella, Anthony J., II, editor. | White, Richard J., editor.
Title: Critical animal studies and activism: international perspectives on total liberation and intersectionality / edited by Anthony J. Nocella II and Richard J. White.
Description: New York: Peter Lang, [2023] | Series: Radical animal studies and total liberation; vol. 11 | ISSN 2469-3065 (print) | ISSN 2469-3081 (online)
Includes bibliographical references and index.
Identifiers: LCCN 2022049441 (print) | LCCN 2022049442 (ebook) | ISBN 9781636670928 (hardcover) | ISBN 9781433199431 (paperback) | ISBN 9781433199417 (ebook) | ISBN 9781433199424 (epub)
Subjects: LCSH: Animal rights—Political aspects. | Animal welfare—Political aspects. | Veganism—Political aspects. | Critical theory.
Classification: LCC HV4708. C738 2023 (print) | LCC HV4708 (ebook) | DDC 179/.3—dc23/eng/20221024
LC record available at https://lccn.loc.gov/2022049441
LC ebook record available at https://lccn.loc.gov/2022049442
DOI 10.3726/b20288

Bibliographic information published by the **Deutsche Nationalbibliothek.**
The German National Library lists this publication in the German National Bibliography; detailed bibliographic data is available on the Internet at http://dnb.d-nb.de.

Cover design by Peter Lang Group AG

ISSN 2469-3065 (print) ISSN 2469-3081 (online)
ISBN 9781433199431 (paperback)
ISBN 9781636670928 (hardback)
ISBN 9781433199417 (ebook)
ISBN 9781433199424 (epub)
DOI 10.3726/ b20288

Published by Peter Lang Publishing Inc., New York, USA
info@peterlang.com - www.peterlang.com

This publication has been peer reviewed.

Table of Contents

Acknowledgements

Anthony and Richard would like to thank everyone who has assisted in the production and publishing of this book. We are especially grateful to Kim Socha for their contribution to the Introduction, and for making other key editorial interventions. Special mention must go to the authors for writing such tremendous chapters, and to Danni McGhee, S. Marek Muller, and Tony Quintana for their extremely thoughtful Foreword and Preface, respectively. We would like to thank all the contributors as well Nathan Grande, María Marta Andreatta, Anja Radaljac, Aljaž Krivec, Michael Allen, Erica Von Essen, Terry Hurtado, Michael Allen, Erica Von Essen, Alex Hinchcliffe, Carlos Garcia, and Kiana Avlon. We would like to thank Peter Lang Publishing particularly Dani Green, Jackie Pavlovic, and Naviya Palani. We are also indebted to the inspiration we draw more collectively from those involved with ICAS, Peace Studies Journal, Transformative Justice, Salt Lake Community College, Green Theory and Praxis Journal, Journal for Critical Animal Studies, Critical Animal Studies Academy, Critical Animal Studies Association, Critical Animal Studies Society, Wisdom Behind the Walls, Arissa Media Group, Eco-ability Collective, Arissa Media Group, Save the Kids, and Poetry Behind the Walls. Finally, we would like to thank our friends and family. We hope that this book helps bring forward a world deeply rooted in inter-species social and spatial justice: a world that we all so desperately desire.

Dedication

News of the tragic death of the long-term intersectional vegan activist Regan Russell (1955–2020) emerged as this book approached its final stages of editing. Regan was fatally hit by a slaughterhouse truck while she protested outside Fearmans Pork Inc. in Burlington, Ontario. We dedicate this book both to her memory and to all those who continue to fight for the greater freedom and liberation of all, wherever you may be.

Foreword

DANNI MCGHEE

Years ago, I met a man who was vegan, and he suggested I give it a try. I thought he was illogical, and I was seriously confused. I could not wrap my brain around the thought of never eating chicken, seafood, cheese, or eggs since they were a large part of my daily diet. I even recall seeing his food, which was a plate full of leafy greens, sprouts, tofu, quinoa, and other vegetables. I immediately said, "I could never go vegan if I have to eat like that!"

Four years later, I was nearly 200 pounds, suffering from irritable bowel syndrome (IBS), joint pain, low energy, terrible sleeping patterns, depression, anxiety, and brain fog. I started the year off by attending group fitness classes 6 days a week and incorporating "healthier" meals according to a standard American diet. After about 5 months of dedication to my workouts and eating plan, I had lost 25 pounds, but then suddenly, my weight loss plateaued. I was still working out 6 days a week and not cheating on my meal plan, but the scale was not budging. Then my friend tagged me on a post on social media where a woman was promoting a 21 day plant based vegan challenge. The challenge host was a beautiful Black woman who was extremely fit and toned. I don't want to reinforce body norms, glorify certain body types, or body shame, but for me, health and fitness are important, especially because I had IBS.

On July 14, 2014, I started the challenge ready to embrace all the amazing recipes that were given to the group. There was also an online community group to keep everyone motivated, share recipe ideas, and support each other as we embarked on a new way of eating. Within 3 days, I lost 4 pounds, and I could not believe it. How did this happen so quickly when I had been struggling for weeks? Then I learned more about digestion and realized some of the foods I thought were healthy were actually extremely harmful to my digestion. I had been suffering with digestive distress for seven years and had no idea that I needed to change my diet to improve the IBS symptoms I experienced daily. The doctors only provided me with a prescription instead of a solution to get to the root of my issue.

The following week of this challenge, the group host posted a list of a dozen documentaries about food nutrition, the planet, and the animals. I recognized one of them; I had been gifted *Forks Over Knives* back in 2012 by two complete strangers that I met while at work. I never watched it but always kept the DVD with me. As I watched *Forks Over Knives*, I was on an emotional rollercoaster between tears of sadness and moments of happiness. I was sad because for the first time, I realized that I had been feeding the conditions I was suffering with, but I was extremely happy because now I understood the connection between food, my health, the Earth, animals, and human rights. This was such an "Ah ha!" moment for me, and I wanted to know more. Over the next two days, I binged on every documentary that was out at the time. I believe in those 2 days, I watched 10 documentaries! I was so intrigued by this information, as I had never heard any of this before in my 31 years of life. As I dived deeper into understanding the full scope of veganism, my mind started to open up to this concept of compassion towards animals, sustainability for the planet, and eating for optimal health. Within those two days, I knew it was my duty to be vegan for the animals, the planet, and my future, and since then, I've never looked back.

At that moment, I thought back to when I told my friend "I could never go vegan!" as I now am fully committing to this lifestyle. As they say, never say never because one day your eyes may be opened to some new information that can change everything. Since transitioning, I have lost 65 pounds; I no longer suffer from IBS, joint pain, depression, anxiety, or low energy. Along with so many other positives, veganism has changed me for the better.

Like those documentaries I watched, this intersectional, grass-roots, total liberation book by scholar-activists is an eye opener for any who will read it. Veganism for me was initially just about my health, but quickly turned into much more—racial justice, environmental justice, social justice, animal justice, and economic justice. As a person who said they loved animals, I was not fully living up to that claim because of the choices I made on my plate, clothing, and lifestyle. This book takes you on a journey to understanding the depths of the importance of animal rights as the authors in the book share the views of individuals from different parts of the world who are making waves across the planet. I loved reading their inspiring words because they show how us as humans can come together for total liberation and be in solidarity with those who are oppressed at the hands of human supremacy.

There is a lot of work that still needs to be done for total liberation of all beings, and it is our responsibility to be a part of the positive changes we want to see. As stated by Dr. Martin Luther King Jr., "Injustice anywhere is a threat to justice everywhere", so let this book and the stories shared here inspire you to dig deeper into why you choose what you eat, what you wear, what you buy, and what activities you participate in. It's all matters.

Preface

S. Marek Muller

The year is 2022 and everyone is tired. Since 2020, the COVID-19 pandemic has ravaged human cultures and brought to the forefront the intimate interconnections of human and nonhuman animal lives. Meat production has waxed and waned as slaughterhouse workers simultaneously kill nonhuman animals and find themselves in increased danger of death by contagion—all while their corporate supervisors go about their lives without risk to their health or livelihoods. Meanwhile, U.S. American news outlets decry East Asian "wet markets" as inhumane and unsanitary vectors for disease, with politicians dubbing COVID-19 the "China Virus" as a means of deflecting Western culpability in both the global pandemic and the cruelty of industrialized animal agriculture. For ordinary citizens worldwide, strolls into pristine "nature" have become the focal point of group activities to substitute close quarters, reminding humans of the mammals, reptiles, birds, insects, and other species surrounding them at any given moment. Once inside their homes, "pandemic puppies" are all the rage as families, quarantined from public life, have sought friendship in the tiny paws, beaks, and tails of companion animals.

Critical animal studies (CAS) has never been *un*important. The fast and furious spread of COVID-19 has simply rendered the field *more visible* to a public traditionally disinterested in critical studies of more-than-human exploitation under capitalism. We can endlessly guess as to why. Perhaps the boredom of quarantine has led some to spend increased time spent online and find our radical vegan spaces. Perhaps the job losses, evictions, and other economic losses borne of the pandemic have led publics to the conclusion that unchecked capitalism is unsustainable. Perhaps the viral videos of and protests against police brutality pushed some to make the inevitable connection between racialization and animalization, between how discourses of whiteness (combined with the speciesist depiction of not-quite-human-enough humans as disposable) justify violence against BIPOC populations. Perhaps populist political slogans that deem immigrants "vermin" and transgender people "unnatural" have forced some to confront how binaries such as human/animal and nature/culture are not only problematic, but also insufficient for understanding the complex relationships between humans and across species.

The timeliness of Anthony Nocella's and Richard White's collection cannot be overstated. Now more than ever is the time for theory-to-activist approaches to scholarship as opposed to theory for theory's sake. CAS is one of the few academic fields that requires of its scholars a firm commitment to *telos* and to *praxis.* It eschews careerists, negates neoliberalism, and contests capitalism. Further, it is the only field that does so with a central focus upon *species* as an identity category. CAS takes seriously the existential and political importance of the (non) human subject in tandem with the intersectionality of race, ethnicity, gender, sexuality, class, disability, and species. In so doing, it offers scholars and activists the opportunity to become scholar-activists committed to a radical vegan ethic of "total liberation."

A common critique of radical vegan theory and praxis is its embeddedness in Western ontologies, epistemologies, and axiologies—in other words, its inextricability from normative whiteness. At worst, this criticism is merely a deflection put forth by scholars and/or laypersons determined to stay complicit in the global animal-industrial complex. Nonetheless, there are legitimate criticisms to be made of both vegan organizations and vegan academics for engaging in colonizing rhetoric and ignoring the systemic inequities in human society that impact our relationships to the more-than-human world. For this reason, this collection's international perspective on CAS is not only timely, it is essential. For CAS to keep its commitment to "radical decolonization" between and across species, scholars must grapple with the politics of citation and the elevation of certain voices/knowledges/cultural traditions over others.

This edited collection brings together a diverse series of voices. In keeping with the radical roots of CAS, the authors consist not only of professional academics but also on-the-ground activists. They are full professors, graduate students, artists, nutrition coaches, and more. They are experts in nutrition, anarchism, punk subcultures, literary critique, political history, vegan ethics, and more. Contributors offer a necessary global perspective on environmental and social justice issues, with authors writing from the United States to Slovenia to Colombia. Readers will find no shortage of situated knowledges in this compendium of criticism and will surely gain a multidisciplinary, cross-cultural perspective on the necessity of total liberation.

Introduction: Critical Animal Studies: Taking Action at a Time of Crisis

Richard J. White and Anthony J. Nocella II

Introduction

The opening years of the 21st century beared witness to the emergence of an unapologetically "critical" approach to animal studies: an approach which aimed to embrace and articulate "the essentially emancipatory character of the animal rights movement" (Nocella et al., 2014, xxiii). In the intervening time from then to now, Critical Animal Studies (CAS) has developed in depth, momentum and visibility in ways that are nothing short of remarkable. Beyond question, CAS has provided a unique catalyst for diverse radical communities from around the world to carry the fight for inter-species social justice. Many of these groups are united by their commitment to a praxis informed by those inter-disciplinary constellations of stars that burn brightly in the reflective light of total liberation (see Anonymous, 2019; Socha, 2012; Nocella et al., 2015; White & Springer, 2018).

Regrettably, despite all of these interventions, the need for CAS at this precise moment is greater than it has ever been. We use the word "regrettable" deliberately because one of the core visions that drives CAS scholar-activists is that of an evolved human society, one that neither oppresses animals (including humans), nor seeks to exploit and harm the planet upon which its existence depends. Yet in these dystopian times—where crisis begets crisis in ways that threaten to end the world as we know it—one might believe the changes are for progressive visions, not to mention the possibility of successfully enacting a "revolutionary politics of total liberation for the twenty-first century" (Best, 2014, xi), retreat further and further into "utopian" horizons. However, while there exists the possibility of a future, we are consoled and inspired by the ever-present possibility of change. It is this emboldened, positive and determined spirit that runs through the global perspectives of total liberation and intersectional activism advanced through the pages in this book (Nocella & George, 2019).

This Introduction is divided into three sections. The first addresses and reflects more fully on the question "What is CAS?" Responding to the ongoing COVID-19 pandemic, the discussion moves to address what it is—or what it might mean—to take action at a time of unprecedented crisis. In the second section, we will argue the necessity of rejecting "old" norms and enacting new insurgent approaches that contain the seeds of solidarity, and the promise of a future within which all life can be valued and given both freedom and support to flourish. Finally, the third section draws attention toward how the book is organized, offering a brief summary of the contributions that each chapter intends to make.

What Is Critical Animal Studies?[1]

CAS was co-founded out of the Center for Animal Liberation Affairs (CALA), which was founded in 2001. CALA was created to challenge the stigma of animal rights activists as being terrorists. In 2006, CALA changed its name to the Institute for Critical Animal Studies (ICAS). ICAS was founded and continues to be coordinated and directed by activist-scholars who are vegan, intersectional in their politics and in support of total liberation (Pellow, 2014); they actively work to end not only speciesism, but also racism, sexism, homophobia, transphobia, ableism, classism, stateism, Zionism, sizeism, and other forms of oppression (Brueck, 2017).

CAS scholars always need to be mindful of the importance of avoiding hijacking and appropriating terms from other movements for their own purposes. In the (critical) social sciences for example, such appropriation has been routinely done with the (mis-)use of "intersectionality". It is imperative, as a minimum, that recognition of the initial meaning of the term, and its emergence as a way of better articulating and addressing racism, sexism, and classism is fully recognized (Crenshaw, 1989). Embracing intersectionality

1 Parts of this section are taken directly from *Radical Animal Studies* (2021), co-edited by Anthony J. Nocella II and Kim Socha, with some adaptations.

in engaged praxis, CAS strives to be fully-supportive of other social justice movements like Standing Rock (Estes, 2019; Gilio-Whitaker, 2020; Estes & Dhillon, 2019) and Black Lives Matter (Khan-Cullors & Bandele, 2018). This takes many forms, not least by attending protests and conferences; publicizing such events on social media; donating resources and money, if able; and speaking about racial justice at animal rights forums (Kendi, 2019). CAS also has an ethical imperative to promote literature that comes from marginalized communities, such as *Brotha Vegan: Black Men Speak on Food, Identity, Health, and Society* by Omowale Adewale and A. Breeze Harper (2021), *Sistah Vegan: Black Female Vegans Speak on Food, Identity, Health, and Society* by A. Breeze Harper (2010), *Aphro-ism: Essays on Pop Culture, Feminism, and Black Veganism* by Aph Ko and Syl Ko (2017), and *Veganism of Color: Decentering Whiteness in Human and Nonhuman Liberation* by Julia Feliz Brueck (2019).

ICAS challenges the scholarly tendency to be safe, jargony, abstract, and detached; we're wary of opportunists, careerists, and welfare reformers. ICAS is a haven for those who want to be radical and take risks for animal liberation. ICAS is a fully-volunteer anarchist-based international collective for total liberation publishing books, journals, articles, and reports; it organizes campaigns, conferences, protests, and webinars (Nocella et al., 2015). ICAS challenges academics to be radical activists in more than their words (Canning & Reinsborough, 2017).

To understand what CAS stands for, also requires an awareness of how CAS emerged as a response to the field of Animal Studies (AS) or Human-Animal Studies (HAS). As Waldau (2013) explains, a primary goal of AS is to put nonhuman animals in the "foreground" of human intellectual endeavors, which is a novel and important goal. However, despite best efforts, humans always seem to become the center of attention, as scholars are prompted to "explore humans' possibilities with other animals in personally relevant ways" (p. x). Thus, an AS proponent may use the field to investigate human-animal relations or explore animality in humans. AS may be practiced by a neuroscientist studying primate conduct in captivity or an art historian documenting the changing depiction of wolves and human responses to them in the Western visual arts. AS was founded in the 1970s on the concept of studying nonhuman animals for human benefit. When applied to the sciences, AS can support vivisection and animal testing, which harm, torture, and kill nonhuman animals. In sum, it is not focused on animal liberation in any radical, socially relevant way.

HAS, popular in the social sciences, is even more human-focused as "an interdisciplinary field that explores the spaces that animals occupy in human social and cultural worlds and the interactions humans have with them. Central to this field is an exploration of the ways in which animal lives intersect with human societies" (DeMello, 2013, p. 4). An HAS student, therefore, can look forward to careers in zoos, veterinary medicine, and laboratory sciences. Unlike AS, there is *nothing* even potentially liberatory about HAS. In fact, as a field, it is part of the problem that CAS has sought to remedy: the view that nonhumans are a means to human ends.

In stark contrast, CAS adheres to 10 principles that all proponents of it were, and still are, expected to support and respect. At the very least, scholars and activists should build off this foundation and try not to contradict the principles. In 2007, Best, Nocella, Kahn, Carol Gigliotti, and Lisa Kemmerer, developed "The Ten Principles of Critical Animal Studies," which follow here:

1. Pursues interdisciplinary collaborative writing and research in a rich and comprehensive manner that includes perspectives typically ignored by animal studies such as political economy.
2. Rejects pseudo-objective academic analysis by explicitly clarifying its normative values and political commitments, such that there are no positivist illusions whatsoever that theory is disinterested or writing and research is nonpolitical. To support experiential understanding and subjectivity.
3. Eschews narrow academic viewpoints and the debilitating theory-for-theory's sake position in order to link theory to practice, analysis to politics, and the academy to the community.
4. Advances a holistic understanding of the commonality of oppressions, such that speciesism, sexism, racism, ableism, statism, classism, militarism and other hierarchical ideologies and institutions are viewed as parts of a larger, interlocking, global system of domination.
5. Rejects apolitical, conservative, and liberal positions in order to advance an anti-capitalist, and, more generally, a radical anti-hierarchical politics. This orientation seeks to dismantle all structures of exploitation, domination, oppression, torture, killing, and power [by humans to each other and other animals] in favor of decentralizing and democratizing society at all levels and on a global basis.
6. Rejects reformist, single-issue, nation-based, legislative, strictly animal interest politics in favor of alliance politics and solidarity with other struggles against oppression and hierarchy.

7. Champions a politics of total liberation which grasps the need for, and the inseparability of, human, nonhuman animal, and Earth liberation and freedom for all in one comprehensive, though diverse, struggle;
8. Deconstructs and reconstructs the socially constructed binary oppositions between human and nonhuman animals, a move basic to mainstream animal studies, but also looks to illuminate related dichotomies
   between culture and nature, civilization and wilderness and other dominator hierarchies to emphasize the historical limits placed upon humanity, nonhuman animals, cultural/political norms, and the liberation of nature as part of a transformative project that seeks to transcend these limits towards greater freedom, peace, and ecological harmony.
9. Openly supports and examines controversial radical politics and strategies used in all kinds of social justice movements, such as those that involve economic sabotage from boycotts to direct action toward the goal of peace.
10. Seeks to create openings for constructive critical dialogue on issues relevant to Critical Animal Studies across a wide-range of academic groups; citizens and grassroots activists; the staffs of policy and social service organizations; and people in private, public, and non-profit sectors. Through—and only through—new paradigms of ecopedagogy, bridge-building with other social movements, and a solidarity-based alliance politics, it is possible to build the new forms of consciousness, knowledge, and social institutions that are necessary to dissolve the hierarchical society that has enslaved this planet for the last 10,000 years. (pp. 4–5)

In the chapters that follow, aspects of all the principles are evident to some extent. We must always be cognizant of the fact that "Domination" and "oppression" are nouns as well as actions—"to dominate," "to oppress", and adjectives—"oppressive" and "dominative"—as in the mindsets of those who have power over others whether by happenstance/history, physical strength, access to resources, access to weapons, financial status, skin color, gender, species, etc. A critical goal of CAS is to expose these malleable mindsets posing as indelible facts, making single-issue politics an ethical impossibility and total liberation a primary objective. And as highlighted in Principle #10, we cannot do this alone.

Critical Animal Studies: Taking Action at a Time of Crisis

We write this Introduction amidst the traumatic landscapes brought about by the COVID-19 epidemic. Deemed a global emergency by the World Health Organization (Sohrabi et al., 2020) by 22 December 2021 over 274,823,095 cases of COVID-19 had been reported, a figure which includes the recorded deaths of 5,362,986 people (ECDPC, 2021). Interpreting this crisis through a CAS lens, the coronavirus stands as another irrefutable example of the pretentious arrogance, immense stupidity, and hollow emptiness of anthropocentrisim and the human-animal divide it perpetuates. It also exposes the myopia of single-issue politics, for the coronavirus crisis is also itself a product of far broader and deeper malevolent frameworks that continue to oppress, exploit and commodify humans, nonhuman animals and the Earth (Brueck, 2019). These malevolent frameworks—as will be visited in the book—operate in ways that both condition our capacity to *think* (e.g. speciesism, carnism, neoliberalism) as well as to act in a (capitalist, statist) society. Wadiwel (2015) persuasively argued that "our systems of violence toward animals [should be treated] as constituting a war" (p. 3). Our ongoing failure to successfully resist and end this war has the direst consequences for us all, for the interspecies violence "out there" inevitably returns to *homosapiens* in ways that bring havoc and enormous suffering within the boundaries that ostensibly demarcate "human" lives from posthuman worlds. The story of coronavirus, in so many ways, embodies the metaphor of "chickens coming home to roost": a devastating consequence that emerged directly from our relentless brutalization and subjugation of other species and the natural world (and we can't help but notice how often these deadly zoonotic diseases arise from our mistreatment of actual chickens, making the old metaphor all the more prescient).

COVID-19 is the related disease of SARS-CoV-2, also a zoonotic disease. It first emerged having "apparently succeeded in making its transition from [nonhuman] animals to humans on the Huanan seafood market in Wuhan, China" (Velavan & Meter, 2020, p. 278). Unsurprisingly, the coronavirus of 2020 is the latest example of a long list of interspecies diseases to have infected humans. Other Zoonotic diseases include anthrax, Arenavirus infection, avian influenza, babesiosis, botulism, brucellosis, Campylobacteriosis, cowpox, cryptosporidiosis, echonococcosis, Escherichi Coli (E.Coli), giariasis, leptospirosis, listeriosis, monkeypox, plague, Q fever, rabies, salmonellosis, Schmallenberg virus, Sindbis fever, swine influenza, toxoplasmosis, trichinellosis, tularaemia, Variant Creutzfeldt-Jakob disease (vCJD), yellow fever and yersiniosis. These examples potentially constitute merely the tip of a deadly iceberg. Indeed, as de Sadelee and Godfroid (2020, p. 210) conclude, "Domesticated animals and wild fauna thus constitute a reservoir for almost 80% of emerging human diseases" (de Sadelee & Godfroid, 2020, p. 210).

At this moment in time, it is impossible to predict with any degree of accuracy what the "post-COVID-19" future may look like or, indeed, if that future is at all possible. What *is* certain is that we will have to act in ways that fully grasp the enormity of living with these interspecies diseases. As Mattar and Gonzalez (2020) observe:

> Zoonotic diseases represent 78% of the diseases considered emerging and reemerging. Viruses participate in these zoonoses in a high proportion and new viruses frequently appear producing high morbidity and mortality; with the aggravating circumstance that there is no treatment. (p. 1)

This stance should not be mistaken for cultivating a fatalistic or resigned posture. Given the increasing depth of knowledge that we have about the conditions upon which these diseases emerge from and thrive, it stands to reason that we should be hopeful that *all* effects to minimize and eliminate these conditions will be made. Of course, one of the most significant enablers (as well as a dreadful illustration of the broken relationships between humans and other species) is the consumption of animal corpses and animal secretions: aka the "meat and dairy" industry (see ProVeg, 2020). Pulling no punches, and stated with absolute ringing clarity, Dutkiewicz et al. (2020) identify both the problem and a possible solution:

> The principal driver of zoonotic diseases (such as the virus Sars-Cov-2, which spread from animals to humans) is industrial animal agriculture. When food production encroaches on wild habitats, it creates opportunities for pathogens to jump to livestock [sic] and humans. Industrial agriculture also breeds its own diseases, like swine flu and avian flu, on hellish factory farms. And it contributes to antibiotic resistance and climate change, both of which exacerbate the problem. … We need to have an honest public discussion on how to produce our food. Individually, we must stop eating animal products. Collectively, we must transform the global food system and work toward ending animal agriculture and rewilding much of the world.

Such clear, rational, evidence-based analysis and practical responses designed to critically address a catastrophic problem have been echoed elsewhere. Significantly as Garcés (2020) notes:

> It is not a matter of feasibility, but of political and social will. Now is the time for policymakers to stop bailing out Big Meat and conducting business as usual; they must make the tough decisions necessary to create a safe food system. Corporations must shift their supply chains to improve animal welfare while

> growing the market share of plant-based products. Consumers should embrace alternatives to animal products that are just as delicious but far more sustainable. It is up to all of us. (p. 2)

Yet as long as these and similar voices of reason are talking to a neoliberal state and a capitalist market economy, they will be disregarded (see Cohen, 2020; Nibert, 2017; White 2017). Already, in a desire to return to destructive life-denying states-of-being that define "the old normal," governments and capitalists across the world have responded by *extending* their capacity for violence and cruelty toward nonhuman animals and increasing the contempt to which they show toward marginalized communities and peoples.

Any interruption or threat to the main operation of the agricultural industrial complex—and the death it brings to billions of farmed animals—has led to urgent avoidance action being taken by the state. Such a damning observation is not hyperbole: if you are in any doubt, consider the following illustrations:

- Millions of US farmed animals (including at least 20 million hens and pigs), have been killed by means of suffocation, drowning, shooting, gassing, anesthetic overdose and blunt force trauma (i.e. "slamming piglets against the ground" (Kevany, 2020, n.p.). In the US city of Chicago, farm workers injected pregnant sows so that they would abort their babies (Polansek & Huffstutter, 2020).
- In Iowa, Direct Action Everywhere, in collaboration with Iowa Select Farms employee whistleblowers, "exposed pigs shrieking in agony as they're blasted with steam and heat exceeding 140 degrees in a barn with the ventilation ports closed. It's a process animal agriculture industry insiders call 'Ventilation Shutdown' or VSD…" (Direct Action Everywhere, 2020).
- The Dutch and Spanish government ordered the destruction of a million mink lives on fur farms over the possibility of coronavirus risk to humans (see Kevany, 2000; Reuters, 2000).

CAS scholars, by embracing an intersectional approach to activism and focusing on a politics of total liberation, have long recognized and sought to make visible the physical and psychological harms that *humans* also endure in the slaughterhouses and other spaces of violence (see Nocella et al., 2014; White & Springer, 2018). The causal link between these industrial places of animal abuse and rates of COVID-19 infections in humans has become clear, with major outbreaks occurring in the UK, Spain, Germany, France, Brazil, Canada and the US (see Reuben, 2020). Such was the extent of infection rates among employees, that Middleton et al. (2020) concluded, "These businesses failed in their duty to workers and the wider public health" (p. 1). Dyal et al. (2020) note that: "COVID-19 cases among U.S. workers in 115 meat and poultry processing facilities were reported by 19 states. Among approximately 130,000 workers at these facilities, 4,913 cases and 20 deaths occurred" (p. 557).

Therefore, despite being fully aware of the significant human incidences of COVID-19 cases recorded in meat and poultry processing facilities, the dominant government response has been to keep these places fully operational. To effectively force these workers back to work is a shocking indictment on how the political and economic neoliberal elite sees human lives as expendable. Of course, the narrative was to frame these practices as "essential," and those who operate within them as "key workers," a status usually afforded to frontline healthcare and education workers (Corkey et al., 2020, n.p.). In the U.S., Swanson and Yaffe-Bellany (2020) reported that

> President Trump on Tuesday [April 28th 2020], declared meat processing plants "critical infrastructure," in an effort to ensure that facilities around the country remained open as the government tried to prevent looming shortages of pork, chicken and other products as a result of the coronavirus. ... The action comes as meat plants around the country have turned into coronavirus hot spots, sickening thousands of workers, and after the head of Tyson Foods, one of the country's largest processors, warned that millions of pounds of meat would simply disappear from the supply chain. (n.p.)

The pressure upon highly marginalized and exploited workers to return to work, and the overt threats of the consequences if they did not comply, were also explicit. Reflecting on Trump's declaration, Eric Scholosser (2020) drew attention to several deep truths relating to the political economy generally and the specific implications at work:

> By issuing that order, Trump helped an industry that has long been a strong supporter of the Republican Party. He reduced the likelihood that meat prices would greatly increase in the months leading up to the 2020 presidential election. And he confirmed what critics of the large meatpackers have said for years: Some of these companies care more about profits than the lives of their workers, the well-being of the communities where they operate, and the health of the American people. Adding insult to injury, Kim Reynolds, the governor of Iowa—where major outbreaks of COVID-19 have been linked to meatpacking plants—announced that slaughterhouse employees who refuse to show up for work will be ineligible for unemployment benefits. While running for governor, Reynolds accepted hundreds of thousands of dollars in campaign funding from donors close to the meat industry. (n.p.)

This top-down stance, underpinned by a desire to keep old norms entrenched, is a familiar one repeated the world over.

CAS scholar-activists are deeply conscious of the need to recognize the animal plight outside of the meat and dairy industry and draw attention to how other animals' lives have been subjected to further abuse, misery and extreme acts of violence as a direct consequence of Covid-19. For example, as well as being morally abhorrent, CAS scholars have long critiqued the unreliability and failure of animal models in the sciences. It is not surprising to see business booming for the "scientific" animal research industry as they benefit from the additional multi-million-pound investment in the race to successfully create a vaccine against SARS-CoV-2. In England, animal experiments are currently taking place that involve mice, ferrets, pigs, monkeys and other nonhuman primates. Writing for *The Ecologist* on animal testing and COVID-19, Hogervorst (2020) emphasized this truth:

> Having lived through Covid-19, I can tell you that it's no joke. We need a vaccine, treatments, and cures—and we need them fast. As a scientist, I know that's exactly why we must stop relying on cruel, inaccurate animal tests. Experimenting on animals is unethical, and it's wasting precious time, money, and lives. (n.p.)

Other examples of abuse resulting from the pandemic include animals incarcerated in zoos being allowed to starve to death or facing the prospect of being fed to each other (Hartley-Parkinson, 2020, n.p.); companion animals, particularly in China, being abandoned and/ or beaten to death (see Campbell, 2020; Wharton, 2020); "wild" animals such as bats being persecuted; and the rise of poaching of endangered species "as tourists stay away and many park rangers are left out of work" (Moulds, 2020, n.p.). Individually and collectively, these examples, while tragic and traumatic in equal measure, are utterly predicable. For, as Arcari (2011) sums up:

> When things go to shit, animals are on their own, which is what makes their entrapment in capitalist political economies so doubly heartless. That this animal-industrial complex is so directly implicated in the COVID-19 pandemic and the climate crisis, with myriad animals being substantial victims of both, only emphasizes the cycles of violence that result from capitalist commodification. (n.p.)

Critical Animal Studies: Fighting for a New Normal in the Shell of the Old

The COVID-19 crisis, and the shattering of the old normal that has followed its wake, provides a real opportunity for change and must be grasped with both hands (see Cudworth et al., 2021). CAS has the potential to make a vital contribution to the battle for hearts and minds in ways that cannot let those whose vested interests in exploitation, oppression, domination and subjugation, part of the old normality, continue to shape and influence future pathways. The old ways will inevitably lead directly to what the eco-communitarian anarchist writer John Clark (2019) refers to as "the *Necrocene*, the "new era of death" (p. 11). The paths that a CAS praxis imagines, envisages and enacts are those that have a deep reverence for all life, one rich in interspecies justice and solidarity.

What is certainly essential, if we are to embrace these bold futures successfully and collaboratively, is that we open up new popular imaginaries in what is possible and practical. This is why, for example, dedicating time and energy to raise greater public consciousness around the meat and dairy industry is vital: the spotlight of attention that COVID-19 crisis has shone on these abusive industries must become brighter and more powerful. Hopefully, this new awareness will give enough cause for consumers "to reflect on how they get their meat, what they are prepared to pay for it, and what conditions they expect the animals and the workers to endure so they can have it" (Middleton et al., 2020, p. 1).

The other side of this coin, of course, is to continue to educate and agitate for a revitalized vegan praxis to come to the fore. How can people be empowered to embrace veganism through choice, not necessity? How can we influence the narrative of veganism as a radical praxis, not a "consumer-based" lifestyle, as capitalist appropriation of the term "vegan" has sought to do? Indeed, how can we extend the radical spirit of veganism in ways that critically recognizes and takes seriously the cost of "vegan" food production across human communities and more-than-human communities, not least insects, and the vitality of the soil itself (Gunderman & White, 2020; West, 2020; Colling, 2020).

In addition to asking the right questions, it is imperative that new solutions that can address and inform our collective responses are sought. For example, CAS scholars, particularly those inspired by a radical feminist and/or anarchist praxis, propose that these solutions lay beyond the state and the capitalist markets (see Nocella et al., 2015; White, 2015). Here there is an urgent need for post-capitalist and post-statist approaches which recognize the value of prefigurative praxis, intersectionality and a truly global politics of total liberation.

Organization of the Book

While firmly rooted in the here and the now, the pages of this book contains both the seeds of a desired future and the ideas and praxis that—we hope—can be taken forward by others. The possibility of new futures founded on new empowered and emancipatory norms will not just happen: they must be fought for and created by each and every one of us. We would be mindful here of the words of Frederick Douglass (1857):

> If there is no struggle, there is no progress. Those who profess to favor freedom, and yet depreciate agitation, are men who want crops without plowing up the ground. They want rain without thunder and lightning. They want the ocean without the awful roar of its many waters. … This struggle may be a moral one; or it may be a physical one; or it may be both moral and physical; but it must be a struggle. Power concedes nothing without a demand. It never did and it never will. (p. 22)

Change and progress take hard work, and when the change-makers do not have access to the very things that allow others to determine how the world works—money, power, easy access to the masses (all things that, indeed, the change makers may be critical of)—change is even harder. But as Douglass and other freedom fighters have taught us, change is possible, though there is rarely a clean, direct line towards progress. For instance, 163 years after Douglass penned the above observation, African Americans are still demanding the most basic of rights and privileges ostensibly granted to them in 1865.

Our book opens with "Exploring the Motivations and Coping Strategies of those who bear Witness to The Animal Condition: A focus on Sheffield Save Movement Activists, UK". Co-authored by two critical animal geographers, Alex Hinchcliffe and Richard J. White, their chapter begins by drawing attention to forms of direct action inspired by the Save Movement, paying attention to the activists, other participants, and the often-overlooked but always complex, precarious, and highly contested spaces of activism that are present therein. The main body of this chapter presents qualitative-based research findings that explore the activists' motivations, experiences and coping strategies when confronted with the violence and suffering they witness. Broader questions are also included. For example, how do these activists intersect with other social justice movements? How effective do they feel their activism is? These findings collectively unearth new and important insights that should be of interest and relevance for others who fight for total liberation on the front line.

Chapter 2, "Performing Veganism: Building Bridges amongst Academia, Activism and Community" is written by María Marta Andreatta. Exploring the significance of performance ethnography for the field of CAS, Andreatta shows how it acts as an important strategy of inquiry that enables and encourages the co-participation of researchers, communities, and activists. Crucially, this union has the potential to bond theory and praxis in important and complex ways. For example, in addition to promoting collaborative research and writing, Andreatta shows how performance ethnography entails a political commitment and encourages interdisciplinarity while avoiding elitist language. Applying such an approach carries with it the great potential of reaching new and wider audiences to stand against abuse and exploitation and contribute meaningfully to the quest for social justice.

"Becoming Vegan in Slovenia: Some Reflections on Theory and Activism" by Anja Radaljac and Aljaž Krivec is the third chapter, which begins by drawing attention to their experiences of trying to better understand and articulate their emerging vegan praxis, particularly on a theoretical level (e.g., speciesism and carnism). In Slovenia, this proved a frustrating process, and through describing how they responded to these setbacks, Radaljac and Krivec offer guidance to others who are making similar journeys. The makes a series of persuasive arguments concerning the relationships between theory and activism. What can be done to influence the public around issues of animal abuse that they are unwilling to recognize? This question opens an engaging discussion about how animal rights can be made more visible in Slovenia. Reflections are made on public dialogues in media and political communities around animal rights, speciesist backlashes, and the importance of embracing an intersectional justice approach. The chapter ends with a considered reflection on the challenges that vegan communities and activists should prioritize if they are to progress and fulfill the radical promise and potential of animal liberation.

The fourth chapter is Nathan Grande's "Strategic Empathy, Intra-Sectional Demonstrations, and Animal Activism: In Pursuit of Total Liberation." Grande makes a persuasive argument for harnessing strategic empathy as a practical approach in multiple scenarios, whether by activists "on the street' or in academic settings by scholar-activists, teachers, and creative practitioners. In addition to focusing on current (mis)uses of empathy, the chapter explores the dark side of empathy, or tactical empathy. In distinction, the strategic empathy proposed in this chapter is theorized as an extension of Lori Gruen's "engaged empathy." Photographic and video technologies are identified as fundamental tools for implementing strategic empathy and pursuing a politics of total liberation. The chapter lays out guidelines that will be of interest for activists who engage in vegan outreach and anti-speciesist advocacy as well as creative teacher-practitioners.

Kiana Avlon is the author of Chapter 5, "Challenging the Ideologies behind the Animal Agricultural Industry: A Case for Critical Animal Studies and Ecofeminism." The chapter demonstrates how ineffective it is to contend with expressions of animal abuse and exploitation (e.g. animal agricultural industry) without paying attention to recognising and dismantling the powerful ideologies that legitimize and normalise these industries. Particular attention is given to speciesism and the cluster of belief systems (e.g., anthropocentrism, androcentrism, and rationalism) that surround it. As an illustration of the powerful way in which ideology informs action in everyday life, Avlon offers an extended discussion and reflection of speciesism and neoliberal capitalism. As with the best of CAS approach, it is never sufficient merely to describe when positive solutions might be presented to address the problems identified. In this context, the chapter concludes with a persuasive set of arguments made for CAS and ecofeminist approaches to be drawn on to inform a liberatory framework.

Chapter 6, "'Before We Talk about Freedom: Let Us Free Our Slaves': An Activist's Reflections on Anarchism, Nonhuman Animals and Total Liberation" is written by Carlos Garcia. The chapter brings a range of persuasive arguments to encourage anarchists to embrace veganism as a core element of their activism and the fight for total liberation. In doing so, the chapter draws attention the significant limits of any anarchist praxis—and other leftist movements—which fails to take seriously the plight of other animals. Indeed, Garcia goes further and draws an uncomfortable spotlight on the range of hollow and miserable excuses that such anarchists use to justify such exclusion. The chapter ends by reflecting on an interesting and important critique of capitalism and class when thinking about Total Liberation and inter-species violence.

The penultimate chapter, Chapter 7, is Terry Hurtado's "Animal Victims in the Colombian War". Here, Hurtado offers a chilling and unique overview of the toll that over 50 years of war has had on humans, nonhumans, and the natural world in Colombia. He catalogues the ways human and nonhuman lives have been used strategically and violently in a long quest for what each willing participant sees as the right and proper outcome of the conflict. Hurtado boldly attempts to account for the myriad ways animals have been victimized by the all-too-human endeavor of slaughtering each other in the name of ideology. He not only asks the question, "What if we began to literally count animals as victims of war in our international humanitarian laws?"; he also begins to answer it by augmenting the standards and policies of those laws to include nonhuman victims as both strategies within and casualties of human-made conflicts.

The final chapter of the book is "On the *Dharma* of Critical Animal Studies: Animal Spirituality and Total Liberation" by Erica Von Essen and Michael Allen. The authors pose a series of searching questions, including ones that invite closer attention toward important relationships between CAS and spiritual growth. Their reflections take us on a fascinating journey that encompasses religious traditions, myths, and fables to neuroscience and cognitive ethology. Exploring the deeper implications present within a politics of total liberation, a searching dialogue around whether such a politics must necessarily be exclusively human is presented. If other animals can also contribute to the total liberation of all species, what radical implications follow from this?

Taken as a whole the book offers new ideas and expressions of hope, some more practical some more and theoretical, about how the world can change for the better. As editors, we are especially excited to offer the words and works of a uniquely international gathering of CAS scholar-activists from Argentina, Slovenia, Colombia, Basque Country, and Sweden, as well as the U.K. and U.S. Please read the works of these scholar-activists with a curious and critical mind. Take what works, question what doesn't, and use this to help inspire further ever radical and alternative conceptions beyond what's on offer here, and that could make all the difference in the world.

References

Adewale, O., & Harper, A. B. (2021). *Brotha vegan: Black men speak on food, identity, health, and society.* New York, NY: Lantern Books.

Albert, M., & Chomsky, N. (2014). *Realizing hope: Life beyond capitalism.* London, UK: Zed Books.

Anonymous (2019). *Total liberation.* London: Active Distribution

Arcari, P. (2020). COVID-19 shows why we need to 'cease and desist' from commodifying animals. *Medium, Age of Awareness.* Retrieved from https://medium.com/age-of-awareness/covid-19-shows-why-we-need-to-cease-and-desist-from-commodifying-animals-c042e6eb5be5

Best, S. (2014). *The politics of total liberation: Revolution for the 21st century.* London: Palgrave Brueck, J. F. (2017). *Veganism in an oppressive world: A vegans-of-color community project.* London: Sanctuary Publishers.

Brueck, J. F. (2019). *Veganism of color: Decentering whiteness in human and nonhuman Liberation.* London: Sanctuary Publishers.

Campbell, C. (2020). 'They are overwhelmed.' China's animal shelters can't cope with the number of pets abandoned due to COVID-19. *Time.* Retrieved from https://time.com/5793363/china-coronavirus-covid19-abandoned-pets-wuhan/

Canning, D., & Reinsborough, P. (2017). *Re:imagining change: How to use story-based strategy to win campaigns, build movements, and change the world.* Oakland, CA: PM Press.

Clark, J. P. (2019). *Between Earth and Empire: From the necrocene to the beloved community.* Oakland: PM Press.

Cohen, N. (2020). Surely the link between abusing animals and the world's health is now clear. *The Guardian* 11 April 2020. Retrieved from https://www.theguardian.com/commentisfree/2020/apr/11/surely-the-link-between-abusing-animals-and-the-worlds-health-is-now-clear.

Colling, S. (2020). *Animal resistance in the global capitalist era.* Ann Arbor, MI: University of Michigan Press.

Corkery, M., Yaffe-Bellany, D., & Swanson, A. (2020). Powerful meat industry holds more sway after Trump's order. *The New York Times.* April 29th. Retrieved from https://www.nytimes.com/2020/04/29/business/coronavirus-trump-meat-plants.html?action=click&module=RelatedLinks&pgtype=Article

Crenshaw, K. (1989). Demarginalizing the intersection of race and sex: A Black feminist critique of antidiscrimination doctrine. *University of Chicago Legal Forum,* 1989: 139–168.

Cudworth, E., Boisseau, W., & White, R. J. (2021), "Guest editorial", *International Journal of Sociology and Social Policy, 41*(3/4), 265–281. https://doi.org/10.1108/IJSSP-04-2021-514.

de Sadeleer, N., & Godfroid, J. (2020). The Story behind COVID-19: Animal diseases at the crossroads of wildlife, livestock and human health. *European Journal of Risk Regulation, 11*(2), 210–227.

Direct Action Everywhere (2020). Breaking: Gruesome Footage Shows Pigs Roasted Alive At Iowa's Leading Pork Supplier Amid Coronavirus Crisis. June 29th 2020. Retrieved from [https://www.directactioneverywhere.com/theliberationist/2020-5-28-breaking-gruesome-footage-shows-pigs-roasted-alive-at-iowas-leading-pork-supplier-amid-coronavirus-crisis

Douglass, F. (1857). *Two Speeches by Frederick Douglass; one of West India Emancipation, delivered at Canandaigua, Aug, 4th and the other one the Dred Scott Decision, delivered in New York, on the occasion of the anniversary of the American Abolition Society, May, 1857.* Rochester: C.P. Dewey Printer.

Dutkiewicz, J., Taylor, A., & Vettese, T. (2020). The Covid-19 pandemic shows we must transform the global food system. *The Guardian.* Retrieved from https://www.theguardian.com/commentisfree/2020/apr/16/coronavirus-covid-19-pandemic-food-animals

Dyal, J. W., et al. (2020). COVID-19 among workers in meat and poultry processing facilities — 19 states, April 2020. *Morbidity and Mortality Weekly Report, 69*(18), 557–561. Retrieved from https://www.cdc.gov/mmwr/volumes/69/wr/mm6918e3.htm

Estes, N. (2019). *Our history is the future: Standing rock versus the dakota access pipeline, and the long tradition of indigenous resistance.* Brooklyn, NY: Verso.

Estes, N., & Dhillon, J. (2019). *Standing with standing rock: Voices from the #NoDAPL movement.* Minneapolis, MN: University of Minnesota Press.

European Centre for Disease Prevention and Control (2022). *COVID-19 situation update worldwide, as of week 49, updated 22 December 2021.* Retrieved from https://www.ecdc.europa.eu/en/geographical-distribution-2019-ncov-cases.

Garcés, L. (2020). COVID-19 exposes animal agriculture's vulnerability. *Agriculture and Human Values,* 1-2. Retrieved from https://doi.org/10.1007/s10460-020-10099-5

Gilio-Whitaker, D. (2020). *As long as grass grows: The indigenous fight for environmental justice, from colonization to Standing Rock.* Boston, MA: Beacon Press.

Gunderman, H., & White, R. J. (2020). Critical posthumanism for all: A call to reject insect speciesism. *International Journal of Sociology and Social Policy.* Vol. ahead-of-print No. ahead-of-print. https://doi.org/10.1108/IJSSP-09-2019-0196

Harper, B. A. (2010). *Sistah vegan: Black female vegans speak on food, identity, health, and society.* New York, NY: Lantern Books.

Hartley-Parkinson, R. (2020). German zoo faces feeding animals to one another as it runs out of cash. *Metro.* Retrieved from https://metro.co.uk/2020/04/15/german-zoo-faces-feeding-animals-one-another-runs-cash-12558117/.

Hogervorst, J. (2020). 'Animal testing and Covid-19'. *The Ecologist: The Journal for the Post-Industrial Age.* 16th June. Retrieved from https://theecologist.org/2020/jun/16/animal-testing-and-covid-19

Kendi, I. X. (2019). *How to be an anti-racist.* New York, NY: One World.

Kevany, S. (2020a). Millions of US farm animals to be culled by suffocation, drowning and shooting. *The Guardian* Tuesday 19 May. Retrieved from https://www.theguardian.com/environment/2020/may/19/millions-of-us-farm-animals-to-be-culled-by-suffocation-drowning-and-shooting-coronavirus

Kevany, S. (2020b). A million mink culled in Netherlands and Spain amid Covid-19 fur farming havoc. *The Guardian.* Retrieved from https://www.theguardian.com/world/2020/jul/17/spain-to-cull-nearly-100000-mink-in-coronavirus-outbreak

Ko, A., & Ko, S. (2017). *Aphro-ism: Essays on pop culture, feminism, and black veganism from two sisters.* New York, NY: Lantern Books.

Middleton, J., Reintjes, R., & Lopes, H. (2020). Meat plants—a new front line in the covid-19 pandemic. *BMJ* 370. doi: https://doi.org/10.1136/bmj.m2716 (Published 09 July 2020).

Moulds, J. (2020). 5 ways the coronavirus is affecting animals around the world. World Economic Forum. Retrieved from https://www.weforum.org/agenda/2020/04/coronavirus-animals-wildlife-biodiversity-tiger-boar-pandas-zoos/

Nibert, D. (Ed.). (2017). *Animal oppression and capitalism.* Conneticut: Praeger.

Nocella, A. J. II, & George, A. E. (2019). *Intersectionality of critical animal studies: A historical collection.* New York, NY: Peter Lang Publishing.

Nocella, A. J., II Sorenson, J., Socha, & Matsuoka, A. (2014a). Introduction: The emergence of critical animal studies. In A. J. Nocella, J. Sorenson, & A. Matsuoka (Eds.) (2014) *Defining critical animal studies: An intersectional social justice approach for liberation*. New York: Peter Lang.

Nocella, A. J. II, Shannon, D., & Asimakopoulos, J. (2012). *The accumulation of freedom: Writings on anarchist economics*. Oakland, CA: AK Press.

Nocella, A. J. II, Sorenson, J., Socha, & Matsuoka, A. (2014b). *Defining critical animal studies: An intersectional social justice approach for liberation*. New York: Peter Lang.

Nocella, A. J. II, White, R. J., & Cudworth, E. (2015). *Anarchism and animal liberation: Essays on complementary aspects of total liberation*. North Carolina: McFarland Press.

Pellow, D. N. (2014). *Total liberation: The power and promise of animal rights and the radical Earth movement*. Minneapolis, MN: University of Minnesota Press.

Polansek, T., & Huffstutter, P. J. (2020). Piglets aborted, chickens gassed as pandemic slams meat sector. *Reuters Business News*. April 27th 2020. Retrieved from https://www.reuters.com/article/us-health-coronavirus-livestock-insight/piglets-aborted-chickens-gassed-as-pandemic-slams-meat-sector-idUSKCN2292YS?fbclid=IwAR0TNHZMx-ERvxbh_G_FoP-mDjjDX0lDAOOYt0GnLU7GaXgLJTQ1YgQRSi0

ProVeg, E. V. (2020). *Food & pandemics report: Part 1 – making the connection: Animal-based food systems and pandemics*. Report. Berlin.

Reuben, A. (2020). Coronavirus: Why have there been so many outbreaks in meat processing plants? *BBC News*. Retrieved from https://www.bbc.co.uk/news/53137613

Reuters (2020). Dutch farms ordered to cull 10,000 mink over coronavirus risk. *The Guardian* June 6th. Retrieved from https://www.theguardian.com/world/2020/jun/06/dutch-mink-farms-ordered-to-cull-10000-animals-over-coronavirus-risk

Salim, M., & González, T. M. (2020). Coronavirus: Chronicle of an announced zoonosis. *Journal MVZ Cordoba, 25*(2), 1–3. Retrieved from https://doi.org/10.21897/rmvz.2048

Socha, K., (2012). *Women, destruction, and the avant-garde: A paradigm for animal liberation*. Boston: Brill Rodopi.

Sohrabi, C., Alsafi, Z., O'Neill, N., Khan, M., Kerwan, A., Al-Jabir, A., Iosifidis, C., & Agha, R. (2020). World Health Organization declares global emergency: A review of the 2019 novel coronavirus (COVID-19). *International Journal of Surgery, 76*, 71–76.

Swanson, A., & Yaffe-Bellany, D. (2020). Trump Declares Meat Supply 'Critical,' Aiming to Reopen Plants. New York Times. April 29th. Retrieved from https://www.nytimes.com/2020/04/28/business/economy/coronavirus-trump-meat-food-supply.html?auth=login-email&login=email

Velavan, T. P., & Meyer, C. G. (2020). The COVID-19 epidemic. *Tropical Medicine & International Health: TM & IH, 25*(3), 278–280. Retrieved from https://doi.org/10.1111/tmi.13383

Wadiwel, D. J. (2015). *The war against animals*. Boston: Brill Rodoph.

West, C. (2020). *The garden of vegan*. London: Pimpernell Press Limited.

Wharton, J. (2020). Pets 'rounded up and slaughtered to stop spread of coronavirus'. *Metro* Retrieved from https://metro.co.uk/2020/02/21/pets-rounded-slaughtered-stop-spread-coronavirus-12277644/?ito=cbshare

White, R. J. (2015). Critical animal geographies and anarchist praxis: Shifting perspectives from the animal 'question' to the animal 'condition'. In K. Gillespie, & R.-C. Collard (Eds.), *Critical animal geographies: Power, space and violence in a multispecies world*. London: Routledge.

White, R. J. (2017). Rising to the challenge of capitalism and the commodification of animals: Post-capitalism, anarchist economies and vegan praxis. In D. Nibert (Ed.), *Animal oppression and capitalism*. Conneticu: Praeger.

White, R. J., & Springer, S. (2018). Making space for anarchist geographies in critical animal studies. In: J. Sorenson, & A. Matuoka (Eds.), *Critical animal studies: Towards trans-species social justice*. London UK: Rowman and Littlefield International.

1. *Bearing Witness to the Animal Condition. Exploring the Complex Motivations, Experiences and Coping-Strategies of Sheffield Save Movement Activists (UK)*

ALEX HINCHCLIFFE AND RICHARD J. WHITE

Introduction

> Animals in the food system are interesting for developing a theory of witnessing because the power imbalance between human and nonhuman animals is so great, as nonhuman animals are fundamentally ownable, commodifiable, and killable in service to human interests. In witnessing animal suffering in the food system, then, even the act of caring deeply for animals becomes a subversive political act of acknowledging an animal's subjectivity and her embodied experience. (Gillespie, 2016, p. 573)

The Save Movement's call to bear witness in ways that recognises the 'plight' of animals (Wolch & Emel, 1998), or 'the animal condition' (Pedersen & Stănescu, 2012), is gaining in momentum across the landscapes of non-violent direct action (see Nocella et al., 2014; Nocella et al., 2015; Pellow, 2014). Typically, Save Movement activists aim to strategically (and legally) occupy key sites that signify the transition between ostensibly 'non-violent', 'visible' and 'public-spaces' from those spaces that are altogether more 'violent', 'hidden', and 'private'. This is certainly true whenever vigils are organised in near proximity to slaughterhouses, and the activists bear witness to the transportation and unloading of non-human farmed animals. Unsurprisingly, Save Movement vigils are highly contested, unpredictable, complex and precarious spaces. Much of this can be accounted by the presence of a number of animal bodies flowing through it at any particular moment: from human activists, slaughterhouse workers, security guards, police officers, truck drivers and members of the general public to the involuntarily, coerced and cowed appearance of other nonhuman animals. These, in turn, become places filled with extreme emotions (anger, resentment, fear, anguish, despair, hope), that capture a heightened atmosphere of tension, compromise, negotiation, and resistance (Jones, 2013). In this way, the inter-species activist geographies seen here have much in common with many other forms of direct action birthed in the name of social and spatial justice.

Situated in this broader context, and despite being very much an emergent area of enquiry across the social sciences, critical researchers have begun the important task of unpacking more fully key coping strategies of social justice/total liberation activists. This nascent research has brought a number of significant insights and reflections to light (e.g. Gillespie, 2016, 2018; Socha & Blum, 2013). However, within this body of literature, there is precious little research explicitly focused on the (UK) Save Movement: with the work of the researcher-activist Alex Lockwood (2016, 2017, 2018, 2022) being a notable exception. Responding to this lacuna, the chapter aims to help address these gaps in knowledge and understanding by drawing explicitly on a qualitative case study focused on Save Movement activists in the UK city of Sheffield. More specifically, the research draws attention to the findings that emerged from qualitative primary research that addressed these three central questions:

1. What are the main experiences of activists Bearing Witness?
2. What are the key motivations of activists who Bear Witness?
3. What are some of the important coping strategies employed by these activists?

The intention of the chapter then is two-fold. Firstly, to offer deeper and more nuanced understanding regarding the activist geographies harnessed through The Save Movement. Secondly, by drawing close attention to the types of activism and activists involved, the hope is that these insights can be used to highlight good practice, tactics and strategies that might helpfully inform other forms of inter-species social justice activism and liberation movements.

Following a brief reflection on the research methodology that informs and underpins the research, the chapter will then introduce the Sheffield Animal Save Movement more fully. The key findings from the research are then grouped into three central themes: (1) the 'encounter', focusing on the activists experiences of Bearing Witness; (2) the rationales that activists draw on not only to attend a vigil, but do so repeatedly having already experienced the suffering and misery that takes place first-hand; and (3) the coping strategies that activists draw on to help cope with their experiences and negative emotions. The chapter continues by making several key reflections that emerge from these findings, before drawing to a conclusion.

A Note on the Methodology

The qualitative research methodology used to inform the chapter draws on a range of complementary methods. Beginning in the summer of 2017, a series of one-to-one interviews with prominent Save Movement activists, as well as the use of 'activist diaries,' were used as a means to elicit insights into original, complex, unique and personal reflections of those fighting for liberation on the front lines. In addition to the oral testimonies of the activists' experiences, participants were also invited to bring photographs which were particularly meaningful to them. Some of these are included in the chapter. Recognising the important *social* dimension of *Bearing Witness* activism, a series of complementary focus-groups were set up in the hope of encouraging more reflective forms of discussion around key themes. A final key approach was the use of ethnographic research, drawing extensively from the first-hand experiences by one of the authors (Alex), who has been highly active within the Sheffield Save Movement since its inception in 2016. Where appropriate, in the interest of maintaining confidentiality and anonymity, pseudonyms have been used instead of actual names.

The Save Movement and Sheffield Animal Save

Founded in 2010 in Toronto, Canada, the Save Movement has multiplied rapidly in recent years. New chapters can be found across Africa, North America, South America, Asia and Australia, New Zealand, and Europe (including Denmark, France, Germany, Italy and Spain). Indeed, there are now over 70 Save Movement groups active in the UK (The Save Movement, no date). Common across all Save Movement groups is the call to 'Bear Witness'. The explicit reasons for doing so are two-fold: first, to express an inter-species solidarity and justice in the present moment, and secondly, to document with photographs, video footage and personal testimony the suffering of nonhuman animals and use this in the future to raise a deeper consciousness around a broader public. Anita Krajnc, founder of The Save Movement, advocates for a love-based, Gandhian approach much like the civil rights movement (Krajnc, 2012), indicating the ideology guiding the movement. All Save

Movement groups are governed by a set of guiding principles and a code of conduct (see Box 1).

Box 1: The Save Movement's Code of Conduct

Code of Conduct

Our aims are to show love and compassion to animals in their final moments and raise awareness of their wrongful and unnecessary suffering and exploitation.
This code of conduct aims to give clear guidelines to vigil attendees.
The Save Movement (TSM) wants to ensure:

1. A welcoming, peaceful and safe environment for all those who attend.
2. No increase of anxiety or stress to the animals to whom we bear witness.
3. The principles of TSM are upheld.

When attending vigils, please adhere to the following:

1. At all times be mindful to keep a safe distance from the trucks when they are in motion, especially when they are turning.
2. Listen to, and respect the instructions of any TSM marshals who are there to ensure the safety of vigil attendees.
3. Respect the boundaries of any coned areas implemented by TSM to ensure safety.
4. Refrain from any violent, loud or threatening behaviour either verbal or physical towards slaughterhouse workers, security, police or truck drivers and members of the public.
5. Minimize loud noises or shouting in the presence of animals so as not to heighten their anxiety or stress. Do not use megaphones in close proximity to trucks. Approach them slowly with love and respect.
6. Respect other vigil attendees. We are all there for the animals and to build the animal rights community.

7. Non-compliance of the above or disrespectful behaviour of any kind will not be tolerated and we may ask individuals persistently violating the principles to leave the vigil. *

*Please note we accept that from time to time breeches of these guidelines may occur. The important thing is to always be striving towards upholding these ideal principles at all times. It is the duty and responsibility of all those who attend to ensure a safe and peaceful vigil experience for the group as a whole. Above all, stay safe, stay mindful, and stay committed to those who need us to hear their voice.

Source: The Save Movement (no date) "Memorandum of Understanding"

Sheffield Animal Save held their first vigil in January 2017 at Woolley Brothers slaughterhouse near Sheffield. The vigil attracted over 25 activists. Since then, the group has increased the frequency of their events: in 2018, vigils were being held once a week at multiple locations both within, and close to, Sheffield. One of these strategically focused on the N. Bramall and Sons abattoirs. In 2017, these abattoirs were the subject of an Animal Aid undercover investigation. The video footage of the nightmarish scenes recorded there was subsequently picked up by local and national media, drawing public attention toward a range of egregious forms of animal cruelty (Burke, 2017). Examples of abuse included, but were not limited to:

> Fearful sheep... running in circles to evade being stunned and in another incident slaughtermen are seen laughing as an animal is twitching on the floor, having just been shot. At one point the udder of a spent dairy cow explodes. (Animal Aid, 2017, para 3)

Over the last 18 months, while many of the vigils have been attended by a large number of activists, a core group of regular activists, those who rarely miss an event, has emerged. Their commitment is unwavering, doubly so in times of adversity, as when activists are exposed to the well below-freezing temperatures of an English winter. It is this group whose views were drawn on extensively as part of the research methodology.

To come across this huddle of people, holding signs with animal rights messages on them at 7 am on a cold, frosty January morning, outside what appears to be an indeterminate 'ordinary' location, a passer-by may be forgiven for thinking 'why on earth are these people there?' It is to this question that the chapter will return shortly. Before doing so, an important contextual question needs to be considered: what is it like to *be* there?

Part I: The Encounter

At the designated site, Save Movements activists stand in empathetic solidarity with every cow, pig, sheep or chicken as they pass through (i.e. are transported as "living stock" on slaughter trucks to be deposited and unloaded). The activists bear witness in full knowledge of the violence and suffering that has been always-present in these other animals' lives to this point and will again in the near future. This *near future* violence, they know, will be catastrophic enough to result in intense suffering, pain and ultimately the loss of life. The activists also know that, since their birth, these farmed animals that pass before them have been incarcerated, denied even the most basic of natural instincts, not least the freedom of space and movement. Born into a speciesist world, they never had a hope of living anything close to a natural and free life. In order to be transported to their deaths, these animals are crowded onto trucks and trailers and have no access to food or water during this time. Too many times they are forced to endure all kinds of extreme weather, from blistering heat in summer months to the piercing cold throughout the winter. Unsurprisingly, in such conditions many farmed animals often don't survive the journey, perishing from heat, cold or stress-induced pneumonia (Dunayer, 2001). During extreme cold winter days, it was not uncommon for Sheffield activists to witness pigs, barely alive, arriving at the slaughterhouse gates with their bodies frozen to the vehicles.

Irrespective of the weather, the cramped, appalling conditions that the animals occupy in the slaughter trucks are nothing new to them. Perhaps the journey to the slaughterhouse is the only novel experience for many animals that, hitherto, have existed inside of dark, pitiful sheds during their unnaturally short lives. Certainly, time spent in daylight, fresh air and travelling are all unknowns. Activists talked about not being able to detect any positive reactions in these animals' faces that might reflect the novelty of the experience; their eyes betray their anxiousness and fear. The miserable disposition of animals arriving for slaughter is a common observation, as Kranjc (2012) states, "You can immediately discern confusion, fear, and pain in their captivating eyes." Their spirits are crushed and broken just as surely as their bodies will shortly come to be.

Having witnessed the arrival of the farmed animals, the Save Movement activists then observe the often brutal and merciless process of unloading the

Photograph 1: Sheffield Activists Bearing Witness

animals from trailers into pens where they are held before going to slaughter. This "living stock" must be moved as quickly as possible, their commodified lives valued only in capitalist terms, and for the workers [and their owners], time is money (for powerful reflections on the entanglement of animal oppression and capitalism see Nibert, 2017a, 2017b). No exceptions are made, regardless of however weak, injured or ill the animals may be. Activists from Sheffield Animal Save have witnessed slaughterhouse workers repeatedly kicking young pigs from trucks and violently prodding cows with long metal poles in efforts to force them into the slaughterhouse. This behaviour is reportedly common amongst workers at the N. Bramall and Sons slaughterhouse, as mentioned earlier. Activists, when interviewed, often reported witnessing slaughterhouse workers' wanton cruelty to other animals, as well as experiencing inflamed levels of aggression and hostility directly to their own persons. Indeed, examples were given of Save Movement activists having personal items stolen by slaughterhouse workers, activists being sprayed with a high pressure water hose and activists being doused in blue dye used in the slaughterhouse to mark inedible body parts.

Finally, the farmed animals are seen standing huddled and isolated in front of the slaughterhouse. The *sensory* dimensions of space—particularly sounds and smells—betray the hidden horror that lives within the slaughterhouse itself. One of the most nauseous is the foul and noxious stench of—quite literally—death. The chicken slaughterhouses in particular create an odour so objectionable that it becomes almost visible in the atmosphere, a point that activists from Save Movement groups that bear witness to chickens will regularly draw attention to and reflect on. Concomitant with the smell are the piercing screams of those animals who are facing—or enduring—their own deaths. It is a heart-breaking sound for activists who are present, one which burns deeply into their soul and which, once heard, can never be forgotten. It is a sound that is born at the very moment our human dominion over other animals is at its most violent; a terrible terrifying cry that is, undoubtedly, the same as humans make when subjected to such torture and brutality. It is primeval sound, something beyond words. Thus, in their last moment of life on this earth, their final breaths scream of injustice, anguish and misery, a futile cry for help that will never come.

To bear witness to this once is incredibly hard; activists speak of having to resist every instinct to either flee or to intervene directly (and illegally) to end this inter-species nightmare. To come back and bear witness to this is to open yourself to a hellish dystopia that wrenches and guts your heart again, and again, and again. Not surprisingly, the distressing nature of attending a vigil and bearing witness to callous acts of cruelty and brutality carried out just meters away was keenly felt by the respondents. An increasing sense of dread and unease was commonly experienced by activists as a Save Movement vigil approached. This sense of foreboding never goes away no matter how many vigils an activist had previously attended.

For first time activists though, their worst fears and expectations never prepare them for what they encounter. Rachael, for example, spoke openly of the trauma she experienced: "I attended my first vigil at the beginning of June for their [Sheffield Animal Save] five-day event … I found the first day to be one of the worst experiences of my life and I almost vomited". Lily also reflected on how her thoughts are taken over by knowledge that the animals that will be slaughtered, and also animals are being slaughtered nearby at that particular moment in time. She recalled a particularly traumatic experience she went through with Manchester Pig Save, when bearing witness to pigs being transported to slaughter: "[F]rom Manchester Pig Save where you can hear the gas chambers, when I first saw that I broke down, I think most people do at their first Save." The feeling of helpless is also closely linked to frustration, a connection Alex drew attention to in his activist diary:

> My frustration is often the over-riding feeling I experience during and after attending a Save Movement vigil; frustration at the fate faced by billions of animals across the world, at the apathy exhibited by the majority of society towards their plight but predominantly at the minimal impact I am able to make in

> that moment. Each truck passing by packed with innocent animals destined for slaughter is another reminder that thus far, for these animals at least, our efforts to advocate on their behalf have ultimately been in vain, leading to intense feelings of guilt and failure.

This dystopian reality is a particularly bitter pill to swallow and process, and is recounted by other respondents. For example, Rachael spoke of: "[T]he feelings of helplessness, overwhelming frustration and sadness [that] are difficult to deal with". Indeed, for many activists, the tremendous feelings of sadness, anger and frustration are exacerbated by the inability to be able to actually do anything (legally) to directly help those animals escape the abuse.

Repetitive emotional distress is also experienced by activists, not least those who record and re-watch vigil film footage or photographs. Two of the research participants were creating a documentary film concerning the Save Movement at the time they were interviewed and spent a lot of their time at different vigils with different Save Movement groups. Interestingly, for them, the mental and emotional burden didn't come so much during the event, but rather afterwards as they worked through the material they had collected. As Joshua describes:

> It could be days and weeks after when you're going through everything else, that's when it hits you more and more because you have to go over it and over it and over it instead of it just happening in real time where you can deal with it all at once, it just comes back again and again, that's the weird thing about filming; it's easier on the day but worse after.

For these activists, being focused on the task at hand and thinking (semi-professionally) about 'the right' camera angles and achieving a good shot meant they didn't fully appreciate the emotional nature of their subject and surroundings in these moments. However, upon re-visiting the material, it was then that sadness, frustration and anger hit them. Naomi revealed how difficult she finds it to process the realities of the animal's fate:

> It's the editing part that's the really hard part, and I think that's because I know that they're not here anymore, like that animal that I was with is now not here, like sometimes I just can't even comprehend that.

For Save Movement activists, their mental state may justifiably be framed as representing a type of 'post-traumatic stress'. Indeed, a number of the research participants reported thoughts constantly preoccupied with images and memories of vigils, with some even revealing they had experienced breakdowns and nightmares as a result. In short, it is impossible to underestimate the (emotional) stress and pain that activists endure, and this suffering became apparent throughout the research. This was something that Alex also drew attention to in his activist research diary:

> Faced with the devastating reality that animals are being slaughtered in the billions despite our best efforts, coupled with seeing the distressed, confused and hopeless faces of these individuals moments before they endure an unimaginable fate, it is no wonder that myself and other activists often experience overwhelming feelings of guilt, born out of frustration and helplessness. This in turn can often lead to activists charging themselves with not doing enough for the cause. This feeling of moral duty can often cause more feelings of guilt, leading to activists struggling with the thought that they aren't active enough. (23rd August 2017)

Indeed, throughout his diary, a common theme Alex reflected on was a deep sense of guilt that emerged through not doing enough activism. One illustrations of this was when he had to spend time away from the city: "feeling ready to get back to Sheffield and get back doing stuff; feeling guilty about not getting involved with activism recently."

This entry was written when Alex went on a family holiday for a week. The sense of guilt at missing activist events was undoubtedly exacerbated by social media, which documented what vigils had taken place in his absence. This feeling of inadequacy is a familiar refrain echoed by others. As Rachael noted:

> I always feel so guilty that I'm not doing enough. It's such a conflict because I genuinely believe that doing vegan outreach and street activism is the best use of my time and resources and I know I cannot do everything but when I see other people doing so much I can't help but feel guilt.

In this sense, the space in which activists occupy is never, or rather no longer 'out-there'. It is a space which has become internalised—a haunting and traumatic space, one which affects engagement with others (activists spoke of intensified negative feelings of frustration and alienation toward non-vegan friends and family) and society more generally. On a profound level, it becomes impossible to fully leave this space, as you cannot unsee what you have seen, and these memories are powerful enough, quite literally, to affect everything thereafter (see photograph 2). As a prominent Sheffield Save Movement activist, Megan McGrath, noted:

> The stench of animal faeces from the transportation trucks is something that lingers long after leaving, along with the sights of the skeletons, heads and organs of the animals that not minutes ago we stroked being forklifted into a skip as waste. (McGrath, 2017, n.p.).

Photograph 2: Bearing Witness—a Haunting and Traumatic Encounter

Exploring the Motivations of Save Movement Activists, or Why We Continue to Stand Outside Slaughterhouses at 6 AM

Given the profound emotional and psychological distress involved, seeking to find out why Sheffield Animal Save activists return to bear witness brings to light a complex range of motivations. For example, there was a broad consensus in both the focus groups and interviews that *not* acting on their heightened consciousness around the suffering of animals and the violence that befalls them was simply not an option. Not only was this a key expression of their unconditional commitment to critical vegan praxis, but also because of a strong sense that other forms of *indirect* action—signing petitions, for example—was nowhere near enough. Indeed, these feelings, particularly antipathy toward appealing to government to end animal suffering, run true across many animal rights activists. Here, and in the broader context, activists often speak of a *desire* to draw attention to the injustices they see by taking direct action (Herzog, 1993). For Sheffield Animal Save activists, the motivation to take direct action through bearing witness went beyond a desire, and was framed instead as a 'moral duty': an obligation to act on behalf of animals.

Unpacking this appeal to a moral duty and understanding the rationales that underpin it is revealing. For some activists, this moral duty was rooted in overwhelming feelings of guilt and shame associated with their past, specifically their speciesist worldview, and how this manifested itself through the consumption of animals' bodies. Peter captured these complex emotions perfectly when reflecting that:

> I owe it to the animals…spending most of your life eating animals, to me it feels like when I go to the vigils it's a motivation to wake up, to go there and bear witness and give them one final moment of comfort.

In addition to drawing on the past failures, where attending vigils allowed individuals to express remorse for their complicity in animal abuse, there were other complex factors at work when an identity of self (ego) was replaced by the collective identity of 'human'. Thus, over-riding motivations for attending the vigils were less about personal histories (forgiveness?), but were driven by a sense of shame for *being human*. As Naomi reflected in her interview:

> I think it's about being there for the individual animal, *and apologising that you were part of that*, and showing everybody that isn't already vegan … to bring it into everybody's consciousness.

Alex also reflected in depth on this question in relation to his own commitment to attending vigils, one which centred around a 'moral obligation':

> When being woken at 4:30 am in the freezing winter months and facing the prospect of standing for 5 hours in the cold outside of a slaughterhouse, staying in a warm bed seemed particularly comforting. Thinking about the derision and abuse from slaughterhouse workers, the general public and police, made this feeling of inertia even stronger. But I always remind myself of the animals that died as a result of my past actions, and I also have an ongoing moral obligation to act, given that I knew the fate that these animals would soon face. This helped massively in my involvement with Sheffield Animal Save. Additionally, the idea that if everyone took the easy, comfortable option and didn't show up, that the animals on route to slaughter that morning would face their horrific fate without a single moment of potential comfort or connection.

It is important that reflections that draw on highly personal reasons as motivations for being present in these places of misery should not be seen as indulgent or virtue signalling. Indeed, throughout the research timeline, many activists, when being asked to focus on their own activist biographies and negative experiences on vigils, realized these were things they had rarely thought about. Held against the immense suffering and trauma of the animals they had bared witnessed to, there was a real reluctance to discuss their own suffering. The core of their activism was never about them, it was always—and will always be about the other animals.

The activists were there *because* of those living animals, both to express an inter-species solidarity and, wherever possible, to try to physically connect or comfort them in some ways. The opportunity to make physical contact was heavily negotiated. The slaughterhouse staff and police did allow a short window of time, while the animals were still inside the slaughterhouse trucks, for activists to approach the animals and communicate with them and/or take photographs. This desire for positive connection rather than just 'passive observation' is instructive, for it underpins a persuasive re-framing of the Save Movement as both an intrinsic and instrumental space of activism.

The intrinsic (as an end in itself) dimension of Bearing Witness has often been underplayed, particularly by those who are sceptical as to what part of the "Save" Movement actually "saves" nonhuman animals. While this is an important critique, it is important that the motivation to try and help the animals condemned to slaughterhouse is never lost nor marginalised. With this in mind, perhaps the 'Light Movement', rather than 'Save Movement' would be a better description, since these vigils shine a critical light on some of the darkest socio-spatial human-animal encounters, Ruby drew attention to this as a primary reason for attending vigils:

> When I was looking at them, they needed something more other than a camera shoved in their face, like at Manchester pig save I was comforting them, singing to them, doing whatever I can, just to make them count.

Embracing a spirit of inter-species solidarity, one rooted in a feminist (Kemmerer, 2011; Gaard, 2002) or anarchist praxis (Nocella et al., 2015;

Photograph 3: Beyond Witnessing—the Need for Physical Connection

Socha, 2012; White, 2015, 2017), meant that activists were continually questioning what animals are going through, listening for an answer and aiming to respond to that individual (Adams, 2016; Gillespie, 2018; Socha, 2013). The idea is to make some form of connection with an animal, either through taking their picture and sharing it on social media or by attempting to comfort them through physical contact (gently stroking) or through talking and trying to sooth them was a common refrain. This is consistent with one of the core central aims of the Save Movement, the act of trying to help an animal who is suffering, which, Lockwood (2018) argues, looks to provide "momentary solace and succour, including with water and fruit, to the animals". Thus, through bearing witness to the victims of the animal abuse industry on their final journey, the Save Movement activist intention, albeit too brief and too temporary, is to transform spaces of fear—permeated by the sounds and smell of suffering beings—to ones which contained inter-species compassion, kindness and solidarity (see also Silvennoinen, no date).

Participating in The Save Movement is motivated by a number of important future-orientated goals. One of these is the power of connecting with the individual animal, rather than talking about species in the abstract. The commitment and resolve that this individual connection brings with it is such an important factor: the fight for *someone,* the subject of a life (Regan, 2004) and not some*thing*. Lily articulated this when concluding that:

> individually catching an image of the animals, connecting with them and looking in their eyes: having that moment of connection [means] you will never forget that animal, nor will you allow them to be forgotten…[you can] show the world that their meal had a face… a name and a story.

Carol Adams (1990) coined the term 'absent referent,' which is the literal being who disappears in the eating of dead bodies. By documenting the plight of animals and sharing their individual stories, the Save Movement ensures that, for some animals at least, the fact that they were a living being with an interest in their life is forced into the public domain and thus not forgotten.

Coping Strategies: The Importance of Activist Friends and Communities

A strong emphasis on the collective human expressions of solidarity and support within the Save Movement was highly valued as a coping strategy. In common with many social justice movements and expressions of direct action, the appeal of bearing witness *in solidarity* is an important facet to the

Save Movement. As Kranjc (2012) argues, the Save Movement works in ways that "touches the collective spirit" and "nourishes community support while sustaining the activists and building the movement".

The opportunity to unite with others, and offer and receive support was vitally important for those who engage in the Save Movement. That said, many activists recognised that their coping strategy was, arguably, one of not coping but of seeking ways to downplay and ignore the mental stress and burden placed on them through bearing witness. An attitude of 'just keep going' was frequently invoked. As Ruby said: 'I don't really think about it before or after, I just kind of get on with it'. This attitude of trying to block out any negative feelings or emotions relating to bearing witness resulted in individuals trying to distract themselves in order *not* to think. Rachael, for example, spoke of how she once had 'a complete breakdown', with tears streaming from her face during a vigil. To avoid this, her coping mechanism revolves around getting on with filling time with everyday tasks, such as routine housework and caring for family:

> You kind of go on auto pilot though don't you? You know you've got to go so you just go, and then I come home and I'll wash pots and pick kids up from school, as if I've not done it, because if I don't … if I think about it too much, I just go wow, so it's better for me to just carry on.

Other coping strategies included trying to find ways of channelling frustration and exasperation into positive, productive energy in order to create better futures. Activists spoke of harnessing their sadness and anger and allowing it to motivate them, hence redirecting it into other forms of advocacy and activism. Lily epitomised this resolve when noting that:

> I try and use my sadness to think well, fuel something, knowing that I'm doing something that will help some animals somewhere … using my sadness to fuel something else, that's kind of the way I cope with it.

This is a very positive approach to mental stress, with a focus on using it for good and allowing it to drive oneself to keep on working for nonhuman animals. This pragmatic approach of holding the interests of those one is trying to help as the most important thing was echoed by another activist, Jake, who reminded himself of the victims of the animal abuse ("livestock" industry) when he was struggling:

> It's just generally thinking about what's happening out there, thinking about the animals that we're out there for. That's what brings me back if I have any negative experience.

For some, the sense of moral duty highlighted earlier seems to help activists carry the mental burden, allowing them to recognise the reason they partake in Save Movement vigils and use their frustration and sorrow to drive their future activism. From personal experience, I (Alex) found that putting things into perspective by comparing my own personal mental and emotional suffering with that of the victims of the livestock industry was a useful strategy. This allowed me to frame my own mental distress in the context of the far worse suffering of another being, leaving me with the resolve to carry on fighting on their behalf.

Finally, another popular coping strategy used by Sheffield Animal Save activists involved talking openly about what happened at the vigil and any associated feelings or emotions. The reasoning behind this was that talking to one another in essence shared the burden with others and allowed time for strategies for coping with these feelings to be devised. For many, the simple act of talking about their feelings with others was beneficial enough to warrant as a method of dealing with negative thoughts and mental stress from activism with the Save Movement. Pennebaker (1997) championed this line of thought, arguing that in relation to negative, distressing situations, keeping our thoughts and feelings to ourselves can be detrimental whilst disclosing them to others is a healthy, beneficial act. Natasha described her coping strategy as follows:

> Well we often go for a cup of tea, a cup of tea works wonders. If we're going to one [a vigil] in a different city we'll make sure we go to a nice vegan café. But for me because I live in a house with three other vegans I just find it so important to talk it out afterwards because when I haven't it's really played on my mind and I get nightmares and stuff.

For Natasha, spending time with other activists in a non-activism setting seemed to be an optimum coping strategy. This was echoed elsewhere, for example in Kelly's conviction that: "I think the only strategy I can say we have is doing something nice and social afterwards and lifting each other's spirits."

It is clear that it is of vital importance for activists to bind together as a community in efforts to cope with mental distress and feelings of sadness, anger and frustration. Whilst some activists also noted strategies that were personal and involved self-reflection, it is worth mentioning that during the focus group with activists from Sheffield Animal Save, there was unanimous agreement from all of the research participants that the time we had spent talking about all things relating to Sheffield Animal Save had been a very positive experience, allowing activists to discuss with and listen to others with similar experiences to themselves.

Coping Strategy: Friends and Family

It is clear then that feelings of frustration and guilt often go hand in hand with one another. Feelings of frustration can also be brought about when talking to family and friends about attending Save Movement vigils. By mainstream standards, waking up at 5 am to go and stand at the side of a road outside of a slaughterhouse is a rather unusual way to spend a morning. The process of becoming vegan and the subsequent task of informing friends and family of one's new (critical) lifestyle can be troubling in itself, with many acquaintances not understanding why someone would make such a decision and often reacting in such a way that mocks, ridicules and derides the person changing their lifestyle (Socha, 2012). A particular theme for younger vegan activists is the assertion that this moral awakening is just a phase, one that will soon pass within a few months.

Reflecting on my (Alex) own experiences my parents were sceptical as to how long my new lifestyle would last given my past history of obsession with new things before quickly losing interest. 7 ½ years on, though, I think they have accepted this isn't a phase. With a loved one going vegan, the issues of animal exploitation in everyday life are thrust right to the fore and become unavoidable subjects for friends and family to confront; this may expose any unease or discomfort they feel at the thought of eating animals, which can often lead to defensive reactions. Given this often heated response to simply learning of a loved one's new lifestyle, it is no surprise that telling friends and family about attending Save Movement vigils can often bring about tense and fraught environments full of misunderstanding, unwillingness to talk constructively, and inevitably heated arguments.

In the context of coping strategies, many research participants reported a general negative, unreceptive response from friends and family toward their activism with the Save Movement. As one respondent, David, said:

> My mum said, it's ok you being vegan, but you going outside these slaughterhouses and protesting or demoing, you're forcing your opinions on other people. The rest of them [family] are generally very defensive, they won't even try a vegan meal, they won't even taste it, they don't want to know … they'll shut you up if you talk about it.

This was perhaps an extreme reaction, with other research participants citing more indirect derision and mockery from family through indifference, strange looks and rolls of the eyes. Some activists reported that friends and family took them more seriously and respectfully due to their obvious commitment to the cause by consistently bearing witness to animals. Where genuine understanding and tacit support from social networks were present, this made an important difference in terms of extending and deepening activists' coping strategies. Where this support was absent, feelings of isolation and alienation were more pronounced.

Final Thoughts and Reflections

If trends in the recent past are anything to go by, then The Save Movement will continue to grow as a means of expressing inter-species solidarity and raising public consciousness toward the plight of farmed animals. By exploring the complex experiences, motivations and coping strategies of activists involved with the Sheffield Animal Save movement, the intention of the chapter has not only been to offer a timely window into this form of activism, but also to offer insights which might provide deeper connections across other animal rights based activism more generally.

Through drawing attention to particular spaces and bearing witness to the final moments of the animals that pass through them, the chapter has sought to impress upon the reader how The Save Movement activists seek to confront cruelty and raise consciousness across a broader public. By exposing these violent geographies, Save Movement activists are challenging the idea that the barbarity, death and panic associated with slaughterhouses are absent from our supposedly 'civilised' society (for discussion on the need for social *and* spatial justice see White & Springer, 2018). As Gregery and Pred (2007) state of the uncovering of everyday violence: "They show that terror and torture are not the exclusive property of others, but inhabit the central structures of our own society too" (p. 5?). In addition to this, by being present at the sight of another's suffering and attempting to help, to care, through offering kindness, sympathy and support means that the farmed animals' final moments are not comprised solely of fear, bewilderment and terror. In this way, Save Movement activists introduce a radical inter-species expression of love and solidarity to an otherwise unrepentantly speciesist space. What we do to them, ultimately, we do to ourselves. As Save Movement founder Anita Kranjc (2012) recognises:

> Looking at the pigs, touching their snouts as they push through the air holes to nudge and sniff our hands, hearing them grunt to communicate with us and each other, strengthens our resolve to do all we can to help them.

In this sense, bearing witness is an important and radical practice that potentially re-envisions our relationship with nonhuman animals. Indeed, as Lockwood (2018) states, the interspecies solidarity shown can assist us in rethinking the boundary between human and nonhuman. This promise notwithstanding, the act of bearing witness does come though at a significant price for the activists themselves, which needs to be better recognised (Gorski & Chen, 2015). The negative physical, emotional—and social (if activism results in the alienation of friends and family)—environments that individuals unwillingly enter demands new coping strategies. With this in mind, it is heartening to see initiatives emerge that are explicitly and unapologetically designed to help encourage new networks of support and care to be found within animal activist groups. For example, in October 2018, Save Movement activists were invited to attend an "activist burnout & self-care workshop" in Leicester (Aherne, 2018), where:

> There will be a number of speakers on the day ranging from counsellors to mental health nurses. There will also be a short yoga & meditation/mindfulness session to end the day. Workshops & talks will cover a range of areas from trauma, post-traumatic stress disorder, compassion fatigue.

Finally, though the emphasis on Sheffield Animal Save Movement activists draws on a highly situated and localised evidence base, we hope that their experiences and reflections offer important synergies that other inter-species social justice movements can recognise, express solidarity with, and learn from. Indeed, if this chapter has helped in some small way to bring new insights into activist solidarity and understanding, and perhaps encourage the reader to join their local Save Movement event, then it will have more than served its purpose.

Acknowledgement

We would like to acknowledge that this research was supported by Staff Student Research Project Funding in 2017 from the Department of Natural and Built Environment, Sheffield Hallam University, UK.

Dedication

Dedicated to Regan Russell, a Save Movement activist killed on June 19th 2020 whilst attending a Toronto Pig Save vigil. Rest in power.

References

Adams, C. J. (1990). *The sexual politics of meat.* London: Bloomsbury.

Adams, C. J. (2016). *Carol J. Adams – Politics and the absent referent in 2014.* Earthling Liberation Kollective. (Available at https://humanrightsareanimalrights.com/2016/01/01/carol-j-adams-politics-and-the-absent-referent-in-2014/ [last accessed 02.09.2018]).

Aherne, D. (2017). The Save Movement UK, Animal Rights Activist Burnout/ Self-care workshop. Eventbrite. (Available at https://www.eventbrite.com/e/the-save-movement-uk-animal-rights-activist-burnoutself-care-workshop-tickets-50454694349# [last accessed 27.11.2018])

Animal Aid (2017). Nightmarish scenes uncovered in UK slaughterhouse. *Animal Aid.* (Available at https://www.animalaid.org.uk/nightmarish-scenes-uncovered-uk-slaughterhouse/ [last accessed 26.11.2018]).

Burke, D. (2017). Undercover secret video inside Sheffield slaughterhouse shows "nightmarish" animal "cruelty". The Star. (Available at https://www.thestar.co.uk/news/video-undercover-secret-video-inside-sheffield-slaughterhouse-shows-nightmarish-animal-cruelty-warning-graphic-content-1-8353043, [last accessed 26.11.2018]).

Dunayer, J. (2001). *Animal equality.* Maryland: Ryce Publishing.

Gaard, G. (2002). Vegetarian ecofeminism: A review essay. *Frontiers: A Journal of Women Studies, 23*(3), 117–146.

Gillespie, K. (2016). Witnessing animal others: Bearing witness, grief, and the political function of emotion. *Hypatia 31*(3), 572–588.

Gillespie, K. (2018). *The cow with ear tag# 1389.* University of Chicago Press.

Gorski, P. C., & Chen, C. (2015). "Frayed All Over:" The causes and consequences of activist burnout among social justice education activists. *Educational Studies, 51*(5), 385–405.

Gregery, D., & Pred, A. (2007). *Violent geographies: Fear, terror, and political violence.* Oxon: Routledge.

Herzog, H. A. Jr. (1993). "The Movement Is My Life": The psychology of animal rights activism. *Journal of Social Issues, 49*(1), 103–119.

Jones, O. (2013). "Who milks the cows at Maesgwyn?" The animality of UK rural landscapes in affective registers. *Landscape Research, 38*(4), 421–442.

Kemmerer, L. (2011). *Sister species: Women, animals and social justice.* University of Illinois Press.

Kranjc, A. (2012). Bearing Witness. *We Animals.* (Available at http://weanimals.org/blog.php?entry=168 [last accessed 02.09.2018]).

Lockwood, A. (2016). *The Pig in Thin Air: An Identification.* Lantern Books.

Lockwood, A. (2017). The save movement, empathy and activism. *Animal Studies Journal, 7*(1), 104–126.

Lockwood, A. (2018). Bodily encounter, bearing witness and the engaged activism of the global save movement. *Animal Studies Journal, 7*(1), 104–126.

Lockwood, A. (2022). A "Useful Uselessness: Vegan Geographies of Bearing Witness at the Slaughterhouse Gates. In P. Hodge, A. McGregor, S. Springer, O. Veron, & R. J. White (Eds.), *Vegan geographies: Spaces beyond violence, ethics beyond speciesism.* Brooklyn: Lantern Publishing.

McGrath, M. (2017). The hills are alive with the sound of slaughter. *Forge Press* (Available at http://forgetoday.com/press/the-hills-are-alive-with-the-sound-of-slaughter/ [last accessed 26.11.2018]).

Nibert, D. (Ed.). (2017a). *Animal oppression and capitalism. Volume one: The oppression o nonhuman animals as sources of food.* Connecticut: Praeger.

Nibert, D. (Ed.). (2017b). *Animal oppression and capitalism. Volume two: The oppressive and destructive role of capitalism.* Connecticut: Praeger.

Nocella, A., Sorenson, J., Socha, K., & Matsuoka, A. (Eds.). (2014). *Defining critical animal studies: An intersectional social justice approach for liberation.* Peter Lang.

Nocella, A., White, R. J., & Cudworth, E. (Ed.). (2015). A*narchism and animal liberation: Critical animal studies, intersectionality and total liberation.* McFarland Press: Jefferson.

Pedersen, H., & Stănescu, V. (2012). Series Editors' Introduction. What is "Critical" about Animal Studies? From the Animal "Question" to the Animal "Condition". In K. Socha, *Women, destruction, and the avant-garde: A paradigm for animal liberation.* Rodolph Press: Amsterdam.

Pellow, D. N. (2014). *Total liberation: The power and promise of animal rights and the radical earth movement.* Minnesota: University of Minnesota Press.

Pennebaker, J. W. (1997). *Opening up: The healing power of expressing emotions.* New York: The Guilford Press.

Regan, T. (2004). *Empty cages: Facing the challenge of animal rights.* Rowman & Littlefield.

Silvennoinen, A. (no date) *Changing the Face of Animal Activism.* Artefact. (Available at http://www.artefactmagazine.com/2017/12/05/changing-the-face-of-animal-activism/ [last accessed 27.11.2018]).

Socha, K. (2012). *Women, destruction, and the avant-garde: A paradigm for animal liberation.* Rodophi Press: New York.

Socha, K. (2013). The "Dreaded Comparisons" and Speciesism. In K. Socha, & S. Blum (Eds.). (2013). *Confronting animal exploitation: Grassroots essays on liberation and veganism.* McFarland.

Socha, K., & Blum, S. (Eds.). (2013). *Confronting animal exploitation: Grassroots essays on liberation and veganism.* McFarland: Jefferson.

The Save Movement (no date) *Memorandum of Understanding.* (Available at http://thesavemovement.org/start-a-save-group/mou/ [last assessed 22.11.2018]).

The Save Movement (no date) List of Save Groups (available at http://thesavemovement.org/list-of-save-groups/ [last accessed 27.11.2018]).

White, R. J. (2015). "Critical animal geographies and anarchist praxis: Shifting perspectives from the animal 'question' to the animal 'condition'." In K. Gillespie, & R.-C

Collard (Eds.), *Critical animal geographies: Power, space and violence in a multispecies world.* Routledge: London.
White, R. J. (2017). Rising to the challenge of capitalism and the commodification of animals: Post-capitalism, anarchist economies and vegan praxis. In D. Nibert (Ed.) *Animal Oppression and Capitalism* (pp. 270–293). Conneticut: Praeger.
White, R. J., & Springer, S. (2018). Making space for anarchist geographies in critical animal studies. In J. Sorenson, & A. Matuoka (Eds.), *Critical animal studies: Towards trans-species social justice.* London: Rowman and Littlefield International.
Wolch, J., & Emel, J. (1998). Preface. In J. Wolch, & J. Emel (Ed.), *Animal geographies: Place politics, and identity in the nature-culture borderlands*. London: Verso.

2. *Performing Veganism: Building Bridges amongst Academia, Activism, and Community*

MARÍA MARTA ANDREATTA

Introduction

Although academic research and teaching on animal liberation and veganism have been conducted for several decades in Europe and North America (Best, 2009), these are still emerging topics in Latin American universities. In fact, practices and discourses on veganism are relatively recent in my country, Argentina, as well as in neighboring countries, although they have become more visible in the past few years because of the size of vegan groups in virtual social networks (Andreatta, 2016; Navarro, 2014). Researchers from diverse fields of knowledge, such as Philosophy (González, 2016; González & Ávila Gaitán, 2014), Literature (Yelin, 2013), the Political Sciences (Ávila Gaitán, 2017), Cultural Studies, Communication (Navarro, 2016), Law (Pezzetta, 2018), and Health Sciences (Andreatta, 2017) throughout Latin America not long ago started studies on veganism, animal liberation, and related topics.

One of the challenges that we face as scholars is that our work can transcend the boundaries of academia, and this is particularly difficult in issues related to animal liberation, since this is, at best, little known, and, very often, frankly unpopular among both academics and the general population. In effect, animal abuse and exploitation are perceived as secondary issues, and problems such as poverty, exploitation, inequality, and violence that are part of the daily life of the human communities of our countries are considered the most urgent. However, this line of reasoning fails to understand that the animal issue is one more injustice that arises when some have more power than others (Andreatta, Pezzetta & Rincón Higuera, 2017).

Performance ethnography (PE) is a non-traditional strategy of inquiry that makes possible the co-participation of researchers, communities and activists in experiences that bring together theory and praxis in complex, contradictory and meaningful ways. Moreover, PE encourages interdisciplinarity, collaborative research, and political commitment, at the same time as it avoids elitist language, seeking to reach wider audiences to reflect on injustice and oppression. In this essay, I take up again and go further with the analysis started in a previous publication (Andreatta, 2016) on the significance of PE for critical animal studies (CAS).

Performance Ethnography

Originating in the 1980s and 1990s in the context of the so-called *crisis of representation* (see Denzin & Lincoln, 2005, pp. 18–19), PE is a strategy of inquiry that brings together and puts into action concepts and methods from Performance Studies and Ethnography. While the latter entails participant observation with the aim of describing and understanding a culture by studying social interactions in their original contexts, the former provides elements from Cultural Studies, Communication, Sociology, Anthropology, and Psychology, as well as from the Arts (Drama, Literature, Dance), and so on (Alexander, 2005; Given, 2008). PE aims to explore human behavior as it occurs in real life, behavior that is considered performative since is "socially constructed, enacted, emergent, repeatable, and subversive" (Alexander, 2005, p. 414). From this perspective, human actions are "similar to a theatrical event" (Given, 2008, p. 608), a cultural performance recreating the socio-cultural norms of a community but reconstructing them at the same time. For Alexander (2005), PE "is, literally, the staged re-enactment of ethnographically derived notes," as well as an "approach to studying and staging culture" (p. 411). He also poses that PE has the possibility of "inciting culture" (p. 411), meaning that the re-enactment of the lives of individuals of a particular culture would cause in audiences a critical understanding and a response that eventually lead to social change. In other words, PE seeks to describe and interpret a culture through an embodied experience, coming to know through *doing* by combining sciences and arts.

According to Denzin (2013), PE favors an experiential and participative epistemology, values intimacy, and involvement as ways of understanding, and enables vulnerability towards one's own and others' experiences. Moreover, PE is a site "where context, agency, praxis, history, and subjectivity intersect" (Langellier, 1999, as cited in Denzin, 2013, p. 16). Thereby, he proposes a performative (auto)ethnography—blurring traditional limits between researchers and participants—in which texts move from "the personal to the political, the autobiographical to the cultural, the local to the historical" and "offer kernels of utopian hope of how things might be different, better" (Denzin, 2014, p. 25). As a method, PE puts critical sociopolitical imagination into action to understand the politics and practices shaping human experiences (Denzin, 2003, as cited in Alexander, 2005). However, from this perspective, understanding the world is not enough, since the final goal is to achieve "a performative politics that leads the way to radical social change" (Denzin, 2003, p. 259). Such a proposal brings together performance inquiry and critical pedagogy, seeking not only to critically analyze and understand culture through *doing*, but also to use collectively built knowledge to change the world.

Ultimately, PE aims to analyze, and challenge established meanings; promote an ethical dialogue by reflexively clarifying a moral position; engender resistance by offering utopian glimpses of how different the world could be, *showing* instead of *telling*, emphasizing the rule that "less is more"; display interpretive and representational adequacy; and encourage political commitment. Doing PE involves the firm conviction that it is not possible to guarantee absolute methodological certainty in Social Sciences, that all research reflects the researcher's point of view, that any observation is loaded with theory, and that there is no chance of constructing a value-free knowledge (Andreatta & Martínez, 2017).

As a strategy of inquiry, PE can be applied at any stage of the research process, that is, for generating research material, for analyzing and interpreting it, and for representing results. However, limits between field work, analysis and results tend to blur when applying PE. At the data collection and/or generation stage, the researcher can look for real life situations or provoke cultural dramatizations. For instance, creating a theatrical piece together with participants entails a different and powerful way of producing knowledge, as well of understanding their reality. Such a play should arise from activities and dialogues that are "spontaneous, intuitive, tacit, experiential, embodied and affective, rather than simply cognitive" (Given, 2008, p. 609). Continuing with this example, when creating and acting a play, interpretation and analysis are occurring simultaneously. Acting a role implies that the performer works on two levels: as a character in fiction and as an actor observing the situation from the real world. Fluctuating between these two realities and organically adding theory to this process allows the performer–participant, researcher or student—to reach new understandings and meanings.

To (re)present the results of the research, PE draws on different popular artistic expressions, such as poetry or music, with ethnodrama being one of the most widely used (Given, 2008). Saldaña (2005, as cited in Given, 2008) distinguishes between ethnotheater and ethnodrama, the latter being the written script and the former the live performance. An ethnodrama can be built from the reduction of data obtained in fieldwork into categories that then become the acts of a play. The dialogues can result from interviewees' narrations, or the action can be set as a monologue based on one interviewee, placing within the script theory regarding the issue addressed in the play (Saldaña, 1999). Moreover, ethnodramas can also involve the audiences in post-performance feedback (Denzin, 2014).

When applying PE, the researcher can decide the way she appears (or not) in the performative text. Alexander (2005) draws a distinction between *auto*ethnography in which the researcher plays herself, and a PE in which the characters are *others*. When *others* perform, the researcher takes a secondary role, remaining "offstage." In the "student-in-class centered" type of PE, based on descriptive data about a certain culture, students must develop a script with the goal of achieving greater understanding through embodied experience, given that they probably have not lived through those practices before. In addition, this performance encourages discussion and critical reflection on the practice and culture.

For instance, in order to comply with a classroom assignment, a group of North American students conducted ethnographic interviews to Mexican migrant street-side vendors, developed a script, and performed it. Thus,

> Through the performance and written reflective essays, the students articulate and claim a new understanding of the lives of *particular others*. The efforts of street vendors are not seen as what is casually assumed or asserted to be their culture, but acts of survival and sustenance grounded in their current predicament and their relation to space, place, and time. (Alexander, 2005, p. 413)

Another form of PE can be "audience-centered," in which audiences are invited to participate in the performance, thus allowing access to knowledge not only through passive observation, but also by *doing* and actively taking part. "Group field study work" is another approach to PE in which interviews and research notes are shared in a public performance and presented to diverse audiences "in the form of scripts, poems, short stories, and dramas" (Alexander, 2005, p. 421–422).

On the other hand, *auto*ethnography entails an "internalized ethnographic practice" (Alexander, 2005, p. 422) in which the researcher puts herself in a vulnerable position by using her personal experience to critically analyze a culture or certain cultural practices. For Ellis, Adams and Bochner (2010), autoethnography "is an approach to research and writing that seeks to describe and systematically analyze (graphy) personal experience (auto) [...] to understand cultural experience (ethno)", using "tenets of autobiography and ethnography" (par. 1). To be considered relevant and valid social research, autoethnography must make a substantial contribution to knowledge on a specific issue. Additionally, it must generate an empathic and reciprocal bond with audiences, aiming to provoke a reaction that eventually leads to social change (Holman Jones, Adams & Ellis, 2013). According to Denzin (2014), autoethnography is about "reflexively writing the self into and through the ethnographic text," identifying "the space where memory, history, performance, and meaning intersect" (p. 22). Ultimately, the boundaries between researcher and participants blur since the former's personal experience regarding a socio-cultural phenomenon becomes her object of study. This experience is represented as a performative text (ethnodrama, poetry, dance, etc.) that must comprise not only the lived experiences of the researcher-participant, but also the theoretical frame applied in her work.

Furthermore, two or more researchers can participate in a performance autoethnography. In *duoethnography*, two participants overlap their life histories in a dialogical narrative to achieve further understanding of a social phenomenon. On the other hand, in *collaborative writing* two or more authors—"often separated by time and distance" (Denzin, 2014, p. 23)—create an autoethnographic text. In the next section of the chapter, I will analyze some performative works within the frame of CAS.

Performance Ethnography in Critical Animal Studies

Given that CAS is an interdisciplinary project aiming to critically analyze and dismantle domination, oppression and exploitation of human and nonhuman animals, and the Earth (Best et al., 2007; Griffin, 2014), strategies of inquiry should be considered that come from diverse disciplines and theoretical approaches, particularly those rejecting "pseudo-objective academic analysis by explicitly clarifying its normative values and political commitments" and making it possible "to link theory to practice, analysis to politics, and the academy to the community" (Best et al., 2007, p. 4-5). Moreover, "epistemologically and ontologically (...), passion and subjectivity" are more relevant for CAS than "'neutrality' or 'hard data'" (Griffin, 2014, p. 115). In this regard, I believe that PE shares such features and proves to be clearly pertinent to issues within the frame of CAS (Andreatta, 2016).

As a strategy of inquiry within CAS, PE favors a critical but, at the same time, empathic understanding of the practice of veganism as well as of animal suffering. Bringing together science and art in performative texts, issues related to nonhuman (and human) liberation become more accessible to wider audiences, thus constituting a valuable tool for the cause (Andreatta, 2016). Although PE represents just a small part of the research strategies applied in CAS, several researchers and activists have developed performative texts on veganism and the relations between human and nonhuman animals in different contexts.

The ground-breaking *Sistah Vegan*, edited by A. Breeze Harper (2010), assembles autoethnographic texts exploring the intersection of gender, race, class, sexual orientation, and religion, among other identities, through the experience of vegan Black females from the USA. The book is very accessible to people outside academia, which makes it an example of how autoethnography, as a form of PE, can introduce difficult issues to communities not previously aware of them. *Sistah Vegan* displays different vegan voices that show how the notion and practice of veganism can vary from person to person, even within a culture (Yarbrough, 2010). For instance, Michelle R. Loyd-Paige (2010), one of the contributors, focuses her veganism on the health of African Americans:

> I am convinced that eating a meat-based diet—not to mention dairy products, eggs, and fish—is not only hazardous to food animals and harmful for the land but, more important to me, perilous to the health of my people. (pos. 383)

On the other hand, Joi Marie Probus' (2010) veganism is clearly based on animal liberation, and she also refers to the conflict that such a stance represents for her within the Black community:

> (…) in modern times, with our vast resources and diverse options for food and clothing, the continued use of animals is unnecessary. We simply have no need, let alone the right, to eat their flesh or wear their skin. It goes without saying that, as entertainment, their use is even more frivolous. Furthermore, we have no right to use animals as test subjects for consumer products and medical research.
>
> I am the only African American vegan I know, male or female, who chose this lifestyle for purely ethical reasons. To nonvegan African Americans, I am an enigma. After all, we are a culture for whom animal-derived foods are dietary staples. Sure, we have learned to accept the occasional Islamic brother or sister who does not eat pork, but for a Black person to shun chicken and fish, leather and wool? And for what? Animal rights? Hell, we're still working on our rights! (pos. 1314)

These examples from *Sistah Vegan* illustrate the reason why we should talk about *veganisms* instead of *veganism,* since they are "heterogeneous practices of re-existence, impossible to predefine" (González & Ávila Gaitán, 2014, p. 69), which put forth diverse alternatives to speciesism.

I also found the book *Afro-Vegan* to be a very interesting example of a performative text on veganism. Chef and M.A. in History Bryant Terry (2014) recovers Afro-diasporic food "to put its ingredients, cooking techniques, and flavor profiles into wider circulation" (p. 11), connecting gastronomy with history and memory. At the same time, the author advocates for food justice, including access to healthier "and culturally appropriate food in all communities" (p. 12). I consider Terry's work an example of "cooking as inquiry," a form of autoethnography developed by Jennifer Brady (2011) aimed at recognizing "bodies and food as sites of knowledge," engaging researcher/s as researcher-participant/s in a "reflexive, collaborative study that explores the ways in which the embodied self is performed relationally through foodmaking" (p. 321). Thus, Terry's *Afro-Vegan* presents "the breadth and richness of Afro-diasporic food by creating culinary combinations inspired by home-cooked meals, cookbooks, restaurants, websites, narrative histories, scholarly monographs, and travel" (p. 14).

The autoethnographic text of New Zealand activist and scholar Lynley Tulloch (2016) draws on Jacque Derrida, Michel Foucault, and Donna Haraway, and with narrative, short stories, and poetry, she analyzes "institutionalized forms of animal use in late-stage capitalism" and defines the figure of the "meat-eating 'cyborg' (…), central to the Western plot of ever-escalating domination of animals/nature" (p. 28). It is interesting how the author experiments with diverse performative texts to expose her experience both as an academic and an activist for animal liberation and applies Haraway's notion of "cyborg" to explain human-nonhuman relations and her own practice as a cyber-activist. In a passage of one of her autoethnographic texts, she writes:

> I enter the cybernetic world. Electricity spreads through my nerves and jolts me alive as I press the keys. At first I am slow and cautious, still in touch with the human world, enjoying the aroma of coffee.
>
> Then I encounter the meat-eating cyborg.
>
> She sends calves to slaughter and she tells me that is life. Her energy tries to dominate and colonize my body. She tells me I am stupid, unrealistic, disgusting for criticizing the farming industry. How else could I survive, she says, without farmers, without the cyborg?
>
> But I don't want to be friends with the meat-eating cyborg and I am diminished as a war wages on the borders of our existences.
>
> I format firstline indent +10format firstline indent +10m shaking as the meat-eating cyborgs rise up in waves flooding my cyber page and trying to kill my human form.
>
> But I am the cyborg too and the page is the cyborg paper and I am using cyborg technology.

I stare at the other that is me and I am ashamed. (Tulloch, 2016, pp. 33–34)

I too sought to reconstruct and explain my experience as a vegan in the context of the Argentinean hegemonic meat culture, as well as the new vision acquired through the process of transition to veganism. I structured my autoethnography as an ethnodrama, recalling those key moments of my life that brought me to veganism, integrating them with the theoretical framework of CAS (Andreatta, 2015). The following is a short passage of my ethnodrama, describing a usual situation for vegans sharing a meal with non-vegans:

The huge tray of grilled beef reaches 37-year-old Maria Marta, and she immediately passes it to the next guest.
Colleague 3: Why aren't you eating? Are you on a diet?
Colleague 4: Don't you like it?
Colleague 5: Are you a vegetarian?
37-year-old Maria Marta: Not exactly. In fact, I'm a vegan.
Awkward silence. Someone coughs. Everybody stops eating.
Colleague 5: Does that mean that you don't eat any animal food products?
37-year-old Maria Marta: That's right.
(…)
Colleague 4: Oh, dear! Well, I really respect your food choice, but personally I could never be a vegan. I love meat! My choice is definitely different to yours. *(He sticks the knife and the fork in a huge portion of meat).*
The scene freezes. A spotlight illuminates the right side of the stage. A woman (Maria Marta in the present) is standing there and speaks to the audience.
Maria Marta in the present: As a vegan within a hegemonic meat culture, I'm often asked about my way of eating, especially in social situations like this *(pointing at the frozen scene on the left).* I've found that some people are honestly interested in veganism, some just want to reassert their own position about eating animals, and others are aggressive with me, maybe because they feel somehow threatened. One way or another, my presence at a table is always the cause for some remark.
The spotlight on the left side on the stage turns off.
Richard Twine *(voice-over)*: "The vegan does not even have to purposively engage, by arguing against someone's animal consumption, to be a killjoy. Often the known presence of a vegan will be enough to trouble the prevailing happiness order [at the table] and vegans soon become aware of the repetitive scripts that omnivores call upon in such situations… [T]he table is materially and symbolically central for those reiterated performances, disruptions, inquisitions around counter-normative eating practices, around counter-hegemonic ways of valuing other animals" (2014, p. 626). (As cited in Andreatta, 2015, p. 82).

Tulloch and I offer two examples of the potential for PE to display alternative ways of life that are respectful and empathic with nonhuman animals and usually also involving concerns about ecological damage and human health (Andreatta & Camisassa, 2017). Richards (as cited in Griffin, 2014) has argued that one of the ways in which people who do not belong to the dominant culture are controlled and normalized is through their representations in texts, usually in a superficial and/or stereotyped way. PE, and particularly autoethnography, offers the advantage that vegans tell of their own experiences and worldviews with their own diverse voices. They thus enable others outside the vegan culture to have access to worldviews that challenge the mainstream about the human-nonhuman hierarchy, becoming a starting point for communities to reflect on the prevailing anthropocentrism (Andreatta, 2016).

PE is also pertinent to expose the multiple forms of exploitation and subjection that nonhumans suffer and to contribute to ending such situations. Birke (2014) points out that, "at present, we humans assume the responsibility of speaking for animals, of championing what we think are their causes" (p. 84). Hamilton and Taylor (2012) propose a multi-species ethnography that takes nonhumans into account with an active agency in the production of knowledge regarding human-animal relationships. Such a methodological approach implies deconstructing established differences between species and a clear challenge to historically silenced discourses that have relegated nonhumans "to the 'natural order' of things" (p. 49). These authors also highlight the relevance of "sensory observation and experience" (p. 49), including visual methods, which would be conducive to performative works that allow nonhuman voices to be heard, by means of, for instance, images or narrations, not in a stereotyped or satirical way, as is usual, but considering their complexity and particularities (Lámbarry, 2014). Ávila Gaitán (2017), in turn, advocates for openness to stylistic creativity, for example, to *animal-writing* (Yelin, 2013), or the exploration of the whole body's potential to generate knowledge, as well as an alliance between CAS and community proposals involving worlds in motion where the "human" turns out to be, at best, only one of its components.

Griffin (2014) comments that "static and moving images, illustrating the horrors of animal exploitation" (p. 123) have long been used for the animal advocacy movement. For instance, the illustrations of Sue Coe (as cited in Griffin, 2014) and the photographs of Jo-Anne McArthur (as cited in Griffin, 2014) are effective ways to explore and expose animal suffering and exploitation. In Argentina, there is remarkable work by activists such as the art movement *Voicot* (2016), which fights for animal liberation by using photography and other artistic forms to expose animal abuse in Argentinean factory farms, as well as organizing virtual seminars with Ibero-American activists/scholars, and graphic artist Airam (n.d.), whose powerful illustrations display key meaningful connections between humans, nonhumans, and the Earth.

Visual methods involving photographs and film provide important support for exposing oppression, abuse, and exploitation of nonhuman animals. Presented in a conventional way, for example, as a traditional scientific essay, such issues may not give rise to the same level of impact and empathy as images can (Andreatta, 2016). Griffin (2014) argues that "informed by academic research and practice," the documentary film "has been a valuable tool within the animal advocacy movement" (p. 121), but also warns that "images can be interpreted in multiple ways; not always those intended by the creator" (p. 124). Furthermore, Messina (2018) alerts us to the bad science behind some of these visual products, in which passion for animal liberation and good intentions combined with, for instance, "poor understanding of nutrition science and research" (para. 8), could end up having the opposite effect to that which they seek. Indeed, exaggeration and misinformation about veganism in relation to health and disease can, in the long term, make people "reinforce any negative view they may already have of vegans" (par. 32). PE must encompass esthetic merit as well as scientific accuracy if the goal is to make a significant contribution to animal liberation.

A Few Final Thoughts

The link between animal exploitation, activism and academic research is a key element of CAS (Taylor & Twine, 2014), and PE opens a range of possibilities to address such issues and their interconnection, promoting high levels of empathy and understanding that other strategies of inquiry hardly provide. By avoiding academic language, PE entails the possibility of progressively engaging members of different communities in the fight for animal liberation, not only to expose situations of abuse and exploitation, but also favoring reflection on the power structures that underpin this state of affairs. Moreover, PE is a useful tool to show how veganism can take different features in different contexts, according to local and multicultural perspectives, thus leading to multiple ways of achieving total liberation. All of us working in the field of CAS should consider the application of PE, in view of its great potential for transcending the boundaries of academia and contributing to social change for the benefit of humans, nonhumans, and the Earth.

References

Airam (n.d.). Activismo ilustrado [Illustrated activism]. Retrieved from https://activismoilustrado.com/category/ilustraciones/

Alexander, B. K. (2005). Performance ethnography: The reenacting and incitation of culture. In N. K. Denzin, & Y. S. Lincoln (Eds.), *The SAGE handbook of qualitative research* (3rd ed., pp. 411–441). Thousand Oaks, CA: Sage Publications.

Andreatta M. M. (2015). Being a Vegan. A performative autoethnography. *Cultural Studies Critical Methodologies, 15*(6), 477–486.

Andreatta M. M. (2016). Veganismo, etnografía performativa y estudios críticos animales [Veganism, performance Ethnography and critical animal studies]. *Revista Latinoamericana de Estudios Críticos Animales, II*(II), 35-52.

Andreatta, M. M. (2017). ¿Veganos en riesgo? Un análisis de los cuestionamientos habituales a la calidad nutricional de la alimentación vegana [Vegans at risk? An analysis of usual criticisms of vegan diet]. In A. Navarro, & A. G. González (Eds.), *Es tiempo de coexistir: perspectivas, debates y otras provocaciones en torno a los animales no humanos* (pp. 50-73). Alejandro Korn: Editorial Latinoamericana Especializada en Estudios Críticos Animales. Retrieved from https://goo.gl/CPfGrJ

Andreatta, M. M., & Camisassa, C. M. (2107). Vegetarianos en Córdoba: Un análisis cualitativo de prácticas y motivaciones [Vegetarians in Cordoba: A qualitative analysis of practices and motivations]. *Revista de Ciencia y Técnica de la Universidad Empresarial Siglo 21, 10*(2), 1-21.

Andreatta, M. M., & Martínez, A. (2017). Alimentación cotidiana y normas de género: Un etnodrama [Food in everyday life and gender norms: An ethnodrama]. *Aposta. Revista de Ciencias Sociales, 73*, 9-29.

Andreatta M. M., Pezzetta S., & Rincón Higuera E. (2017). Presentación [Introduction]. In M. M. Andreatta, S. Pezzetta, & E. Rincón Higuera (Eds.), *Crítica y animalidad: cuando el Otro aúlla* (pp. 7-8). Alejandro Korn: Editorial Latinoamericana Especializada en Estudios Críticos Animales. Retrieved from https://goo.gl/H13r3a.

Ávila Gaitán, I. D. (2017). El Instituto Latinoamericano de Estudios Críticos Animales como Proyecto Decolonial [The Latin-American Institute for Critical Animal Studies as a decolonial project]. *Tabula Rasa, 27*, 339-351.

Best, S. (2009). Rise of critical animal studies: Putting theory into action and animal liberation into higher education. *Journal for Critical Animal Studies, VII*(1), 9-52.

Best, S., Nocella, A. J., Kahn, R., Gigliotti, C., & Kemmerer, L. (2007). Introducing critical animal studies. *Journal for Critical Animal Studies, 5*(1), 4-5.

Birke, L. (2014). Listening to voices. On the pleasures and problems of studying human-animal relationships. In R. Twine, & N. Taylor (Eds.), *The rise of critical animal studies: From the margins to the center* (pp. 71-87). London: Routledge.

Brady, J. (2011). Cooking as inquiry: A method to stir up prevailing ways of knowing food, body, and identity. *International Journal of Qualitative Methods, 10*(4), 321-334.

Denzin, N. K. (2003). Performing [auto]ethnography politically. *Review of Education, Pedagogy, and Cultural Studies, 25*, 257-278. doi: 10.1080/10714410390225894

Denzin, N. K. (2013). *Performance ethnography. Critical pedagogy and the politics of culture.* Thousand Oaks, CA: Sage Publications.

Denzin, N. K. (2014). *Interpretive autoethnography.* Thousand Oaks, CA: Sage Publications.

Denzin, N. K., & Lincoln, Y. S. (2005). Introduction: The discipline and practice of qualitative research. In N. K. Denzin, & Y. S. Lincoln (Eds.), *The SAGE handbook of qualitative research* (3rd ed., pp. 1-32). Thousand Oaks, CA: Sage Publications.

Ellis, C., Adams, T. E., & Bochner, A. P. (2010). Autoethnography: An overview. *Forum Qualitative Sozialforschung / Forum: Qualitative Social Research, 12*(1), Art. 10, [40 paragraphs]. Retrieved from http://nbn-resolving.de/urn:nbn:de:0114-fqs1101108

Given, L. M. (2008). Performance ethnography. In L. M. Given (Ed.), *The SAGE encyclopedia of qualitative research* (pp. 608-612). Thousand Oaks, CA: Sage Publications.

González, A.G. (2016). Una lectura deconstructiva del régimen carnofalogocéntrico. Hacia una ética animal de la diferencia [A deconstructive Reading of the carnophallogocentric regime. Towards an animal ethics of difference]. *Daimon. Revista Internacional de Filosofía, 69*, 125-139. Retrieved from http://dx.doi.org/10.6018/daimon/221121

González, A. G., & Ávila Gaitán, I. D. (2014). Resistencia animal: ética, perspectivismo y políticas de subversión [Animal resistance: ethics, perspectivism and policies of subversion]. *Revista Latinoamericana de Estudios Críticos Animales, I*(I), 31-72.

Griffin, N. S. (2014). Doing critical animal studies differently: Reflexivity and intersectionality in practice. In R. Twine, & N. Taylor (Eds.), *The rise of critical animal studies: From the margins to the center* (pp. 111-136). London: Routledge.

Hamilton, L., & Taylor, N. (2012). Ethnography in evolution: Adapting to the animal "other" in organizations. *Journal of Organizational Ethnography, 1*(1), 43-51.

Harper, A. B. (2010). *Sistah Vegan* (English Edition). New York: Lantern Books. Retrieved from Amazon.com

Holman Jones, S., Adams, T. E. & Ellis, C. (2013). Introduction: Coming to know autoethnography as more than a method. In S. Holman Jones, T. E. Adams, & C. Ellis (Eds.), *Handbook of autoethnography* (pp. 17-48). Walnut Creek, CA: Left Coast Press.

Lámbarry, A. (2014). El animal se rebela. La voz animal en la novela *El portero* de Reinaldo Arenas y el cuento *Perro (2)* de Griselda Gambaro [Animal rebellion. The animal voice in the novel *The Janitor* by Reinaldo Arenas and in the short story *Dog (2)* by Griselda Gambaro]. *Revista Latinoamericana de Estudios Críticos Animales, I*(II), 126-144.

Loyd-Paige, M. R. (2010). Thinking and eating at the same time. Reflections of a Sistah Vegan. In A. B. Harper (Ed.), *Sistah Vegan* (English Edition). New York: Lantern Books. Retrieved from Amazon.com

Messina, V. (2018, March). A Vegan Dietitian Reviews "What the Health". *Vegan.com*. Retrieved from https://www.vegan.com/posts/vegan-dietitian-review-what-the-health/

Navarro, A. (2016). *Representaciones e identidades del discurso especista: el caso de la carne vacuna y sus derivados en la Argentina (2000-2012)* [Representations and identities in speciesist discourse: The case of beef and its derivatives in Argentina (200-2012)] (Doctoral thesis, National University of La Plata, La Plata, Argentina). Retrieved from http://sedici.unlp.edu.ar/handle/10915/52068

Pezzetta, S. (2018). Derechos fundamentales para los demás animales. Especismo, igualdad y justicia interespecies [Fundamental rights for other animals. Speciesism, equality and interspecies justice.]. *Lecciones y Ensayos, 100*, 69-104.

Probus, J. M. (2010). Young, black, and vegan. In A. B. Harper (Ed.), *Sistah vegan* (English Edition). New York: Lantern Books. Retrieved from Amazon.com

Saldaña, J. (1999). Playwriting with data: Ethnographic performance texts. *Youth Theatre Journal, 13*(1), 60-71.

Taylor, N., & Twine, R. (2014). Introduction: Locating the "critical" in Critical Animal Studies. In R. Twine, & N. Taylor (Eds.), *The rise of critical animal studies: From the margins to the center* (pp. 1-15). London: Routledge.

Terry, B. (2014). *Afro-vegan. farm-fresh African, Caribbean, and southern flavors remixed.* New York: Ten Speed Press.

Tulloch, L. (2016). An auto-ethnography of vegan praxis and encounters with the meat-eating cyborg. *Review of Contemporary Philosophy, 15*, 28–45.

Twine, R. (2014). Vegan killjoys at the table—Contesting happiness and negotiating relationships with food practices. *Societies, 4*, 623-639.

Voicot (2016). Acciones [Actions]. Retrieved from https://www.voicot.com/home

Yarbrough, A. (2010). Book review: Sistah vegan. *Journal for Critical Animal Studies, VIII*(3), 66-69.

Yelin, J. (2013). Para una teoría literaria posthumanista. La crítica en la trama de debates sobre la cuestión animal [For a posthumanist literary theory. Criticism in the frame of debates on the animal issue]. *E-misférica, 10*(1), 1-9.

3. *Becoming Vegan in Slovenia: Some Reflections on Theory and Activism*

Anja Radaljac and Aljaž Krivec

The article was mostly written in the year 2018. While there were some further developments regarding veganism, animal rights theory and animal rights activism, and some of the facts are outdated, the main issues addressed in the article and the general depiction still stand.

Becoming Vegan in Slovenia: The Beginning

At the end of February 2015, in an effort to do everything we personally could, to stop the exploitation of non-human animals, we became vegan. Before going vegan, we were vegetarians—Anja had been a vegetarian 'on and off' since elementary school, and Aljaž became a vegetarian when we started helping stray cats in Ljubljana (with food and shelter). It no longer made sense that we were helping cats, yet continued to eat the bodies of other animals. We departed from our vegetarian position to become vegan when we were presented with two incontrovertible facts, namely (1) that calves in the milk industry are taken away from their mothers and raised for slaughter and; (2) that all the male chickens are killed in the egg industry. Becoming aware about those two dreadful practices, and how—even as vegetarians—we were still complicit in the brutal and immoral treatment in the lives of other beings, made all the difference, and pushed us to embrace veganism.

Wanting to better understand and articulate our emerging vegan praxis, we searched for any information we could. We hoped to learn more about 'animal liberation', 'carnism' and 'speciesism', as well as finding out more about what other types of animal rights activism exist. Of the three concepts mentioned "speciesism" was the most crucial for us. It called us to really think critically about how this dominant speciesist ideology held in society had been 'internalised' in our own values to that point—not only in always privileging the experiences of fellow human being over non-human animals, but also in our consistencies regarding our treatment across different animal species. For most of our lives we had unquestioningly accepted the dominant cultural form of fragmentation and dissociation we had been exposed to; one where 'caring' for the lives of certain animals (e.g. cats, dogs), is as strongly encouraged as the indifference is to the violence that other animals (e.g. cows, pigs) experience. From there on it was much easier to understand how speciesism and carnism form and animate the problematic intersections with other forms of oppressions. Nevertheless, it remains a 'truth' that it is not always—and not for everyone—easy to grasp. The propaganda that normalizes speciesism, and effectively discourages people in our society from "connecting" the dots is so powerful. 'Speciesism' is certainly not a well known form of oppression in Slovenia, let alone the idea that carnism is a prevalent ideology. There is no critical awareness about how both combine to govern our dominant relationships toward non-human animals (at least in the area of food industry). Similarly, we lack the ability to see how these justify our treatment of animals through the belief that eating meat is natural, normal, necessary, and (sometimes) nice. We hope that our reflections and our experiences on becoming vegan will encourage others to raise their own consciousness, make these connections, and offer some support and solidarity on the journey that they may take in doing so.

Of course, there was a lot of educational material on the internet, particularly via YouTube. We would certainly highly recommend the YouTube channel *Bite size Vegan*[1]; the film *Live and Let Live* (2013)[2] and key lectures by animal rights scholars such as Steve Best[3] or pattrice jones[4]. Online lectures were some of the most important sources of information for us. However, crucially, we didn't find anything about the topics that came from local sources. The main exception was the website for The *Slovenian Vegan*

1 *BiteSizeVegan* is available at https://www.youtube.com/channel/UCluiFIVPKluGkB8TFUVgX5w. Even though Emily Moran Barwick stopped producing new video-material (until further notice), the channel is still an amazing source of veganism/animal rights related information.

2 *Live and Let Live* is available at https://vimeo.com/ondemand/liveandletlive

3 One of the most interesting lectures by Steve Best, where he explains the idea of total liberation, can be viewed here: https://www.youtube.com/watch?v=Pr7Ax_p7ocw

4 A brilliant lecture by pattrice jones, one that certainly takes animal liberation movement one step further, can be found under the title *What's wrong with "rights"? Pattrice Jones at IARC 2013 Luxembourg* (https://www.youtube.com/watch?v=kO97L7hxraY).

Society[5]: which we stumbled upon after an "instinctive" internet search, as you can probably imagine. However, disappointingly, this site offered just a few pages of very basic information about animal-rights, exploitation and the horrors of factory farming. Its content was far more 'consumer based', highlighting practical 'lifestyle' aspects, such as are healthy eating, recipes, shopping guides, restaurant lists and so on. Elsewhere, we found a group called "Za živali!"[6] (a name which we can roughly translate as "For The Animals!"), which offered far more animal-rights based theory and emphasis. It was here where we first came in touch with Gary Francione's work and consequently their abolitionist theory. Overall, despite investing a lot of time and energy, unearthing other *local* academic animal studies papers and books was futile. Consequently, and problematically we were forced to rely on the non-local (mostly British and North American) sources, many of which spoke to contexts and settings that had very little to do with the everyday contexts we were embedded and engaging in.

Early Reflections

We felt that the first part of our mission: to be able to gain deeper knowledge, insights and understanding of animal rights and vegan praxis didn't go well, so we proceeded according to our second instinct: find a community of supportive, like-minded people. In addition to embracing a vegan diet, our commitment to vegan praxis included that we should participate in form(s) of activism and find a way for a political participation in the animal rights community. Therefore we really wanted to find some activist groups in our own country. This was important to us as we believe that veganism should be, first and foremost, a political movement. If we don't *act* on our beliefs and knowledge, and fail to engage with activists struggling for justice and social change, nonhuman animals will continue to be exploited. It is perfectly clear to us that activists must be prepared to 'demand the impossible': we must overthrow all the oppressive structures and for that the dominant economic and political system must change as well.

However, our attempts to find and express solidarity with like-minded vegan activists fell short. We managed to find a few local Facebook groups, but usually there wasn't much going on, at least not in the fields of either activism

5 Their homepage can be found at http://www.vegan.si/ (mostly in Slovene, but some pages are in English).

6 Their homepage can be found at http://www.zazivali.org/ (mostly in Slovene, the only exception being the section "About us").

and/or theory. The 'pinnacle' was (and still is, unfortunately) a Facebook group called *Vegetarijanci, vegani, presnojedci* ("*Vegetarians, Vegans and Raw foodists*")[7]. A lot of people in this online group were (and are) being "vegan" primarily for personal gain, particularly the benefits for their health. Indeed many group members posted arguments condemning animal rights activism as "aggressive", and that "everyone has their own choice on what to eat". Yes, they repeatedly used the term "*what*"; neglecting to understand that animals are not *things* but rather *persons*. We didn't find many activist groups; at that moment we already knew about the aforementioned "Slovenian Vegan Society" and some small-time enthusiasts who mostly organized a bunch of vegan brunches, dinners, picnics and alike. There were, of course, exceptions to the rule, but since there weren't many, their work was not as visible or they may have even been forgotten. Needless to say, when we became vegans almost five years ago, we didn't feel animal rights theory and/or activism were as visible (and engaged) as they should be in Slovenia. There weren't many written or filmed materials about animal rights; we didn't find any local animal rights blogs or vlogs; there was scarce academic work on those subjects and scarce vegan activism groups that would explicitly promote and champion animal rights.

While our experiences were underwhelming on a personal level, more importantly perhaps, particularly in terms of raising consciousness at a public level, debates around veganism and vegan praxis in the mainstream media or in politics was almost entirely absent. One of our country former presidents (Janez Drnovšek) went vegan[8] a few years before the end of his career. This was one of the few exceptions of veganism encroaching onto the Slovenian political landscape. Though his public persona was structured around new-age ideals, one could argue persuasively that there was some ethical regard to it nonetheless. In our media veganism, if mentioned, was reduced to a health-oriented consumerist 'lifestyle'; a trendy plant-based diet promoted either by new-age communities or across so-called "women's magazines"'.

Given the apparent absence of ongoing discussion of animal rights activism/theory in Slovenia, both in the activist communities and in mainstream political discourse it really felt like we were one of the very few looking to attempt to think seriously about these topics. Happily, though there were

7 Link to the Facebook group: https://www.facebook.com/groups/102831523178809/

8 An interesting interview with Drnovšek regarding this question was done by the Croatian animal rights group Prijatelji životinja: http://www.prijatelji-zivotinja.hr/index.en.php?id=565 (in English)

some positive examples that gave us cause for hope and a renewed sense of belief came to light. These included:

- Finding out about a few local groups dealing with animal rights (though some of them even ceased to exist before we went vegan), and we did get to meet a few like-minded people.
- Stumbling upon a free magazine about animal rights called *Osvoboditev živali* (Animal Liberation). *Osvoboditev živali* was first published in 2004.
- Through different (mostly personal) sources we educated ourselves about ALF-like actions which were occuring in the 90's.
- Elswehere we heard about a re-publication of oldest Slovenian vegetarian cookbook—published in 1983—called *101 zelenjavni jedilnik* (roughly translated as *101 plant-based dishes*).
- We came across the information about first vegetarian restaurant in the capital Ljubljana established in 1932 (and a similar one in the holiday town of Bled, which was established around that time or even before), which made us realize that veg(etari)anism has a certain history in Slovenia. When we went vegan there were only two or three vegan restaurants in Ljubljana, now there are many more (10 or so) and some of them are present in other cities of Slovenia and were not four or five years ago.
- We found some books and articles on eco-criticism (for example: *Ekokritika in literarne upodobitve narave*, which can be roughly translated as *Ecocriticism and literary depictions of nature* by Jožica Čeh Steger, on animal-rights from (more or less) Marxist perspective (for example: an essay *Este animal que soy* by Miklavž Komelj). We stumbled across the translation of two children books by Ruby Roth, regarding the animal rights and a Slovenian translation of the book *Eat Like You Care* (Gary L. Francione and Anna Charlton).
- We discovered Slovenian poet Jure Detela (1951–1992). He is known both for his lucid (and to some extent revolutionary on a global scale) approach to animal rights theory and activism, and personally engaging in direct action by freeing animals from the Ljubljana Zoo.

The examples we've listed in these bullet points were crucial for evoking at least two feelings in us: (a) that struggle for animal liberation is something that was happening (long) before contemporary groups and activists even existed and; (b) no matter what we do or don't do, someone is fighting for this cause one way or another. We were not alone!

Moving Forward: Rethinking the Correlation(s) between Theory and Activism

The themes and experiences that we've touched upon so far concern problems of animal rights activism/theory that are relevant globally, and not just limited to Slovenia. For example the struggle to question and address animal rights seriously whether in the mainstream society, or in the corridors of economic and political power, are universal. The reasons for this are also common. The public don't want to know about it, because it makes them think about the (hidden) violence that other animals experience, and also question their ill-gained privileges built on speciesism and anthropocentrism. Capitalist companies and industry who profit from the ongoing (ab)use of non-human animals don't like it because it threatens to negatively affect the profits they make; politicians don't like it (since veganism is unpopular with voters); the media, who benefit financially from advertisements designed to promote the meat and dairy industry, don't like it either. Given this powerful interplay between willful public ignorance and the enormous power of the animal use industries, the consequences are expected: a lot of what animal rights activists say is ridiculed, laughed at, and dismissed by those with powerful vested interests in maintaining the exploitation of other animals. While we, as animal rights activists, feel that this is an appalling state of affairs, it is a (harsh) reflection of the society we live in. Therefore, it has to be dealt with. What the chapter will now explore are ways in which we can strengthen our activism, and the power of the vegan community more generally. Here, one of the main areas that needs addressing, and re-thinking, is the correlation between activism and theory.

In our experiences where activism was present, for example in vegan workshops, cooking workshops, animal rights art performances, there was no critique that framed this activism in the perspective of the wider society we live in. How can this kind of local activism spark changes beyond the immediate community in ways that challenge and overcome speciesist values "out there"? Conversely, where animal rights theory and the question of inter-species justice was discussed (for example at animal studies conferences, and through articles, and lectures) it was too often abstracted from reality. There seemed little attempt or appetite to find its activist potential and implement it.

Furthermore, there lies another problem: remember how we felt we're one of the few people dealing with animal rights at all? While this may had been true in the aspect of some smaller communities we belong(ed) to, it wasn't really the case regarding the whole picture. It is a feeling implemented by the society we live in, and that feeling of isolation and fragmentation can be very damaging for one's struggles in the field of activism. And it is exactly this feeling that the dominant majority wants to reproduce: by making people who question their worldview believing that they are the ones who are extreme, weird, unwanted and irrational. While it's common sense that a strong community, based on solidarity is much needed for this feeling to fade, we also believe that there is a certain amount of self-isolation present. This can lead to individuals once again staging actions that have already been witnessed; actions that and may have proved ineffective. counter-productive and/or being coopted by others in problematic ways. These negative scenario(s) may have been avoided by activists engaging more closely with theory, and using this insight as a way of strengthening their own ability to understand and articulate their (moral) positions re. animal rights and veganism. For example, after reading *Rain Without Thunder* by Gary L. Francione it is much harder to advocate actions that focus on the animal welfare. After finding out about occasions on which neo-nazi groups tried to hijack animal rights movement (see Foggo, 2000), it becomes much clearer that one's movement should have a strict and wide political stance regarding all areas of politics and not only animal rights[9]. Or, for example, after reading about the history of different animal organizations, one should become more aware about one's own positions, since a lot of organizations started with clear intentions advocating animal liberation, but after years or even decades compromised their positions to even support welfare actions taken by multinational companies. A lot of actions by individuals or groups that deal with animal rights clearly don't take this kind of context in the account. In addition, it is also important to critically reflect on the question of "activism" to gauge the effectiveness and impacts of tactics and strategies. What forms of activisms work—how can you demonstrate and evidence their effectiveness. Without knowledge, without proper assessment of (wrong)doings of activism, it is possible that we are doing something counter-productive, when we believe we are doing the best we can to help animals.

Self-isolation, as we perceive it, can be understood as a very wide process and both feeling of being one of the few (who do something) and invisibility of struggles that already exist are part of it. We believe that such feeling stems from the general feeling that is present in the society. A percentage of vegans is small (more or less everywhere), a percentage of public figures (politicians, media stars, widely known intellectuals...) or so to say, "outed animal rights activists" is even smaller. This, arguably, is why the animal rights struggle

9 Sadly, we've had an experience with exactly this kind of problem in our local community (even though the issue was and still is, present on an international scale).

seems like a small, even personal thing and consequently occupies an extreme position on the margins of mainstream society in which you are more or less alone. And this feeling of isolation grows even more, not least when comparing the size of the animal rights movement to the number of animals being used, tortured and murdered every day.

So why did it take us some time to find out about what was already happening regarding animal rights? Because the topic of animal rights wasn't—and this is something that is, thankfully, changing—as all-embracing and inter-connected as it should have been. At one end, the resident vegan community dealt exclusively with just 'food choices'. At the other extreme moral debates around vegan praxis led to self-absorbed theoretical posturing, promoted through academic papers without any real value for activism in practice. While we do believe in 'high-quality' theory, there was too much theory that was uncoupled from 'the real world', allowing no possibility to influence the public consciousness around animal rights, and ultimately bring about a much needed post-speciesist paradigmatic shift.

While the food may have been good and the theory may have been good also (and they have both been important contributions in their own right) this disconnect between the two was profoundly weakening and limited. Any exclusive focusing on veganism as a food choice gave a feeling of vegan praxis being a personal choice without any ethical connotations to it. So, on one hand there was a notion that animal rights don't actually concern you (directly, personally), and on the other hand there was a process of localizing the animal liberation idea which made it seem like it is something not actually present in everyday life, if you even had a chance to hear about it.

The critical position we held is that the notion of animal rights is not *present* enough in the public consciousness, and that is its fundamental weakness. There were rarely interviews or articles in mass media where the general public could become acquainted with concepts of animal rights, speciesism or carnism. "Food-based activism" on the other hand, had successfully repackaged veganism as something belonging to the private sphere. This was something we learned when we talked with people at the open-to-all lectures we gave about speciesism in public libraries. Veganism was perceived as a type of a diet: indeed many never heard of speciesism. But, as it turned out, a lot of people knew the difference between vegetarianism and veganism. Information about veganism did, in fact, already found their way into the broader society before that, they were just not the *right* information. So—there it was. Veganism was known—but not as what it is; it was readily appropriated as sort of a diet.

We believe that vegans who promote vegan food, often do that with best intentions. This is an important distinction to be made with the appropriation of vegan foods by capitalist industries seeking to further their own profit margins. It is not the intention of everyday vegans to promote veganism as a vain, hip lifestyle for rich people. But, perhaps their lack of knowledge about animal rights, animal studies, political studies and history of other political movements, makes them think they are doing something *good*, when, in fact, they are often making the moral question of our treatment of non-human animals invisible once again. Social movements that are acquainted with history and development of other—more or less successful—social movements, do tend to have a better sense of how their actions affect society and what kind of consequences are those actions going to have. A fine example regarding the animal rights movement is Direct Action Everywhere (DxE). Crucially, DxE looked at the development of other social, political movements that did achieve at least some of their goals and tried to adapt their approaches in a way that they would align with their own. It is welcoming to note that DxE has recently become active in Slovenia too. But while this situation was doing nothing for the non-human animals and their rights (at least not yet and not on their own), it did eventually help to open the mass media to the question of healthiness of "veganism" (the term was used as a synonym for plant-based diet). And one way or another: it is crucial to understand that plant-based diet can be healthy (or even healthier), since this means there is absolutely no barrier on our way to adopt it in everyday life.

Making Visible Animal Rights: Mainstream(ing) Debates in Slovenia

In 2011, there was a case of a malnourished baby, who died because their parents didn't want for them to get antibiotics for pneumonia. The problem was that the parents were, by coincidence, consuming plant-based food. Suddenly every media reported that the baby died because they were "vegan". There was, for example, an article in *Slovenske novice* (*Slovenian news*), bestselling Slovenian newspaper, famous for its bombastic titles that published an article titled *Vegana dojenčico stradala do smrti?* (*Did vegans starved their baby to death?*)[10] under the section titled Skrajnosti (Extremisms). At least three other articles mentioned "veganism" in the title, while simultaneously claiming that problems may not have been linked with plant-based diet itself[11].

10 Accessible via: https://www.slovenskenovice.si/crni-scenarij/doma/vegana-dojencico-stradala-do-smrti [last accessed 09.05.2019].

11 Accessible via: https://www.dnevnik.si/1042465103, https://www.rtvslo.si/crna-kronika/starsi-za-leto-in-osem-mesecev-v-zapor-zaradi-smrti-otroka/319778 and https://www.dnevnik.si/1042594087 [last accessed 09.05.2019].

But veganism was mentioned nevertheless and comment sections along with forums, were full of anti-vegan propaganda. Consequently, after a streak of different articles and columns "veganism" gained a very bad reputation; our pediatrics were preaching to the public that plant-based diet cannot possibly be healthy for children and that raising a child on a vegan diet could be considered child abuse (and they still do that, but granted: with a little bit of reservation). This became a very popular argument against veganism; and at this point transspecies ethics or even ecology were rarely mentioned. Veganism was, if we exaggerate a bit, seen as semi-dangerous hip lifestyle that didn't have any political implications.

Yet, it was from this unhappy context that a long-anticipated public dialogue finally happened. A few vegan nutritionists (such as independent scholar, researching scientific literature about plant-based diet, Marko Čenčur, who frequently appears in the media) raised public awareness about a number of relevant contemporary scientific studies. These studies had endorsed nutritional guidelines that argued that plant-based diets are not, in fact, "dangerous", but can be, on the contrary, healthy and can even protect us against some of the most common diseases in Western cultures. As a relevant side issue, as well as form of challenging popular stereotypes about 'unhealthy' vegans, this is an excellent example of how science can be used to inform activism. Imagine if every activist who wanted to show how delicious vegan recipes are to a skeptical public were able to confidently incorporate scientific findings to combat widely held myths about nutritional benefits. But—and we believe this is crucial—when the aspect of health was highlighted, this stirred up debate, which gathered momentum, and led to public dialogue. Suddenly quality spaces were opened up to address the reasons for veganism—and of course to re-represent it as a political movement. First there were a few journalists, columnists and bloggers (for example: Irena Štaudohar and Maja Prijatelj-Videmšek, who were both writing for the main Slovenian newspaper, *Delo*), who set the record straight as far as the ecology goes: after the health debate this was more or less the next "hot topic".

Something became clear at this time—if not before—that promoting vegan as "food activism" had hit a dead end. Though in Slovenia it did successfully lead to a broader political movement for animal rights, in other words much more in keeping with a meaningful vegan praxis. But still the whole "vegan praxis scene" in the mainstream consisted only of few people. These were individuals mostly working as academics, university professors, artists or journalists and critics, all of them semi-working as activists as well, to address those questions in the public sphere and, also, fight in realm of activism.

Individually and collectively their work moved the debate further from the 'health' benefits, and closer to the 'political' question of morality and ethics. In unprecedented examples of public discourse focused on ethical aspects of veganism, it was clear that the majority of people, while accepting the environmental benefits of veganism, were exceptionally hostile when asked to recognize ethical obligations towards non-human animals. Yet the energy and appetite for the debates were there, it didn't burn out and fade away. Around that time philosopher from University of Koper, dr. Tomaž Grušovnik, published a theoretical book about animal ethics and transspecies hospitality (Tomaž Grušovnik: *Etika živali, O čezvrstni gostoljubnosti*, publishing house Založba Univerza na Primorskem, Univerzitetna založba Annales, 2017) published at a similar time frame as an essayistic novel that one of us had written (Anja Radaljac: *Puščava, klet, katakombe*, publishing house Litera, collection Nova znamenja, 2016).

Recent Years: Public Debates and Speciesist Responses to Animal Rights in Slovenia

The last few years have in many ways witnessed the high point of intellectual public debate about animal rights in Slovenia, mirroring trends apparent elsewhere in the world. There were numerous mainstream interviews, lectures, debates and critiques that took place in this period. The public were, generally speaking, responsive, but it still seems that this was (and still is) the topic where we stumbled on one of the neuralgic points of our society. Debates often descended when respondents and attendees tried to publicly shame us (animal rights activists). We have been called "fascist" for advocating for animal rights, namely a right to live freely! We also underestimated just how little if any understanding of speciesism and its intertwinement with other oppressions 'public' individuals had. There was a huge paradigm gap: our opponents were (unknowingly) arguing from an anthropocentric point of view and our anti-speciesist position was not exactly warmly welcomed. This reaction was, of course expected, because at a very serious level it challenged their core beliefs about themselves, their ethics, and their relationships with others (or even The Other), about which they never even thought about before in a similar sense. So, while the public sphere was now open for discussion—a fantastic opportunity to learn and evolve—only a few number of activists for animal rights, were capable of articulating and defending the theories that underpin the moral arguments that for animal rights, and an end to speciesism and anthropocentric thinking.

Regrettably, though more groups—including the Cube of Truth (Anonymous for the Voiceless)—have held workshops and lectures, their presence in Slovenia only occurred later, in the first few months of 2018. The initial public debate happened mostly via social networks and two or three articles in specialized media dealing with questions of arts and culture). On reflection this didn't nearly advance the case for animal rights as it could have done. We surely did our best to present our arguments and build logically consistent 'defense', but it seemed that the question of animal rights was too much of a novelty in our environment (at least this part of environment, namely field of arts and culture), that we were not really heard. Consequently, the debate ended up being messy and destructive; resulting in a lot of comments by non-vegans, proudly telling one to another how they don't care (to put it politely). Around the same time we even had the dubious pleasure to witness two book publications about the traditional slaughtering of pigs at home (called *koline*) with the help of ones family and friends. For those involved this is celebrated as a very happy event, indeed—as our *cultural tradition* which 'should be preserved without a question' as their author proposed (the books in questions are titled *Koline* and *Ni ga tiča čez prašiča!* both written by Dr. Janez Bogataj and published in 2017).

Embracing Intersectionality

It is important to contextualize this debate around animal rights in the context of broader changes in global politics and social justice movements. It took place at roughly the same time as renewed hostile discourses—anti-immigration, racist, nationalistic, homophobic, queerphobic and chauvinistic—started to spread in Slovenia (and elsewhere). In a surprisingly short time the conservative, or rather contemporary type of the right wing part of the public actually took up its own kind of an "intersectional approach" by linking ostensibly different activist groups together. The common thread between this groups was the mainstream opposition they invoked. The public didn't oppose just "animal rights activists"; they were opposed to "lesbian-feminist-pro-immigrant-liberal-vegans" that were/are set to "ruin their culture" (namely culture defined by patriarchal and/or nationalist structure). They were also opposed to "immigrants", people with different cultural backgrounds who are coming (and in most cases fleeing) to different European countries including Slovenia. We think that the question of animal rights did in a way resonate with the public as sort of a movement that should include a lot of other social justice political movements. In this aspect the debate did cut deep and showed that general public does perceive the fight for animal rights similarly to fight against anti-immigration, chauvinist, patriarchal, and queerphobia sentiments, but it also showed how widespread are hate and aggression in our society.

Alas, our feminist, queer and pro-immigration movements didn't necessarily see things the same way: movements that *should* protect the rights of all social groups and stand against oppression, like the feminist movement, didn't necessarily rethink their views on the question of animals. There was (almost) as much shaming from liberal, feminist, queer or pro-migration groups than from right wing conservatives. It was very clear that this topic—of intersectionality and solidarity—was underrepresented in a public sphere, but also in the academia and other social justice movement circles as well.

Everything mentioned in last two paragraphs can be evidenced by taking a better look at some of the local mainstream media. Four or five years ago content on veganism or animal rights from the vegan standpoint wasn't really present (as we've already mentioned). Only gradually were articles about veganism being published. Most of these could be found in more or less liberal media such as *Delo* or *Večer* or aforementioned "health" and "women's" magazines. Such media is likable by the public, since it is not radical and it usually contains mild (or none) criticism of, for example, capitalism. Veganism was represented as something positive, something healthy, ecological and ethical, but not as something urgent or something we should all follow. Or, to put it this way, it was represented as something 'nice' but not something 'serious'. Another extreme was/is right-wing or even far-right media, local examples of such are *Reporter* (classic right-wing media), *Demokracija* (a bit further to the right, linked with Catholicism), *Nova24* (infamous local TV and internet media, linked with international far-right movements and politics such as Orbán's media conglomerates, basing their content on attacking liberal politics, socialism in ex-Yugoslavia and other socialist countries, conspiracy theories, anti-immigrant politics and so on, also linked with the most popular local political party SDS, sympathizing with political figures such as Bolsonaro, Trump, Le Pen, Salvini...). Some of those, especially *Nova24*, started publishing articles on veganism, however all of their content was focused on veganism being a 'stupid', unhealthy, bizarre and 'snowflake' lifestyle choice, without any real political logic behind it. The pinnacle are probably articles directly attacking local politicians or public personas promoting veganism and branding them as totalitarians who try to impose 'what to eat'. Strangely (or not) a right-wing media *Družina*, linked with Catholic Church did not give much attention to veganism, but when it did it represented it as something more or less positive because of its ethical component.

But what was happening with far-left media? For starters we don't really have any far-left media. The magazine *Mladina* or the radio station *Radio Študent*, which sometimes do have far-left content (especially the latter), didn't put much emphasis on question of veganism let alone intersectionality. *Mladina* did publish some articles about veganism from the standpoint of animal rights, and it did put it in the context of left-wing politics. In this way it wasn't entirely against that notion, but later on also published dubious interviews with people claiming that veganism isn't even possible on a grand scale. Disappointingly *Radio Študent* didn't address that question either properly or fully. Far-left movements that don't necessarily possess any media are, on the other hand, more or less on the same page with far-right media, seeing veganism as a personal and wrong-headed lifestyle choice without any real political power or significance (of course there are exceptions to the rule, usually in the communities of anarchists). Of course there are also examples of alternative media sympathizing with veganism as a political movement (*Zdravo Slovenija*, *Cajtng*...), but they are not important players in local media landscape and they often promote conspiracy theories and controversial ideas such as anti-vaccination, pro-Putin politics, new-age elements and such, which can quickly put the question of animal ethics in the background.

One way or another: veganism is under-represented or even mis-represented in local media. We do believe that this is, at its core, a question of interplay between animal rights theory and animal rights activism, and emphasizing the intersections across every other social sphere, in every other social justice movement, the political intention, and theoretical knowledge of activist groups were the key elements of "success". In short every successful movement needs a group of people committed to disrupting exploitative practices directly (on the ground direct action), and also working on how to question these practices theoretically and expose the immoral and unjust assumptions they rely on. Most importantly all this has to be done in ways that educates the public, and changes hearts and minds. It seemed that we didn't have that at the time. So when the debate started in our newspapers and in articles, there was a huge unfilled space where the activist activities should take place to loosen beliefs that majority of people had (and still have) about animal rights.

The Importance of Embracing an Intersectional Approach to Animal Rights Activism

Our experiences have taught us an important lesson: it is vital that the question of animal rights takes place in as many (social justice) spheres as it is possible. Approaching animal rights solely with activism (in a narrow sense, that is) poses a danger of confining ourselves in a notion that animal rights are a thing "of their own" rather than something crisscrossed in our society. The "animal rights" question is a question that can and should emerge when we discuss politics, ecology, philosophy, religion, and everyday life: what we wear, what we eat, how we build etc. It is theory that has an ability to expand the animal question to different dimensions of life and different, already existing, schools of thought. And it is activism that has an ability to make this notions visible, to make them practical and maybe even to set an example and another possible solution to the problem we encountered. Activism can, with its visibility, its demand spark a debate in a field of theory, or rather theories. It makes the question so visible that one has to detect it, reflect it and put it in the perspective. What does this do? It widens the animal rights question once again and gives new options to activism etc. to 'infinity'.

Theory is the one that gives perpetual meaning to activism, making it possible to always be sure of what are the actual neuralgic points, rather than the latter follows its instinct which can be misleading since the question of animal rights (and other questions of social justice) is always under attack to become appropriated and our 'sentiments' and 'feelings' are usually the ones that are being coopted, cheated, adjusted and used to work against us and against the animal liberation, since they are paradoxically also in the heart of the same fight.

And it is not only theory that can bring positive change to activism, but also the other way around. Different schools of thought tend to include question of animals (as it can be seen even by solely listing philosophers such as are Schopenhauer[12], Nietzsche[13], Derrida[14], Adorno and Horkheimer[15], even Žižek[16]. Of course that does not mean that it is visible and it certainly does not

12 An overview of possible reading of Schopenhauer's ethical consideration towards animals is for example presented in an article *Schopenhauer on the Rights of Animals* by Stephen Puryear, accessible on: https://philarchive.org/archive/PURSOTv3 [last accessed 09.05.2019].

13 It is not an easy task to read Nietzsche's work through the lense of animal rights, but one can certainly take into account that Nietzsche did in fact try to address and destroy the notion of human being a kind of non-animal, constantly using examples of the animal kingdom to prove concepts in the realms of humanity. Along with that: story of Nietzsche encountering a horse being beaten (in Turin) and consequently suffering a nervous breakdown, may in some sense prove significant regarding philosopher's views on animal ethics.

14 For example: *The Animal That Therefore I Am* where Derrida famously proposed a term *animot*.

15 Adorno and Horkheimer collaborated on a book *Dialectic of Enlightenment*, in which they did (along with other issues) pose questions regarding animal ethics.

16 Žižek reflects G.K. Chesterton's notion of »monster« and Derrida's quote *Je sais bien mais quand meme* (trans.: I know well, but anyway). For example: https://www.youtube.com/watch?v=pGFVUsYnw8U [last accessed 09.05.2019].

mean it is actually concerned with animal rights and critical animal studies. The loudness of activism has a power to bring those questions forth and it can also redirect the stream of thought to be aligned with animal rights. We are not encouraging (for example) philosophy or sociology to necessarily take a supporting stance on animal rights or even take a stance at all, we're just proposing a possibility of a way of thinking which can regard this question thus researching yet an uncharted territory which may prove to be productive and interesting to the field itself. Thinking about human biology in the context of evolutionary theory is impossible without including non-human animals; reflecting questions of human condition are based on problematic notion of radical disconnection of humans from other animals; ecological thought is inadequate if humankind is perceived as the sole ecological factor and the list goes on.

Critically Reflections on "the Vegan Debates" in Slovenia

The debates in the media about veganism and vegan praxis did lead to another side of power and influence becoming involved: parliamentary politics. In 2017 the Slovenian "Ministry of agriculture, forestry and food" (co)funded a national project title *Naša super hrana*[17] which could be roughly translated as "Our super food". One of project's results was a TV commercial which focused on local meat, marking the latter as "Our super meat", encouraging citizens to ... eat even more meat! That happened regardless of statistics proving that meat consumption in Slovenia is already one of the highest in the world[18]. We believe we don't have to explain what this means for animal rights, or rather welfare, questions of ecology and last but not least: health issues.

However, this development led to a key debate in the national assembly. A representative of one of the opposition parties (Slovenia has a proportional voting system) called *Levica* (trans.: The Left, which is one of the parties 'belonging' to the European Left) wasn't exactly pleased with the advertisement and posed a few potent questions to the Minister of Agriculture, Forestry and Food, pointing out all three "usual suspects" of vegan debate: ethics, ecology and health. The debate which took place in November of 2017 in Slovenian parliament illustrated once again that question of veganism or animal rights in the context of parliamentary politics is always limited by party expectations

17 Link to the project: https://www.nasasuperhrana.si/ (in Slovene) [last accessed 09.05.2019].

18 As of 2009 Slovenia holded 21st place on the infamous list, and it was right there with Germany and Italy. Source: https://en.wikipedia.org/wiki/List_of_countries_by_meat_consumption [last accessed 09.05.2019].

and particular interests. While the representative of *Levica* (Luka Mesec) did pose some logical questions (regarding meat consumption, which is already too high, and questions of ecology and ethics) the answers he received were unsatisfactory and evasive. They were articulated by Dejan Židan, the successful ex-president of one of the Slovenian meat producing company who then served as a president of one of the (more or less left-wing or at least social-democratic) political parties *Socialni Demokrati* (Social Democrats). His answers were more or less addressing veganism/vegetarianism as a free personal choice, overlooking health or ethical issues and claiming that animal agriculture is the most ecological choice in example of Slovenia!

In a matter of a few months we witnessed a debate about animal rights organized by *Levica*. Their members spoke about the issue in the media and added a few animal welfare propositions in the latest coalition treaty (including *Levica* as a kind of a silent partner), something that (at least to our knowledge) never happened before. To be fair: we have reservations about actual changes, since they mostly belong to the field of welfare, rather than rights. We also believe that parliamentary politics is powerless in some aspects, and above all: we still deal with an absolute minority in the national assembly. Veganism is not always proposed, as the popular appeal is toward reductionism and vegetarianism. That said, we are of the opinion that there are three really important outcomes of what was going on, namely:

1. The question of other animals, and our treatment of them has become visible and it has become political in a way majority of people understand politics (meaning: parliamentary politics).
2. Important seeds were sown that focused on ethics, ecology and health.
3. All the debates have shown that at least some people in *Levica* understand animal question as the integral part of the left-wing politics—in one instance posing Jeremy Corbyn as an example. As of 2019, *Levica* has two vegans and one vegetarian serving as their spokespeople in the parliament. All in all they have nine spokespeople in the parliament at the moment)[19].

19 But it has to be said *that Levica* did suffer some internal backlash due to the fact that some of the members proposed veganism as an integral part of left-wing politics. As a result, even though the party still holds a favorable position regarding animal ethics, they are not as loud and clear about the topic as they used to be. Ironically it is now members of *Socialni Demokrati* (especially a parlamentarian Meira Hot) that address the issue of animal rights more frequently. But the focus are now mostly pets and animal shelters.

We do have to acknowledge, of course, that the link between animal rights and left-wing politics was something already present. These synergies were particularly apparent in anarchist communities. Some representatives of LGBTQA community supported animal rights, as did other initiatives and associations such as the aforementioned "Za živali!" already pointing out the intertwinement long before the debate.

We strongly believe this is a result we owe to the allied powers of theory and activism. Activism made animal rights issue visible enough for them to find a way in national assembly, it was the one that has shown that some of us (citizens, voters) take a great interest in them, it was the one that one way or another made some members of parliament *go veg(etari)an* and it was them who took the activist approach, addressing the issue in public, being active by their own initiative. And on the other hand: it was the theory that made them capable and competent to even advocate the issue out there and most importantly: it was the theory that made it possible to incorporate animal question in left-wing politics as such. This is something that can be easily seen even with a quick analysis of the discourse led by pro-vegans in parliament: they addressed ethics, ecology and health, they proposed a notion that animals should be part of our moral community also and that this is something integral to the left-wing idea of politics. It's of course hard to pin-point the actual theoretical works or examples that served as basis for this kind of discourse, but such notions can be found in works by, for example, Paola Cavalieri, Tom Regan, Anna Charlton, Peter Singer, Rosalind Hursthouse, Donna Haraway, Gary Francione, pattrice jones, Carol J. Adams, Steve Best etc. We hope (and believe) this is a first step to a wider debate about the issue, other left or right wing parties are now suddenly in a position to address the issue one way or another if they want to participate in a debate at any level.

Final Thoughts: Where Are We Now and What Should We Do Next?

It is of course impossible to pinpoint what were the most important events that lead to the change of dynamics regarding animal rights question. But we can detect some results. More left-wing politicians now—at least to some extent—are sympathizing with the notion of animal rights, and seeing animal rights as a legitimate political issue. This can be detected when reading leftist media or talking with self-identified leftists). When veganism is shamed or laughed at, the reasons for this abuse have significantly changed. Veganism is not perceived as an 'obscure' fad anymore, but rather a serious political "danger", a notion which can be interpreted as positive, since that means it obviously poses vital questions about our culture, society and human(ity) itself.. Is our community also becoming larger? Sadly the actual statistics are more or less non-existent, one of them offers a data claiming that vegans along with vegetarians represent 2% of Slovenian population. Interestingly, the Facebook group mentioned before (Vegans, vegetarians and raw foodists) consists of 22.000 members. Of course this doesn't mean much, but it shows that veganism and/or vegetarianism is a significant minority at this time.

In 2018 veganism was *remarkably* present. It started with establishing local chapters of international initiatives like DxE (organizing disruption actions)[20]; The Save Movement (organizing so-called vigils)[21]; and Anonymous for the Voiceless (organizing Cube of truth)[22]. It then continued with a proposal to change the ongoing food politics to one that should lean towards veganism, written by two activists addressing the government, gaining visible coverage and support. The initiative was covered in a series of articles in one of our biggest newspapers (but probably the most important one) *Delo* and at roughly the same time another internet based newspaper dedicated to veganism was established. 2018 also brought us workshops regarding vegan activism and workshops for non-vegans who wish to go vegan.

Something was going on in the field of art too. The collected poetry of the afore-mentioned Jure Detela was (finally) published; the Museum of Contemporary Art Metelkova (the most important local museum of such kind) set an exhibition *Heavenly Beings: Neither Human nor Animal*[23] with corresponding events. The exhibition was highly problematic, since it didn't manage to free itself from the notion of animals being used as metaphors for people, or rather: animal abuse being used as a metaphor for human suffering. Nevertheless, the exhibition still managed to address the issue, at least to some extent. In the beginning of 2018 a performer named Betina Habjanič, who dealt with animal rights on many occasions managed to spark a fiery debate about one of her artistic actions (done in the end of 2017). The performance of pulling a pig's corpse through the center of Ljubljana[24] which, of course, has some problematic dimensions since the pig's corpse was once

20 Webpage: https://www.directactioneverywhere.com/ [last accessed 09.05.2019].
21 Webpage: https://thesavemovement.org/ [last accessed 09.05.2019].
22 Webpage: https://www.anonymousforthevoiceless.org/ [last accessed 09.05.2019].
23 Link to the presentation of exhibition (in English): http://www.mg-lj.si/en/exhibitions/2369/heavenly-beings-neither-human-nor-animal/ [last accessed 09.05.2019].
24 Link to the Facebook post posted by Kapelica Gallery (producer of the performance) with a press release (in Slovene) and some photo-material of the event: https://www.facebook.com/pg/Kapelica/photos/?tab=album&album_id=1378691762241266 [last accessed 09.05.2019].

again... used, but it nevertheless addressed the issue of animal rights. It is also safe to say that most of the individuals and organizations that were advocating animal rights long before the recent events, got a little bit more active, and the surroundings are making them more visible.

But what are some still remaining issues and what are the dangers? The theoretical point of view provides us facts and figures, it acknowledges the problems with our attitude towards animals. We now do understand we're dealing with a big political issue, one that is essential part of left-wing politics, we now more or less accept the fact that veganism can be healthy, that animals do suffer and that we just may be on the brink of environmental catastrophe. But we are now stuck between not caring, not having solidarity, not accepting the responsibility and seeing animal rights as an issue reserved for "snowflakes", an identity which is in conflict with our own: carnistic and domineering.

What we need now is to renew and strengthen the bonds between theory and activism. Theory has to detect how our identity is structured, what is the role of caring and solidarity in our culture, it has to consider how much can we actually achieve as individuals, what interventions does the system need to undergo and how to achieve that. And when theory makes a convincing case for the most effective approaches then activists must to carefully acknowledge its findings and direct its efforts in the right directions.

We should try to detect what are the actual neuralgic points regarding animal rights. Can protesting in front of abattoirs, expressing compassion to animals being led to slaughter actually produce any result? Are abattoirs places where people are disconnected from the animals or is it somewhere else? Is it possible that we should protest in supermarkets in front of the meat section, because this is where our link with non-human animals is actually broken? Sometimes activism can, in a way, get carried away simply because it focuses on our own body, feeling *we* possess. We should acknowledge that we as vegans are already the ones who made this change and understand using animals as un-ethical and so it may not be that the feeling *we* have that is the most important, but rather what feelings do non-vegans have and how to address that feelings. But on the other hand we also need to follow a simple, even though frequently forgotten rule: on some level it is not a question of our theory or our activism. It is rather a question of animal liberation and animals well-being and our activism and theory should always be dependent of that.

What it means "to be" engaged in vegan praxis is in danger of being coopted. From a viewpoint of society it doesn't necessarily mean you have to go vegan in order to follow best interests for animals. It doesn't even mean you follow the (ethical) notion of animals being a living beings of their own, even if you do deal with questions regarding animals—this is where activism comes in. And on the other hand: it doesn't necessarily mean that your activism addresses all of the crucial parts of our society. It doesn't mean that you propose a wider social and system change, it doesn't mean you actually see the intertwinement between different (class, gender etc.) struggles. Moreover: it can even mean fighting for animal rights while reproducing other issues and consequently reproducing speciesism in a long term. It can also mean that activism you participate in is already appropriated, stripped to an action that doesn't change anything, that addresses no one (even if it maybe did in the past). Rather, it gained a form in which it represents you as an activist (as a sort of identity), while you can still remain a non-dangerous individual in a society.

The vegan community itself is producing actions and/or ideas that need more attention, and need to adapt to reflect the ever changing circumstances of animal rights movements. This is also true for the case of the vegan movement in Slovenia. We've already mentioned that media such as left-wing magazine *Mladina* or political parties, such as left-wing *Levica* may sympathize with veganism, but on the other hand do not seem to take it as seriously as they could or should (sometimes even expressing doubts about the sensibility of veganism and/or animal rights). Earlier in the chapter we also highlighted a lamentably bland response to a danger of neo-Nazis joining (Slovenian) vegan community.

There are other issues though that need further reflection. For example. after gaining significant media coverage[25] in the beginning of 2019, interest for the issue of animal rights/veganism, now seems to be at a bit of standstill. The number of actions such as graffitiing, disruptions and Cube of Truths declined greatly, although vigils still remained quite popular. Overall the number of articles/events regarding animal rights declined too. Is this some kind of a silent phase which may become louder again? It may be so (or at least we hope that it is so), but we can detect another process at work: a certain shift of focus. It seems that while there are less actions intended for the non-vegan public, there are more for the vegan activists, such as workshops about activism, picnics for activists and such[26],

25 It was at that time that different Slovenian magazines found out about graffitis on animal rights/veganism, vigils done by the save movement and so on … These »incidents« caused a public debate once more and divided a public. Especially the ring-wing media reacted unfavoribly, clearly building their own identity on carnism and speciesism.

26 We believe that the popularity of vigils is representative in this case, since it is very much focused on activists.

[27].

We believe that close cooperation with theory would be crucial to detect such problems and stop actions that can lead to reproducing them, rather than simply *going with the flow*, thus being a subject to public relations techniques and an easy target of only emotion-based activism with unclear intentions, or at the least intentions that do not put animal rights in their center.

Regardless of that, there are some reasonable doubts about the actions vegan community proposes at the moment too. It is true that that may be (or even mostly is) a result of an attempt to discourage veganism, but they still should be taken into critical consideration and reflection. For example:

1. Buying (vegan) products at the supermarket still makes you a buyer in the supermarket, your actions are carried out within the limits of consumer society and your power of changing the circumstances is merely a buyer's choice, still reproducing capitalistic logic.
2. You cannot be completely vegan—it is not possible. Sometimes you accidently step on an insect, hit an animal while driving a car, doing something ecologically non-sustainable (like buying new clothes, flying a plane...) and thus hurting animals once again.
3. Since you fight for the animals, you don't fight as much for people.
4. Non-human animals can hardly be a factor in our law system.

All of the listed concerns may be exaggerations and provocations, but there is still some logic in them. For example in response to:

Scenario (1): it is true that you actions make profit for capitalists. That being the case one should try to source their food elsewhere where possible, and find other way to abolish the current exploitative economic system where possible.
Senario (2): it is true that you cannot live as fully vegan as you could in some other circumstances· In some cases the line between intentionality and unintentionality can be quite thin. The biggest ethical issue we address (using animals for food, clothes, experiments …) isn't that hard to grasp. But how about, for example, hitting a deer, or even a fly while driving? While your action was unintentional, one can always ask themselves if it was necessary to take a ride or even owning a car … With including all animals in our moral community, a lot of issues like this would be resolved by themselves, since the society as a whole would bear in mind animal

27 Such as attacking the internal criticism of animal rights movement or a »strange« process of male activists gaining most of the crucial position in the movement, even though some studies show that women present up to 80% of the vegan community. We fear that the community itself isn't immune to sexism and patriarchal schemes, thus different »leading« figures are able to gain positions with the help of a certain kind of machismo.

ethics, thus considering animal lives while for example building a road, innovating a vehicle and so on.
Scenario (3): It is true that focusing solely on non-human animals can have a negative effect on non-human animals While this may seem like a paradox, we strongly believe that we must integrate question of non-human animals in the idea of total liberation: for humans, for animals and for the Earth. Beside that: it is not just the notion of non-human animals suffering, but also humans oppressing them. We believe that all the oppressions have same roots and when we allow one of them to flourish we also open the door for all the others. In order to fight this in case of non-human animals, we need to address the notion of oppression as such and at the same time abolish the dichotomy between human and non-human animals.
Scenario (4): It is also true that we can hardly expect non-human animals to become equivalent partners in our law system. This being the case we should protect non-human animals by law, liberate them and making it our duty to help them when possible. But we must bear in mind that we can only grant them rights that do have a meaning for them (right to live or right not to be used/abused, are certainly some of those, while having a right to open a business is, for example, not) and we cannot expect them to follow some of the laws meant for people.

All four points often closely follow our ordinary everyday actions, reflect our lifestyle and choices and so veganism as a praxis and a lifestyle can be criticized in such a way; we as vegans are not above criticism. We need to know what our actions mean in reality and question ourselves: (1) How can I (in everyday life) isolate myself from being someone who is solely reproducing the action of buyer's choice? (2) How can we structure our society in a way that excludes animal suffering as much as it is possible? (3) How to address the issue of non-human animals in a way that harnesses total liberation (thus abolishing the dichotomy human-animal), rather than enclosing us in countless circles of gaining/losing successes of our struggles? (4) What place can non-human animals have in our law system to provide: (A) A logical law system, (B) A law system which respects non-human animals as free beings. Most importantly: if we do find out how to do that... how could it be done via activist action and via actions in our everyday life? We believe that we need to understand that every struggle has to deal with circumstances that are constantly changing. Some actions or theories that may have hit the right spot, were revolutionary, productive, maybe even genius in the past, aren't necessarily such at this moment in time. One needs to reflect them, rethink them and dispatch new ones at any time, and this is exactly what strong bonds between theory and activism are able to do and should do, since being loud doesn't mean you have something to say, and saying something doesn't mean anyone hears you.

References

Adorno, T., & Horkheimer, M. (1947) *Dialektik der Aufklärung* (*Dialectic of Enlightenment*). Amsterdam: Querido Verlag.

Čeh Steger, J. (2015). *Ekokritika in literarne upodobitve narave* (Ecocriticism and literary depictions of nature). Maribor: Litera Publishing House.

Derrida, J. (2008). *The animal that therefore I am.* Available at: https://www.e-skop.com/images/UserFiles/Documents/Editor/derrida_cat.pdf [last accessed 09.05.2019]

Detela, J. (2018). *Zbrane pesmi* (Collected poems). Ljubljana: Beletrina.

Drev, M., Tomažič, S., & Drev, T. (2012, year of 1st issue: 1983). *101 zelenjavni jedilnik* (101

Plant-based dishes). Ljubljana: Modrijan.

Foggio, D. (2000). Neo-Nazis join animal rights groups. *The Daily Telegraph.* Available at https://www.telegraph.co.uk/news/uknews/1353870/Neo-nazis-join-animal-rights-groups.html [last accessed 09.05.2019]

Francione, G., & Charlton A. K. (translated by Majaron, E.) (2014). *Etika v kuhinji* (orig. *Eat Like You Care*). Škofja Loka: Planet.

Grušovnik, T. (2017). *Etika živali, O čezvrstni gostoljubnosti* (Animal ethics: About transspecies hospitality). Koper: Založba Univerza na Primorskem, Univerzitetna založba Annales.

Komelj, M. (2010). *»Este animal que soy«* in *Nujnost poezije.* Koper: Hyperion.

Ozmec, S. (4. 6. 2013). *Vegana dojenčico stradala do smrti?* (Did vegans starved their babyto death?). Available at: https://www.slovenskenovice.si/crni-scenarij/doma/vegana-dojencico-stradala-do-smrti [last accessed 09.05.2019]

Puryear, S. (2017). *Schopenhauer on the rights of animals.* Available at: https://philpapers.org/archive/PURSOT.pdf [last accessed 09.05.2019]

Radaljac, A. (2016). *Puščava, klet, katakombe* (The Desert, The Basement, The Catacombs). Maribor: Litera.

Roth, R. (2009): *That's why we don't eat animals: A book about vegans, vegetarians, and all living things.* Berkeley, California: North Atlantic Books.

Whitney, E., & Rolfes, S. (2011). *Understanding nutrition* (12th ed.). Australia: Wadsworth Cengage Learning.

Žižek, S. (23. 9. 2014). *Slavoj Zizek and Animal Rights.* Available at: https://www.youtube.com/watch?v=pGFVUsYnw8U [last accessed 09.05.2019]

4. *Strategic Empathy, Intra-Sectional Demonstrations, and Animal Activism: In Pursuit of Total Liberation*

Nathan Grande

A stranger and I stood a few feet away from a computer that displayed video footage of farmed animals being abused and killed in slaughterhouses. When I asked what he thought about the footage, he stated, "It doesn't bother me, but I know these places are bad for the environment. I'm thirty. I'll be vegan in ten years, when I need to start being healthier." Seeing an opening to probe him about veganism from a health or environmental perspective, I navigated the conversation away from the animals because my goal was to persuade him to commit to a vegan diet challenge.

I stood with several activists outside of a slaughterhouse. A transport full of cows approached us. We ran toward the truck with camera phones and water bottles in hand. We squirted water through the holes of the transport to show the cows a few seconds of kindness, as they would, within minutes or hours, be killed and butchered into chunks of meat for humans to eat. Using both loud and quite voices, we apologized to the cows, who trampled over one another as they moved away from us and toward the other side of the crowded transport. We frightened them. Perhaps our voices and physical presence signified human aggression or the possibility of rough handling, the sort of cow-human interactions that those cows may have been most familiar with. Perhaps we should have spoken more quietly or approached them in complete silence.

At another time, I entered a grocery store with a group of activists. We were there to protest in front of a meat case to disrupt the normalization of farmed animal exploitation by screaming and chanting loudly. As I walked toward the meat case, I passed a father who pushed his young daughter in a shopping cart. I informed him, "We're animal activists. We're gonna get pretty loud in a second. Your daughter might get scared." The father replied, "Well. She has to see this stuff sooner or later. Thanks for letting me know." Later, I realized that I did not seize the opportunity to talk with that father, in that moment, about the plights of farmed animals. I missed the opportunity to try to get him to think and feel more deeply about the life experiences of farmed animals.

In reading these experiences, most likely, you have already associated each form of activism with a currently popular street activist organization. To be clear, it is not my intention to speak out against street activist organizations. And most certainly, it is not my intention to speak out against activists who employ these tactics. I share my experiences, however, to show that, at times, I myself have shifted the focus of my activism away from the life experiences of animal others, even as I try to convince strangers on the street to consider a vegan diet. Often, my conversations have not addressed humans' relationships with animals, as such. Sometimes the life experiences of animals have gone visually unrepresented altogether. As I suspect that my experiences are not entirely unique, I propose that connecting humans with the actual and potential life experiences of other animals must play a greater and more consistent role in our street activism. We must get the public to consider, foremost, that they are in fact in relationships with other animals, and with the multitude of species, and that these relationships are in need of deep consideration and immediate change.

In this chapter, I introduce strategic empathy, which utilizes non-violent and violent video footage to present the life experiences of vulnerable others. Strategic empathy is an approach to street activism that occurs in intrasectional demonstrations, or demonstrations that focus on multiple contexts of exploitation. Strategic empathy is an open and alterable creative practice in which activists operate as narrators and visual media editors. The practice leans away from argumentation and debate and leans toward description and narration as a means to guide the public toward experiencing empathy for animal others. To proceed, I will briefly discuss empathy and two general ways that scholars have thought about its cognitive and affective components. I will then discuss three existent conceptualizations of strategic and tactical empathy. Finally, I will situate strategic empathy for animal activism in theory and action.

Empathy

Although the popular understanding of empathy is simply that one stands or walks in the shoes of another, empathy, as a phenomenon, is more involved. Indeed, what counts as empathy, and what does not, has been debated by scholars and remains open to theorization. Frans de Waal (2009) describes empathy as an unconscious merging of self and other in which "the other's experiences echo within us. We feel [the other's experiences] as if they're our own" (p. 65). de Waal (2009) says that this merging of or movement between self and other is best conveyed by the meaning of empathy's German predecessor, "*Einfühlung* (feeling into)" (p. 65). In 1872, Robert Vischer coined the term *Einfühlung*, which found use in German aesthetics and described an observer's projection of their own emotions or feelings onto an object of admiration and reflection, such as an artistic work; through this interaction with an artistic work, one could come to find aesthetic value and pleasure in the beauty of it (Rifkin, 2009, p. 12). Wilhelm Dilthey applied the meaning of *Einfühlung* outside the realm of aesthetics "to describe the mental process by which one person enters into another's being and comes to know how they feel and think" (Rifkin, 2009, p. 12). Psychologist E.B. Titchener, in 1909, translated *Einfühlung* into the word, "empathy," in which the "pathy" of empathy "suggests that we enter into the emotional state of another's suffering and feel his or her pain as if it were our own" (Rifkin, 2009, p. 12). A subtle but important difference between Dilthey's understanding of *Einfühlung* and Titchener's translation is the emphasis of the former as a mental process in which we come to know the thoughts and feelings of another, and the emphasis of the latter as a participative affective state in which we emotionally feel along with another.

Rifkin (2009) points out that psychologists have debated this difference, the role of affective and cognitive components of empathy, with some psychologists attempting to rid the term of its affective component by "suggesting that empathy is a cognitive function wired into the brain but requires cultural attunement" (p. 13). Without its affective component, empathy becomes a means of assessing another's behavior, thoughts, and intentions in order to respond appropriately to them or as a means of "reading" others for the purpose of establishing social relations (Rifkin, 2009, p. 13). For Rifkin (2009), such views border on situating empathy as a tool for measuring another in order to progress one's particular social interest or to maintain acceptable social relations with others (p. 13). Other psychologists, however, maintain that empathy is fundamentally an emotional, or affective, state that contains a cognitive component. As such, empathy is:

> a total response to the plight of another person, sparked by a deep emotional sharing of that other person's state, accompanied by a cognitive assessment of the others' present condition and followed by an affective and engaged response to attend to their needs and help ameliorate their suffering. (Rifkin, 2009, p. 13)

Lori Gruen (2015) would call this latter understanding of empathy a process "of moral perception" (p. 39). Gruen's work on empathy is the foundation of strategic empathy for street activism, as I discuss in a later section of this chapter.

Frans de Waal further differentiates what counts as empathy, and what does not, according to two types of perspective-taking: empathic perspective-taking and cold perspective-taking. Using his Russian Doll Model, de Waal (2009) depicts empathy as three evolutionary layers; it is not that the earliest form of empathy no longer exists, but rather evolutionary layers have formed around it, making it an existent core of empathy's full capacity (pp. 208–209). The core layer represents emotional contagion and state-matching; the middle layer represents sympathetic-concern and consolation; the outmost layer represents perspective-taking and targeted helping (de Waal, 2008; de Waal, 2009). While giving an in-depth explanation of these layers, what is most relevant to our purpose here is that de Waal (2008) sees these layers as being connected, such that the perspective-taking aspect of empathy is a combination of perspective-taking and emotional engagement, which he calls empathic perspective-taking (p. 285). For de Waal (2009), empathic perspective-taking is "geared more toward the other's situation and emotions," and is a "combination of emotional arousal, which makes us care, and a cognitive approach, which helps us appraise the situation" of the other (p. 100). de Waal (2009) explains this cognitive-emotional balance in context: we hear children screaming from within a burning house, which "pulls at our heartstrings," but we then look around to determine how we might best help the children, whether by looking for a way that they can escape or by calling the fire department or finding out if the fire department has been contacted already (p. 100). It seems that empathic perspective-taking moves us toward altruistic and constructive ends.

On the other hand, de Waal identifies cold perspective-taking as a strictly cognitive engagement with another, without an affective component; it is a "cold phenomenon" that could lead either to constructive or destructive ends, or to helping or hurting others (de Waal, 2008; de Waal, 2009). When one engages in cold perspective-taking, one's entire focus is on what the other might see or know, without concern for the other's needs, wants, and emotions (de Waal, 2009, p. 100). de Waal seems to describe two extreme instances of cold perspective-taking in the context of torturers and serial killers. de Waal (2009) points out that methods of torturing a prisoner "rests on our ability to assume [the prisoner's] viewpoint and realize what will hurt or aggravate them the most" (p. 211). Further, de Waal (2009) suggests that in the case of psychopathic serial killers, for while such individuals engage cognitively with the other (their victim), even understanding their wants and weaknesses, they care nothing about the implications of their behavior and what it means for the other: "they are intellectually capable of adopting another's viewpoint without any of the accompanying feelings" (p. 212). de Waal's analysis of psychopathic serial killers might well apply to a torturer, that is, a torturer understands the wants and weaknesses of another without caring much about the implications of their behavior. As I see it, cold perspective-taking, albeit in different forms and sometimes in far less severe interactions, seems to be what others have conceptualized as strategic and tactical empathy.

Existent Conceptualizations of Strategic and Tactical Empathy

The three conceptualizations of strategic and tactical empathy discussed here show how empathy has been applied to or identified in actual situations in the world. They serve as a means to make sense of interactions or to instruct humans in their interactions with others. Each emphasizes "reading" the other or assessing the other's thoughts, behaviors, and intentions, but without affective participation with the other, who becomes an object of empathy for the purpose of being manipulated, out-maneuvered, or persuaded. Feeling into the place or experience of the other becomes a strictly cognitive matter, rather than a cognitive-emotional one. Existent conceptualizations of strategic and tactical empathy seem to be iterations of de Waal's cold perspective-taking.

Bubandt and Willerslev (2015) conceptualize tactical empathy as an empathic identification with the other which "contains, and in fact is motivated by, seduction, deception, manipulation, and violent intent" (p. 6); it is a practice in which the "other is constructed" as such through empathic mimicking carried out by the empathizer, in order to deceive and even destroy the other (p. 7). Bubandt and Willerslev identify tactical empathy in a case study that recounts Willerslev's observation of a Siberian Yukaghir hunter disguised as a moose. As Willerslev recalls, the hunter rocks back and forth, while wearing a moose-hide coat, "worn with its hair outward, the headgear with its characteristic protruding ears, and the skis covered underneath with a moose's smooth leg-skin so as to sound like the animal when it moves in the snow" (Bubandt & Willerslev, 2015, p. 6). Underneath the moose-hide coat hides the hunter, who carries his loaded rifle. As Willerslev recounts:

> A female moose appears from among the bushes with a young calf. At first the animals freeze in their tracks, the mother lifting and lowering her huge head in bewilderment, seemingly unable to solve the puzzle in front of her. But as the hunter moves closer, she is captured by his mimetic performance, suspending her disbelief, and begins to walk slowly toward him with the large-legged calf tottering behind her. At that point the hunter lifts his rifle, and in quick succession shoots both dead. (Bubandt & Willerslev, 2015, p. 6)

Bubandt & Willerslev (2006) would describe the hunter's engagement with the moose as an instance of "the dark side of empathy," as they claim that empathy is not bound to the conventional virtues of altruism, consolation, understanding, compassion, and care, and therefore, it can be used for violent reasons and for deceiving others (p. 6). Yet to evaluate the case study according to what de Waal says of cold perspective-taking, the hunter, as supposed empathizer, categorically operates under the heading of cold perspective-taking. I say this for two reasons. First, the hunter's sole concern is about what the mother moose sees and hears; the only aim of the hunter's disguise is to fashion himself as the innards of a moose in order to manipulate her perception. Second, the hunter is not emotionally engaged with the mother moose—in her own experience, as she is living in it—at the moment in which the hunter comes face to face with her and her calf. Leading to destructive ends, this conceptualization of tactical empathy seems not to be about the dark side of empathy, but about a form of perspective-taking without an affective engagement with the other, or cold perspective-taking.

Historian Zachary Shore (2014) conceptualizes strategic empathy as "the skill of stepping out of our own heads and into the minds of others. It is what allows us to pinpoint what truly drives and constrains the other side" (p. 3). As Shore (2014) explains, to successfully carry out strategic empathy, one needs to identify the most relevant information in a given situation (p. 3), which can be found in "pattern breaks," or deviations in the routine behavior of another (p. 6). Shore (2014) treats Mahatma Gandhi's response to the 1919 Massacre of Amritsar as a case study of strategic empathy. British General Reginald E. Dyer ordered troops to open fire on roughly 25,000 peacefully assembled Punjabis in a public space in Amritsar, India. The massacre left 400 Indians dead and more than 1,000 wounded. Shore (2014) posits that this particularly violent incident "was a definite break in the pattern of British rule," which provided Gandhi the opportunity to "read the British," and to subsequently form "long-term strategies of resistance to colonial authority" based on that reading (p. 14–15). According to Shore's analysis, what

Gandhi read correctly about this pattern break (the massacre itself) was that it pointed not to an evil Britain, but to a remorseful one: "In the massacre's aftermath a sizeable segment of the British public and its leaders ardently opposed [General] Dyer's form of repression" (Shore, 2014, p. 18).

Gandhi, as Shore (2014) explains, saw clearly that an incident like that at Amritsar would most likely not occur again in India, but if it did, it would not occur without international repercussions that would only aid India's independence from British rule. Thus, Gandhi's political movement of resistance through nonviolence was a matter of correctly reading the enemy (Shore, 2014, p. 23) or an example of successfully employing strategic empathy. It seems that, in Shore's analysis, Gandhi's engagement with British national leaders would have aligned with the understanding of empathy that, as Rifkin (2009) describes, is divorced of an affective component and is instead a means of assessing another's behavior, thoughts, and intentions in order to respond appropriately to them or as a means of "reading" others for the purpose of establishing social relations (p. 13). To be clear, I am not suggesting that Shore's conceptualization is problematic or misguided. I mean only to suggest that is seems to be what de Waal calls cold perspective-taking. Indeed, in terms of responding to national and international tragedies, "cold perspective-taking is a great capacity to have" (de Waal, 2009, p. 100), particularly when it leads to constructive ends and helping others, as Shore's case study would demonstrate if understood as an example of cold perspective-taking.

Finally, Claire Brooks takes legal ownership of strategic empathy by copyrighting the term. For Brooks (2016), "Strategic Empathy©" is "the activation of empathy-based organizational learning into marketing strategy, as a powerful source of competitive advantage" (p. 76). This empathy-based organizational learning occurs in the approximately 17-week, 3-phase Strategic Empathy Process in which marketing teams, in part, explore the thoughts, feelings, and behaviors of consumers (Brooks, 2016). Although Brooks (2016) explicitly points out that empathy is a cognitive-emotional engagement with the other, for her purposes she explicitly adopts "cognitive understanding" as the definition of empathy (p. 3-4). Stripping the affective component from this conceptualization of strategic empathy leaves us with cold perspective-taking.

Each of these conceptualizations applies empathy as a strategic tool in competitive arenas and as a means to achieve some end, whether constructive or destructive. Such arenas are the very places that de Waal suggests complicate the cultivation of empathy in society: "Fostering empathy isn't made easier by the entrenched opinion in law schools, business schools, and political corridors that we are essentially competitive animals" (de Waal, 2009, p.

204). The game of hunting also seems like an unlikely competitive activity in which one would find themselves in empathetic interactions of the cognitive-emotional sort. Certainly, it might be that there is something valuable in these conceptualizations that one might appropriate and apply to activism, as activist Bruce Friedrich (2006) has done in "Effective Advocacy: Stealing from the Corporate Playbook." But that may be a different project for another time.

To be sure, our work on the streets is a sort of competitive arena in which we must contend with opposing cultural norms. And, we too wish to achieve an end: the liberation of animal others from exploitative contexts and from the realm of human indifference. However, strategic empathy for street activism is not a strategy for out-maneuvering, manipulating, or persuading others, per se. Rather, it is a strategy that aims to create moments in which others might experience empathy.

Strategic Empathy for Street Activism: In Theory and Action

Strategic empathy is a technological form of activism that juxtaposes non-violent and violent video footage to present the life experiences of vulnerable others. Strategic empathy is a creative approach to street activism that aims to arouse empathy by mediating the actual and potential life experiences of others who are vulnerable to captivity, abuse, mistreatment, oppression, or exploitation. Strategic empathy is a practice of compassionate narration and explanation that aims to focus humans' attention on how our entanglements with others, indirectly and directly, determines whether or not those others exist in states of violence or non-violence. Strategic empathy is an open and alterable framework of street activism that can be applied and revised by local activists to best suit the goals of their local activism.

The four propositions above are meant to give structure to this initial conceptualization of strategic empathy. While I admit that I have thought solely of animal others when thinking through strategic empathy, I have tried to articulate these propositions in somewhat flexible terms, so that they might be employable in all arenas of activism. For instance, *vulnerable others* and *others*, as written above, can refer to other animals, humans, and the Earth, either individually or collectively. Thus, strategic empathy falls within a total liberation framework. Although my aim in this section is to apply strategic empathy to an example of an intra-sectional animal activist demonstration, the demonstration setup that I describe could easily be reconfigured for an *inter*sectional demonstration in which animal liberation, Earth liberation, and human liberation activists work collaboratively alongside one another in a single demonstration; activists and critical animal studies scholar-activists might wish to explore the possibility of intersectional demonstrations and strategic empathy in more detail.

Intra-Sectional Demonstrations

The practical setup of an intra-sectional demonstration could take many forms and could involve any combination of species and contexts of exploitation. For the purpose of explanation, imagine that your local activist group has convened in a public space in your own city. Your work area consists of three small tables. You dedicate one table to chickens, the second table to elephants, and the third to rabbits. On each table rests two computers which function like a split screen. One computer at each table displays video footage of animals in a violent context: chickens in factory farms and slaughterhouses, elephants in the circus and as hunted and poached subjects, and rabbits in laboratories. The second computer displays non-violent video footage: chickens living at a sanctuary, elephants living at a sanctuary and/or in their natural environment, and rabbits living in the wild or in captive care. Alternatively, perhaps your local activist group has dedicated each table more broadly to a specific context of exploitation. The first table pertains to factory farms, the second to the circus, and the third to laboratories. In this second configuration, you edited sequences of video footage, so that the videos at each table correspond. That is, at the first table, both computers display video footage of chickens for five minutes, then cows for five minutes, then pigs for five minutes. During each five-minute duration, violent and non-violent video footage displays side by side. You edited and aligned video sequences in the same manner for the second table that pertains to the circus; both computers display elephants for five minutes, then rhesus macaque monkeys for five minutes, then tigers. This is crucial: at any given time, passersby should be able to shift their gaze back and forth between two computer screens to see a single species living in violent *and* non-violent contexts, simultaneously.

An intra-sectional demonstration might at first seem impractical and unfocused. It might seem that a single demonstration that includes farmed animals, coerced animal performers, and animals who exist in other contexts of exploitation is a demonstration that would fail to give devoted and particular attention to any one animal rights concern. There are at least two points to consider here. First, an intra-sectional demonstration is the setting for a strategic empathy approach, which focuses on narrating and describing the particular life experiences of other animals, as shown onscreen (I demonstrate one approach to narrating and describing, in the last section of this chapter). Therefore, it might be that these demonstrations focus on what matters most: details of the violent and non-violent life experiences of animal others and our role, as humans, in making those experiences a reality. Second, there is a strategic advantage with the broadened focus of an intra-sectional demonstration, as it could lead to several outcomes, depending on the species or contexts of exploitation represented. For instance, if farmed animals are part of the demonstration, discussions about veganism are inevitable. Indeed, to assess one's entanglements with pigs, for instance, would require one to think about how a pig is shot, stabbed, hung upside down, and ultimately cut or butchered into parts that humans eat. During these demonstrations, discussions about veganism ought to happen and pamphlets or other materials ought to be given freely. Additionally, during the same street demonstration, if passersby are especially disturbed by video footage that displays, for instance, the aftermath of elephant slaughter or the abusive treatment of elephants by circus handlers, we can invite and encourage those passersby to join us in protest at an upcoming or future circus or hunting protest. Or we might inform them that specific organizations that combat poaching could always use additional financial support. A single intra-sectional demonstration could lead to manifold outcomes, from fostering empathy for other animals to educating the public about veganism and potentially increasing the number of activists in a given local community.

For local abolitionist vegan communities that want to experiment with intra-sectional demonstrations, the following question might be an important one to consider: What is the best way to proceed if a person we meet on the streets wishes to become active for non-farmed animals while overlooking the plights of farmed animals? That is, that person has yet to come around to veganism, but might wish to join us at rodeo, hunting, circus, aquatic park, or other protests. I do not want to answer the question conclusively for others, but I will share my own experience.

My path to veganism did not begin as a result of seeing images or video footage of farmed animals being killed or living as captives on factory farms, nor did I know much about or research the plights of farmed animals even after going vegan. Rather, the detail that I saw in one picture of a slaughtered elephant put me on the vegan path. That one slaughtered elephant—sitting in a seemingly restful pose, with her front legs peacefully extending forward, with the flesh behind her face completely exposed, and a chunk of her face dangling from the side of her head—changed my perception of the meat and fish section at the supermarket. Thankfully, it became impossible for me to see chunks of red meat, chunks of chicken, and chunks of fish without seeing a once living being. My singular concern about the wellbeing of elephants quickly grew into a larger concern about the wellbeing of elephants, cows, pigs, chickens, fishes, and all other animals in the world. Perhaps, in a world of entanglements, there are many paths that can lead to veganism and to an abolitionist stance.

The Empathy of Strategic Empathy

The empathy of strategic empathy is grounded in Lori Gruen's work on empathy. Of empathy in general, Gruen (2015) sees it as "a kind of moral perception" (p. 39) and a process that is not necessarily linear (p. 51). As such, the parts of this process include the empathizer's attention getting caught by the wellbeing of the other in a particular circumstance, the empathizer reflectively imagining themselves in the other's particular position, the empathizer judging how the conditions of the other impact the other's psychological state or wellbeing, and the empathizer carefully evaluating the circumstances of the other to determine what information is most relevant for empathizing effectively with the other (Gruen, 2015). As Gruen (2015) sees it, we use our empathy, or moral perception, when new information presents itself or is found, which can occur in "purely narrative or discursive" contexts (p. 40). While Gruen (2015) sees empathy as a type of moral attention, entangled empathy is additionally a "caring perception" (p. 28). As such, we would put aside the common understanding of empathy as standing in the shoes of another. Instead, as Gruen (2015) suggests, "What we need to do when we are trying to empathize with very different others is to understand as best we can what the world seems, feels, smells, and looks like from their situated position" (p. 66). In doing so, we would try to understand one's species-typical behavior and one's individual personality over the course of time, and we would concern ourselves with the particularity of an animal's life, the particularly different types of relationships that we are in with individuals of different species, and "differences in context and differences in particular experiences" as they relate to the other and our place in reference to them (Gruen, 2015, p. 67).

Our moral and caring perception occurs in our entanglements with others, that is, in the inevitable and inescapable "social/natural" relationships that we are in with other human and other-than-human selves (Gruen, 2015, p. 63–64). But it is not simply that we are in relationships as selves with others: "The very elements of our 'selves'—emotions, perception, the feeling of being a particular person—develop through our interactions with others" (Jones & Gruen, 2016, p. 187). Our entanglements, then, play a part in how we become who we are; how we construct our thoughts, desires, identities, attitudes, perceptions, and agency; and how we make sense of living in the world (Gruen, 2015, p. 63–64). Because we cannot escape our entanglements with other animals and humans, as we all exist together as organisms on the Earth, it is sensible to ensure that we are in meaningful or non-abusive relationships with them (Gruen, 2015, p. 64). Importantly, our entanglements are not fixed and are changeable should one discover that certain entanglements constitute an exploitative or abusive relationship for another (Gruen, 2015, p. 64).

In a sense, intra-sectional street demonstrations are a manifestation of various thoughts that Gruen has about empathy, entangled empathy, and entanglements. The non-violent and violent video-footage of intra-sectional demonstrations can open the door for the public to get caught up in the circumstances of animal others, thereby allowing them to evaluate and judge the conditions and places that animal others are put into because of our entanglement with them. The violent video footage presents what is, for many humans, new visual information about how animal others figure in the world. The combination of non-violent and violent footage makes visible the actual entanglements that we are already in with animal others, and the possible entanglements that we ought to strive for, as individuals and as members of a species. By narrating the events shown onscreen, we can describe and give detailed attention to how species-typical behaviors and individual personalities are permitted to be and to flourish in some places, but not in others. We can reflectively imagine, alongside passersby on the street, what the onscreen animal others might see, what they might smell, how they might feel, and what it might be like to be in their situated positions, in particular violent and non-violent places.

One aspect of entangled empathy might seem impractical for street activism. Passersby cannot come to know the personality of one particular nonhuman over the course of time. I wish to make two points here. First, it is useful to remember that empathy, and therefore entangled empathy, is not necessarily a linear process (Gruen, 2015). Therefore, we can do the reflective work with passersby on the streets, while encouraging them to seek out long term relationships with individual animal others, perhaps by visiting nearby animal sanctuaries. Second, even in the absence of a personal relationship, one can be affected by the plights of another. Teya Brooks Pribac (2016) states, "One does not need to know an animal personally, that is, develop a physically and emotionally proximal relationship with the animal, to identify with her/his misery and be deeply affect by her/his death" (p. 194). The video footage of intra-sectional demonstrations gives the public the chance to identify with the misery of animal others and perhaps be deeply affected by their mistreatment, suffering, and deaths, as shown onscreen. If we want other humans to realize their capacity to care about other animals and to connect to their experiences, video footage might be our most powerful tool for activism, as it can allow one to form a mediated connection to another, as that other exists in their particular experience.

As a technological form of activism that relies on video footage, we can think of strategic empathy as a gentler form of direct action and a form of resistance through education. Following Marti Kheel (2006), we would adopt a broader understanding of direct action, one that does not necessarily require physical bravery nor certain danger and one that can occur in everyday courageous acts that challenge and defy "the tyranny of convention" (p. 313). Kheel (2006) reminds us that open rescues "exemplify the kind of direct action that helps individual beings, while also promoting empathy and an understanding of the larger context of animal oppression" (p. 311). The successful outcome of open rescues, then, seems to be twofold. Of course, living, suffering animals are liberated from neglectful and abusive environments and relocated to places of safety, comfort, and care. But it is the video footage of open rescues that provides evidence of a challenge to the tyranny of convention. It is the video footage of the open rescues that can foster empathy, as it puts viewers in a place to identify with the animal others onscreen and to develop an understanding of contexts of animal oppression. However, challenging convention and arousing empathy and understanding, with an eye toward animal liberation, certainly is not limited to video footage of open rescues, nor is it limited to violent footage. Jonathan Burt (2002) argues that filmic or cinematic animals can arouse emotional responses in humans and suggests that documentaries, animal rights videos, experimental and surrealist films, and even family films can play a role in transforming the place of animals in human cultures and the nature of human-animal relations (p. 15). In preparing for intra-sectional street demonstrations, we would want to think about how we can creatively juxtapose different film genres–video footage, broadly. In curating and editing video sequences, our guiding question might be, simply, "How can we edit a video sequence to best ignite an emotional response in others?"

In Strategy and Culture: Utilizing Non-violent and Violent Video Footage in Intra-Sectional Demonstrations

Presenting non-violent and violent video footage during a single demonstration can serve several purposes. Non-violent videos can attract passersby and give them pleasant imagery on which to focus their gaze. Those of us who participate or have participated in Anonymous for the Voiceless (A/V) demonstrations can attest to how passersby express their disgust or sadness about the footage that we present, even as they walk by without stopping. The graphic video footage repels them. During intra-sectional demonstrations, non-violent footage might attract a greater number of passersby, while allowing them to linger for a longer amount of time: watching a pig as he prepares a bed of hay or watching a mother pig interact with her piglets is undoubtedly easier on the human eye, heart, and mind than is a pig confined in a crowded pen on a factory farm or hung upside down by her feet to be bled. Further, non-violent footage is a means of highlighting the sorts of entanglements that are worth moving toward, adopting, and preserving. For instance, giving attention to video footage that displays relationships of care between humans and typically farmed animals might instill new understandings and realizations about one's own relationship with farmed animals. Giving attention to video footage that displays elephants interacting within their family unit might convince some humans that those species-typical relationships must be saved and preserved in natural settings; their status as entertainer or as a captive subject of "education," which strips them of their species-typical sociality, or close community, is called into question. Thus, the non-violent footage of intra-sectional demonstrations is also a means of seeing the kind of life that is available to other animals, but often denied to them, precisely because of our entanglements with them.

On the other hand, the violent footage that we present during intra-sectional demonstrations forces the plights of other animals out from invisibility and into the realm of visibility, concern, and seriousness. In visual entertainment, other animals often are represented in cultural forms that strip them of integrity and respect; memes, films, and silly videos often cater to a human gaze that values the cuteness of animals and that prefers depictions in which animal others are subservient beings of amusement or entertainment (Malamud, 2012). Meanwhile, their inhumane and violent realities go unseen. Discussing the invisibility of farmed animals in particular, Melanie Joy (2010) comments that whether we live in rural or urban places, humans rarely, if ever, encounter the animals who they eat, as many of those animals exist in windowless places of confinement, and when taken to slaughter, many are transported in unidentifiable and sealed vehicles.

Even in language, we render animal others and their plights invisible: "Animals are made absent through language that renames dead bodies before consumers participate in eating them … when we eat animals we change the way we talk about them" (Adams, 1990, p. 21). With the words bacon, sausage, and pork, we render pigs absent in language, while casting their abusive experiences and inhumane deaths further from our thoughts, even as we eat their body parts. Similarly, Susan Nance (2013) calls attention to the paternalistic and anthropocentric rhetoric that has been historically adopted by circus handlers who *educate* and *teach* elephants rather than *train*, which implies "punishment and painful consequences for incorrect behavior" (p. 72). Elephant *captives* become *pupils* (Nance, 2013, p. 91). The word *guide* dulls the sharpness of a bullhook. During intra-sectional demonstrations, activists can work to make animals reappear in language, and in thoughts, in a more accurate way by narrating video footage events as they unfold. Through the use of violent video footage, intra-sectional demonstrations can creatively transform a human gaze from one that sees only objects of entertainment or cuteness or fascination, into one that sees individuals and different sorts of communities who can, and do, suffer because of their species-particular entanglement with our species.

Further, violent footage can create opportunities for other humans to bear witness. In bearing witness, "we emotionally connect with the experience of those we are witnessing. We *empathize*," thereby closing the gap in our consciousness through which violence endures (Joy 2010, p. 138). In instances of "*collective witnessing*...the gap in social consciousness" can close, and society moves in the direction of "an informed public and a system in which values and practices are more aligned" (Joy, 2010, pp. 138-139). As "an act of creation," as Joy (2010) states, "Witnessing can take many forms, including demonstrations, candlelight vigils, banners, lectures, and artistic creations" (p. 139). Some of the creative artifacts of witnessing include the AIDS Quilt, the Vietnam Veterans' Memorial wall, revolutionary or protest music, and the event Earth Hour 2008 (Joy, 2010, p. 139). As I see it, intra-sectional demonstrations constitute an act of creation in several ways. Editing together sequences of video footage for an intra-sectional demonstration puts activists in the role of creative editor. The edited footage itself is a new sort of media artifact. By presenting edited violent and non-violent video footage alongside one another, activists create a unique visual media experience that would otherwise not exist. In doing so, activists create the conditions for empathy to arise in those moments in which humans connect with animal others through bearing witness.

Still, despite our best efforts, violent video footage will remain intolerable for some, and understandably so. Many will walk away when they see the onscreen violence. Others will have to look away. Quite importantly, at times, *we*, as activists, also must look away. At times, we ought to completely disengage from activism that relies on images and video footage of graphic violence. Social media activity could lead one to believe that some animal activists live in an almost constant state of bearing witness, and "bearing witness means choosing to suffer" (Joy, 2010, p. 142). But we must also choose to rest our eyes, hearts, and minds by not bearing witness at every opportunity to do so. And if by bearing witness to the torture, suffering, and death of animals, we have brought about our own grief (Pribac, 2016, p. 193), then we must let our grief happen, we must feel through it, we must express our sadness, and we must not isolate ourselves from others during our grief (Joy, 2008). In *Strategic Action for Animals: A Handbook on Strategic Movement Building, Organizing, and Activism for Animal Liberation*, Melanie Joy (2008) offers practical and useful ways for animal activists to cope with grief brought about by bearing witness.

Narrating and Describing to Reflectively Imagine the Experiences of Other Animals

The combination of non-violent and violent video footage presents a wider picture of our entanglements with other animals and allows us to ground our narrations and descriptions in visual information, which can help us to better articulate what animal others might smell, feel physically, and see around them in captivity, in captive care, or in their homelands. Focusing on such details can allow us to reflectively imagine the experiences of other animals (Gruen, 2015), thereby aligning our activism with the specific desires that other animals would have during specific moments. As a point of concern, we ought to be cautious about projecting our direct desires onto other animals so that we do not neglect the specificity of their own desires and life experiences.

When we project our "direct desires" onto another animal, we might think that they are scared, lonely, or sad, "when in fact it is we who are feeling lonely or sad or imagine the animal will be afraid;" consequently, our own desires and the interests that we have for the wellbeing of that particular animal replace what that animal may actually desire or what might be in their actual best interest (Gruen, 2015, p. 57). I get a sense of this sort of projection in the commonly chanted statements "they want to live" and "they don't want to die." I am not suggesting that such statements do not align with the best interests of other animals or the desires they have for themselves and their own wellbeing. But I cannot help but feel that such statements disguise the strong desires of the activist who passionately utters them: it might be that what we truly mean is that "I want them to live."

What concerns me most about such statements is that they do not capture the explicitness of another's experience and the desires they would have in those experiences: a sick factory-farmed piglet whose hind legs are grasped by a human hand that violently swings her body up in the air, smashes her head into the ground, and throws her convulsing body into a trashcan filled with other dead piglet bodies would have very immediate desires that deserve explicit recognition through words. *She does not want to be grasped by her hind legs and violently hoisted into the air. She does not want to be smashed into the ground. She would prefer to receive care and play and rest freely with other piglets.* If an aim of our activism is to represent "the interests, desires, needs, preferences" and perspectives of animal others (Gruen, 2015, p. 73), describing their experiences in more detail and being explicit about what their immediate desires would be in those experiences might be helpful.

Further, during conversations with the public, there might be an empathetic advantage in reworking our commonly chanted statements to make *our* desires for the wellbeing of others explicitly known. As de Waal notes, "identification with others based on physical similarity, shared experience, and social closeness" make up part of "the motivational structure" of empathy (de Waal, 2008, p. 287). It would seem, as a matter of species, that humans can more easily empathize with other humans than with other animals. Thus, by explicitly proclaiming our desires–"I want them to live. I don't want them to be killed. I don't want him to smash that piglet's head into the ground"–perhaps we can more firmly situate humans in the position to evaluate why they themselves do or do not want the same for vulnerable others, for it might be within a human's capacity to more easily empathize with humans who have wants and desires than would it be for them to empathize with individuals of other species who have wants and desires. Even so, we can work to guide humans toward experiencing empathy for animals by describing and narrating their non-violent and violent experiences, as I attempt to do in following example.

Imagine that you're at an intra-sectional street demonstration. We've set up three small tables with two computers on each table. Two people have stopped to look at video footage of pigs. We approach them. As we would at an A/V demonstration, we ask, "Have you seen videos like this before? What's your take on this?" We listen to their response sincerely. We inform, perhaps passionately, but never accusatorily, "We're talking to people about pigs, elephants, and dolphins. We're showing people the different experiences they have, depending on the relationship that we have with them. The video footage on this computer screen shows caring or good relationships between humans and pigs; this computer screen shows abusive relationships." We listen. We explain, "These pigs are confined in a factory farm. Places like this are where most pigs live before they're killed and cut up, before their bodies become bacon, pork, and sausage at the grocery store. These pigs pretty much live in a world of wood, concrete, and metal. They're usually forced to eat, sleep, urinate, and defecate in the same enclosed area. Imagine living like this your entire life, unable to escape the smell of urine and feces." We listen sincerely. We refer back to the video footage. "She's pregnant. She's forced to live in that farrowing crate; it's about two feet wide, so she can't turn around. She can't walk. She can only stare straight ahead, looking at that concrete wall. She'll be confined in there for several weeks, most likely two months or so. This happens to her a couple times a year when she's forcibly impregnated. Imagine living like this, unable to get free from those bars pushing into your body." We listen sincerely. We look at the other computer screen, "That's Rose. She's gathering hay to make a nest to sleep on. She lives at an animal sanctuary now, but she used to live at a factory farm. If she hadn't been rescued, she would have been killed just like this pig." We point to the other screen. "A worker slit her throat. She's hanging upside down from a hook piercing into her body, but she's not dead yet." We draw attention to open wounds, sores, injured legs, and torn ears, to pigs who chew on metal bars. "Rose is acting like mother pigs do, tending to her piglets by nudging them with her nose; they have this entire grassy area to relax and play on. Rose will never be killed to become the bacon, sausage, and pork that people eat." We talk about veganism. We walk to the second table to talk about elephants. The two passersby talk with another activist about dolphins. We invite them to join us at an upcoming protest or demonstration and give them pamphlets and a list of book, film, and website resources.

Understanding that conversations on the streets can and do go in every direction, the above is for illustrative purposes only, to give a sense of a strategic empathy approach, of what it might be like to reflectively imagine ourselves into an animal other's experience. It might seem that the approach is a description of obvious conditions and events. However, we do not want to take it for granted that the violent and non-violent video footage speaks for itself or that the public sees and notices what we see and notice through activist or vegan eyes. We want to narrate and describe to reorient the human gaze. We want animal others and their experiences to become present in language and to appear in thoughts. We want to listen sincerely to strangers on the street as they make sense of the visual information that we present. In doing all of this, perhaps we can work to create the conditions for humans to judge how the experiences shown onscreen impact the psychological state and wellbeing of animal others, and in turn, to transform their entanglements with other animals.

I encourage you, animal activists, to experiment with the strategic empathy approach and intra-sectional demonstrations. Infuse both with your personal creativity. Build upon and improve the strategies offered in this chapter. And with our raging hopes and urgent demands, let's take to the streets to focus people's attention on the life experiences of other animals.

References

Adams, C. J. (1990). The sexual politics of meat: A feminist-vegetarian critical theory. New York, NY: Continuum.

Brooks, C. (2016). *Marketing with strategic empathy: Inspiring strategy with deeper consumer insight*. Philadelphia, PA: Kogan Page Limited.

Bubandt, N., & Willerslev R. (2015). The dark side of empathy: Mimesis, deception, and the magic of alterity. *Comparative Studies in Society and History, 57*(1), 5-34.doi:10.1017/S0010417514000589

Burt, J. (2002). *Animals in film*. London, UK: Reaktion Books Ltd. de Waal, F. B. M. (2008). Putting the altruism back into altruism: The evolution of empathy. *Annual Review of Psychology, 59*, 279-300. 10.1146/annurev.psych.59.103006.093625

de Waal, F. (2009). *The age of empathy: Nature's lessons for a kinder society*. New York, NY: Harmony Books.

Friedrich, B. (2006). Effective advocacy: Stealing from the corporate playbook. In P. Singer (Ed.), *In defense of animals: The second wave* (187-195). Oxford, UK: Blackwell Publishing.

Gruen, L. (2015). *Entangled empathy: An alternative ethic for our relationships with animals*. Brooklyn, NY: Lantern Books.

Jones, P., & Gruen, L. (2016). Keeping ghosts close: Care and grief at sanctuaries. In M. DeMello (Ed.), *Mourning animals: Rituals and practices surrounding animal death* (187-192). East Lansing, MI: Michigan State University Press.

Joy, M. (2008). *Strategic action for animals: A handbook on strategic movement building, organizing, and activism for animal liberation*. Brooklyn, NY: Lantern Books.

Joy, M. (2010). *Why we love dogs, eat pigs, and wear cows: An introduction to carnism*. San Francisco, CA: Conari Press.

Kheel, M. (2006). Direct action and the heroic ideal: An ecofeminist critique. In S. Best, & A. J. Nocella, II (Eds.), *Igniting a revolution: Voices in defense of the Earth*. Oakland, CA: AK Press.

Malamud, R. (2012). *An introduction to animals and visual culture*. Basingstoke, UK: Palgrave Macmillan.

Nance, S. (2013). *Entertaining elephants: Animal agency and the business of the American circus*. Baltimore, MD: The Johns Hopkins University Press.

Pribac, T. B. (2016). Grieving at a distance. In M. DeMello (Ed.), *Mourning animals: Rituals and practices surrounding animal death* (pp. 193-199). East Lansing, MI: Michigan State University Press.

Rifkin, J. (2009). *The empathic civilization: The race to global consciousness in a world in crisis*. New York, NY: Penguin Group.

Shore, Z. (2014). *A sense of the enemy: The high-stakes history of reading your rival's mind*. New York: NY: Oxford University Press.

5. *Challenging the Ideologies behind the Animal Agricultural Industry: A Case for Critical Animal Studies and Ecofeminism*

KIANA AVLON

Introduction

The animal agriculture industry accounts for the death of approximately 3 billion non-human animals a day (72 billion land animals annually) and more than 1.2 trillion aquatic animals each year (Zampa, n.d.). Now, more than ever, we need to urgently dismantle the core ideologies that legitimize this industry: an industry that claims an *increasing* number of non-human animals, human-animals, and broader ecosystems as its victims. Taking up this challenge the chapter has two principal aims. The first is to emphasize the power of underlying ideologies (hidden belief systems) and demonstrate how these serve to legitimize and inform human-animal's exploitative practices toward non-human animals. Put simply, if these are not recognized nor fully understood then animal liberation will fail. It is my contention, for example, that the heavily subsidized agricultural killing industry is largely held intact at an ideological level by 'speciesism', a form of discrimination based on the belief that human-animals are superior to non-human animals. Speciesism as an ideology normalizes hierarchical relationships based on species membership, and this must always be recognized when exploring forms of "economic exploitation, unequal power, and ideological control" (Nibert, 2014, p. 13). Furthermore, as Matsuoka and Sorenson (2018, p. 1) point out, speciesism is not just a term describing how humans interact with other animals, but it is the "socially, politically, economically, and culturally constructed everyday practices and a body of knowledge that supports such relationships".

A fundamental part of critiquing speciesism involves drawing critical attention toward other belief systems which support and uphold it; particularly, anthropocentrism, androcentrism, and rationalism. Recognizing how these act as root systems that allows speciesist beliefs, and respondent acts to flourish in society, the chapter aims to better understand how these systems engage, interact and reinforce each another. A further ideology to highlight is 'carnism'. Coined by Melanie Joy, carnism also works to legitimize our domination of non-human animals and is, "arguably the deepest, most pervasive and catastrophic in modern Western cultures" (Weitzenfeld & Joy, 2014, p. 4). In response to this critique, the second main aim of the chapter discusses ways in which these ideologies might be challenged. Here, a case for Critical Animal Studies (CAS) and ecofeminism is made. Both ecofeminism and CAS, it will be argued, are key frameworks that can deeply analyze, critique, and guide a paradigm shift that fosters harmonious relations among *all* species and ecosystems.

Assuming that many readers may be more familiar CAS, I want to take a moment early in the chapter to sketch out what ecofeminism represents, and the relevance it has here. Ecofeminism, I believe, offers an alternative way of being and relating to other species that addresses the root causes of speciesism. Ecofeminism, "is not a single movement or philosophy" but a broad term that refers to the "loosely knit philosophical and practical orientation linking the concerns of women to the larger natural world" (Kheel, 2008, p. 8). For Martusewicz et al. (2014) ecofeminists are "[w]omen who look explicitly at the intersection of the oppression of women and other social groups with ecological degradation" (p. 89). Mies and Shiva (2014) assert that "[e]cofeminism is about the connectedness and wholeness of theory and practice. It asserts the special strength and integrity of every living thing." (p. 14). This framework, therefore, studies and challenges the historical and current overlapping oppression of women and nature with the hopes of creating a paradigm shift (Kheel, 2008). While ecofeminism has been critiqued as essentialist for embracing a connection between women and nature, ecofeminists have reclaimed this "pairing of women and nature expressed as a refusal to base society and community on the power hierarchies of a capitalist patriarchy" (Thompson & MacGregor, 2017, p. 47). Federici, for example, offers in depth analyses of how nature and ecosystems are devalued and "eaten up" for capitalist accumulation (2008, p. 32; 2009). As will be explored more fully later in this chapter, ecofeminism allows us the ability to both acknowledge mutual oppression *and* strengthen our resistance through theorizing about the connections of attacks against women and nature. For the moment though the discussion moves to highlight another critical intersection, namely the entangled violence that emerges from neoliberal capitalism and speciesism.

Speciesism and Neoliberal Capitalism

Neoliberal capitalism upholds speciesism in the most brutal and exploitative way possible, through non-human animals being commodified and monetized for human entertainment, clothing, medical and/or food industries (White, 2017). Neoliberalism, the ideology that underpins capitalism, revolves around deregulating the markets so the state relinquishes power to for-profit entities. Unsurprisingly the pursuit of profit over life causes significant and extensive harms, with the ongoing privatization of services directly linked to "social and economic polarisation and inequality" (Gills, 2010, p. 171) for example.

Crucially, the continuation of capitalism relies immensely on keeping separate the world of consumption from (the intrinsic violence and exploitation that occurs in) the world of production. To illustrate, think of a customer shopping in a grocery store. The customer is completely ignorant of the production process behind the items that they see on the shelves. Stopping outside the 'meat' aisle, they have no reason or cause to consider how a once-living being, a sentient being possessed with the capability of experiencing complex emotions and desires, has been transformed into neatly plastic-wrapped slices of meat. The rotting flesh in the grocery store feels utterly separate from the body of the once-alive pig, whose last moments saw her lowered into a gas chamber and thrashed in agony. Or, as the customer takes a block of cheese from the refrigerator, they fail to make a connection between this object and the story behind it: of a mourning mother who was raped repeatedly and had her baby calves taken away time and time again. This is no coincidence, to re-state: the world of capitalist production must be hidden from the world of consumption.

If the capitalist economic system did not detach us from our food supply so successfully, we may start to deeply consider the victims of our consumption choices. Crucially, such enlightenment would entail widening our circle of compassion to not only include the non-human animal victims, but also the human-animals employed by the animal agriculture industry. Dick Gregory (1968) draws attention to the reality that consumers do not know, and certainly do not have to interact with, the person in the packing house who kills animals on their behalf (so that can have chicken meat, cow-meat or pig-meat). As he put it, the "wealthy are protected from such horror" (1968, pp. 69-70). Furthermore, Gregory also asserts that consumers of meat and dairy tacitly endorse the deprived conditions experienced in marginalized communities, which includes kids dying of hunger and the attacks on people's dignity. The meat industry capitalizes on vulnerable and desperate populations that find themselves excluded from decent employment opportunities.

This disturbing reality was evident in the ICE raids in August 2019 on several 'chicken processing facilities' or, more accurately, buildings for dismembering tortured chicken bodies. These ICE raids in Mississippi stand as a testament to the overlapping forms of inter-species oppression of human-animals and non-human animal victims brought together by the animal agriculture industry. Many of the workers who work in the production line or on the kill floor of the slaughterhouse are undocumented and only have access to brutal jobs with little to no safety regulations. This perpetuates a cycle of trauma as these workers must endure the violence of stabbing, electrocuting, shooting, and sexually abusing animals for their flesh and secretions, which is then compounded with the violence of ICE raids during the workday (Nibert, 2014). Slaughterhouse workers have some of the high rates of domestic abuse, substance abuse, PTSD, and other mental illness (Dillard, 2008). Serious physical injuries are also a regular part of the job as Compa's (2004) report on the U.S. poultry and meat industry points out when noting that nearly all of the workers interviewed for this research displayed signs of injuries. Ergo, financial support of the meat and dairy industries are also support of corporations that thrive off of exploiting communities. For this reason, Dick Gregory says, "If you can justify killing to eat meat, you can justify the conditions of the ghetto. I cannot justify either one" which highlights how the oppressions from this industry are mutually reinforcing (as cited in Adams, 2015, p. 25).

Bad Things Come in Threes: Anthropocentrism, Androcentrism, and Rationalism

Anthropocentrism, one of the root causes of speciesism, values human life over everything else. In this power dynamic, man [sic] feels the rightful ownership over other life forms, including nature. The result is that nature "becomes an accessory, instrument, and resource" to man who has tried to separate and elevate himself above all else (Figueroa-Helland & Lindgren, 2016, pp. 6-7). Anthropocentrism can be traced way back to the Enlightenment, when Francis Bacon advanced that "nature's secrets can be extracted from 'her' bosom through technologies that would enable men to dominate the natural order" (Adelman, 2015, p. 11). From an ecofeminist perspective, nature is gendered as feminine because men commodify that of which they rely upon: ecosystems to survive and women for reproduction (Keller, 1985; Mies,

2014). Since economic systems shape how we interact with one another, they influence culture and social value so "an economics of commodification creates a culture of commodification, where everything has a price and nothing has value" (Shiva & Mies, 2014, pp. xvi–xvii). This works to both devalue and exacerbate violence against women and ecosystems.

Anthropocentrism also works to rationalize the colonization of people in the race for land grabs, thereby continuing the ongoing project of resource extraction for a capitalist system that necessitates infinite growth. It manifests itself most insidiously through the privatization of land. The idea that land can be legally owned as property reduces land to a commodified "thing" that then becomes part of the capitalist marketplace. Land grabbing can be defined "as pivoting on a dialectic: of 're-territorialization' via investment in offshore lands for agro-exporting of food, fuel, and bio-economic products, and 'de-territorialization' as host states surrender land and water for export to states defined (through market measures or policy) as food-dependent" (Borras et al., 2015, p. 48).

This commodification of land excludes racialized and marginalized groups as the colonizers steal, commodify, privatize, and exhaust land for its resources. Within an anthropocentric framing–compounded with racism–Indigenous people's sophisticated and ecologically sound management of land is misrepresented and demeaned. Their land is referred to as "territorium nullus" meaning empty or virgin land. By framing the land in this way as wasted, colonizers rationalized their actions as worthwhile owners: using the land "productively", namely for the purposes of developmentalism and industrialization (Mies, 2014, p. 150). As McMichael (2017) explains, Europeans thought that "non-European native people or colonial subjects were 'backward' and trapped in stifling cultural traditions...it was easy to take it to the next step, viewing the difference as 'progress'—something colonizers had—to impart to their subject" (p. 27).

The colonizers effectively stole and controlled the land to extract all possible resources for monetary benefit. When social and reproductive labor are disregarded as non-labor, Shiva (2014) describes the effects as rebranding appropriation and robbery as development and improvement. Theodore embodied this line of thought in 1889 when he said, "the settler and pioneer have at bottom had justice on their side; this great continent could not have been kept as nothing but a game preserve for squalid savages;" Shiva (2014) draws upon this quote to point out how native use of land was disregarded and how the colonizers believed they were justified to appropriate the land (as cited in Mies & Shiva, 2014, p. 33). This privatization of the natural world extends to encompass non-human animals. Non-human animals are, under law, considered property. Consequently, rescues of non-human animals are criminalized through ag gag laws and rescuers are branded as 'ecoterrorists' who trespass and steel commodities, rather than compassionate people who rescued beings from places of torture and slaughter.

The belief that only humans are uniquely capable of rational thought is also a key part of anthropocentrism. Christian and Jewish beliefs that "only 'man' is made in the image of God" results in only viewing "men (and, by extension, women)… as 'persons' who are unique and irreplaceable creations worthy of dignity" (Kheel, 2008, p. 6). Animal testing, the consumption of non-human animal flesh and secretions, and using non-human animals for entertainment are a testament to this carnist belief that all other beings are here for human-animals to use. The violence against non-human animals is made palatable through the absent referent–a term from Adams' (2015) which is a result of the way language "renames dead bodies before consumers participate in eating them" (p. 21).

Referring specially to using non-human animals as "food", Adams (2015) observes that language is employed to distance the animal from the end product so flesh, tendons, and muscle turns into "meat" which allows the consumer to separate the dismembered body from the food. Nonetheless, Adams (2015) reminds us that no one can consume meat without necessitating the killing of an animal so "the absent referent permits us to forget about the animal as an independent entity; it also enables us to resist efforts to make animals present" (p. 21). Moreover, the rhetoric surrounding the consumption of animal bodies is constructed in such a way that it makes it easy for the consumer to disassociate the pig from the pork and the beef from the cow. Even when we are reminded this "food" comes from a living being, anthropocentrism makes it convenient to dismiss any guilt about unnecessarily robbing an individual of their life, since it is not a human life.

Cunningham (n.d.) looks at how the absent referent is constructed in the dairy industry: where the role and lived experiences of the cows in this industry remains invisible. The origin of the milk includes a forced pregnancy, the separation of a baby calf from their mother, and the eventual slaughter of the cow, yet dairy advertisements focus on selling milk products through sexualized images of the female body. Davis (2004, p. 11) encapsulates the overarching danger of the absent referent by reminding us of the phrase, "We're treated like animals". This indicates how each of their individual lives does not count and they are made absent as most do not hear this phrase and then question what that means about how we treat non-human animals.

Another root cause of speciesism is androcentrism. Androcentrism creates "a global gender hierarchy that privileges males over females and European

Judeo-Christian patriarchy over other forms of gender relations" (Spivak, 1988; Enloe, 1990 as cited in Grosfoguel, 2011, p. 9). Carolyn Merchant uses an ecofeminist lens to trace androcentrism back to Francis Bacon in the 1600s. Bacon largely influenced how nature is perceived by describing nature as "a common harlot" (as cited in Thompson & MacGregor, 2017). Adams (2015) writes that "in a patriarchal, meat eating world animals are feminized and sexualized; women are animalized" so the interrelated objectification of women and non-human animals prevails (Adams, 2010, p. 304). Patriarchal narratives that associate meat with strength are used to justify the myth that men must eat meat: as Adam's notes: "the literal evocation of male power is found in the concept of meat" (p. 11). Since patriarchy is tied to an entitlement to meat-eating as an expression of hegemonic masculinity, violence against women and non-human animals is obscured through the absent referent as metaphors distance "the violent transformation of living to dead" (Adams, 2010, p. 304). This dissociation between meat and the animal it was taken from makes meat "a free-floating image, used often to reflect women's status as well as animals" (Adams, 2015, pp. xxiv–xxv).

In addition to this Adams' study of the absent referent illuminates an intersection between how women and non-human animals are, in many ways, stripped of their personhood and used as objects for male consumption. Albright (2002) concurs that the absent referent reduces women and non-human animals to passive objects by removing the characteristic from the image or identity which, in turn, makes it "psychologically easier for consumers to subjugate women and animals" (p. 928). This subjugation is evident as men have "controlled, raped, not given any credibility, [and] not taken seriously" women, non-human animals, and nature. This complete disregard and assumed right to colonize others' bodies is exemplified in the mutilation and domestication of "their cycles [and] their entire beings... conformed to human's needs" (Adams, 1991, p. 127). Ergo, the dynamic between the absent referent and androcentrism interacts in such a way that women, non-human animals, and nature are rendered as objects for male control.

Rationalism is another root cause of speciesism, as its logic of hierarchy is used to rationalize and justify exploitation. This thinking and resultant actions have been entrenched in western thought since the Classical period of Ancient Greece. Val Plumwood (1990), for example, traces dualism right back to Plato who launched the dichotomy of reason versus nature. Since rationalism privileges white, cishetero males of European origin/descent, it creates a hierarchical logic where one way of knowing is deemed superior to all others. A rationalist framework instrumentalizes the "passive object" for human gain (Figueroa-Helland & Lindgren, 2016); as Martusewicz et al.

(2014) explain, "the first term in this string of oppositional pairs is always presented as superior and independent of the second, while the second term is always inferior to and at the mercy of the first" (p. 90).

Commenting on the overlap between women and nature, Shiva & Mies (2014) writes that "women all over the world, since the beginning of patriarchy, were also treated like 'nature', devoid of rationality, their bodies functioning in the same instinctive way as other mammals" and the tools of oppression include "science, technology, and violence." (p. Xxii). In other words, being rational is achievable only by man so those who operate from a place of emotion or instinct are naturally inferior and, therefore, rightfully subjugated. In terms of the commodification of non-human animals, Alloun (2015) calls for alternative collective and political actions to hold the economic and political systems that underpin animal exploitation, as well as the hegemonic cultural ideology of carnism. But bluntly, under a rationalist framework, the "rational" men are superior to "emotional" women, "instinctual" animals, and "wild" nature (Figueroa-Helland & Lindgren, 2016).

Rationalism can be traced to Descartes who advocated a stark split between mind and body. It is predicated on dualisms in which the term on the left is deemed superior and has the authority to subjugate the term on the right. In the following pairs, the word on the left is the active subject who acts upon the passive object: man/nature, man/woman, human/animal. This heavily influences how human-animals view the earth. Stewart-Harawira (2005) examines how René Descartes' ideas promoted efforts to maximize the use of tools of manipulation, in order to minimize human effort for extracting the "fruits of the earth" for human consumption. Looping back to the human/animal example, dualism ties into rhetoric so closely because human-animals try to separate themselves from other species. As Kheel (2008) describes, "[t]he term 'animal,' for example, is usually employed with little awareness that humans are also animals" (p. 6).

For this reason, altering our language and way of thinking that encourages us to reflect on the fact that humans are animals, can help us unlearn the damage of anthropocentrism and the value of all life. Plumwood (2003) argues that dualism not only hyper-separates and ranks the term on the right relative to the one on the left, but also instrumentalizes the tool on the right so it is seen as an object at the service of the one on the left. Mathews (2017) describes the term on the right is also homogenized or viewed collectively providing the example of "all sentient life on the planet… lumped together under the category 'animal' which is assumed to be a different category than 'human'" (p. 58). Moreover, creating these distinct categories and hierarchical ranking of values has become the hegemonic system for judging the value of all life and ways of knowing where one particular identity and framework is placed on a pedestal and the rest are devalued and mechanized in service of the active subject. Kheel (2008) asserts that hegemonic masculinities with associated traits of rationality, universality, and autonomy are privileged in this system. In contrast, their counterparts–emotion, particularity, and relation and dependence are viewed as inferior. It is crucial to counter rationalism as it informs hegemonic systems such as western science, capitalism, and coloniality (Figueroa-Helland & Lindgren, 2016).

Western science is informed by rationalism. This effectively creates "the other"–whether it is women, non-human animals, or nature–viewed as disposable objects at the whim of men's experiments. Francis Bacon, often considered the "father of modern science" aimed to "'wrestle secrets from nature's grasp' and to veal the 'secrets locked in nature's bosom'" and this view, "for many feminist analysists… is not just rhetorical excess" as these intentions are quite tangible in how western science operates (Seager, 2017, p. 37). This can be interpreted as man's insecurity that he is reliant upon the reproductive labor of women and nature to sustain life, so in response he tries to control and mechanize these cycles to fit into the patriarchal capitalist marketplace; in other words, men "want to be creators themselves" (Keller, 1985 as cited in Mies, 2014, p. 45). In terms of the animal liberation movement, I would argue that rationalism has a stronghold in which arguments are perceived as the strongest. While there is value in debunking speciesism, carnism or other toxic ideologies through appealing to reason and logic, it becomes a serious problem when this overshadows and dismisses any approaches rooted in empathy and care. This is a key reason why, as will be discussed in more detail shortly, drawing on CAS and implementing ecofeminist approaches becomes so important.

Finally, while appearing distinct and separate, we must always be aware of the interconnected natures of anthropocentrism, androcentrism, and rationalism, and how these inform—and are informed by—the hegemonic neoliberal order. Adams (2015), for instance, investigates how the construction of gender informs the political landscape providing the example of politicians who attack "welfare queens" but do not launch a "cowboy welfare kings" attack about the ranchers who's businesses are heavily subsidized by the government (p. Xxix). Another example is the former agriculture secretary, Ezra Taft Benson, who said to President Eisenhower in response to Rachel Carson's critique of insecticide manufacturers that "We can live without birds and animals, but, as the current market slump shows, we cannot live without business. As for insects, isn't it just like a woman to be scared to death of a few little bugs! As long as we have the H-bomb everything will be O.K." (Stoll as cited in Seager, 2017, p. 39). These two examples illustrate how the underlying ideologies that surface in economic and political contexts are elements of anthropocentrism, androcentrism, and rationalism. For this reason, any guiding frameworks that address speciesism must grapple with the overlapping beliefs that uphold this exploitation.

Implementing CAS and Ecofeminist Approaches

CAS and ecofeminist approaches are vital to (a) understand each root cause of speciesism; (b) analyze the intersections, and (c) deconstruct the underpinning economic and political forces that bolster speciesist ideologies. While many fringe groups take an intersectional approach to veganism by including critiques of patriarchy and the economic system, for example, this cross-analysis is depressingly lacking in much of the mainstream animal liberation movement. Critical Animal Studies (CAS) has much to offer here, not least through its intersectionality approach. This allows us to (1) incorporate broader critique of the economic and political landscape, and (2) explore alternative ways of organizing such as anarchism that challenge toxic hierarchies. As Best et al. (2007) write, CAS

> Advances a holistic understanding of the commonality of oppressions, such that speciesism, sexism, racism, ableism, statism, classism, militarism and other hierarchical ideologies and institutions are viewed as parts of a larger, interlocking, global system of domination (p. 2).

Anarchist political thought comes into play as a means to address these converging problems and reject the exclusion that results from unnecessary hierarchies. It also lends itself to taking a stand against speciesism since the hierarchical nature of this ideology puts human-animal life above non-human animals (see Nocella et. al., 2015). Furthermore, anarchists recognize that speciesism cannot be dismantled with consumption choices alone, especially when consumption remains within the capitalist marketplace which will always be exploitative (Werkeheiser, 2013). Anarchists' stance against exploitative hierarchies ties into ecofeminism which studies the connection between the oppression of women and nature and expand upon this to posit that speciesism is "an intentional parallel of sexism [and] the root of our exploitation of non-humans" (Werkeheiser, 2013, p. 168).

Both ecofeminism and CAS teach us valuable lessons about recognizing the appropriation of social movements. Appropriation attempts to undermine the potential that social movements have to radically challenge mainstream hegemonic norms or vested interests. To add insult to injury, it can become highly profitable for businesses when capitalism successfully appropriates social movements into consumer goods. This can be observed in the vegan movement when capitalist monopolies pander to the rise in plant-based foods by offering options instead of fully transitioning their products to veganic for the benefit of the non-human animals, their consumer's health, and the prospect of avoiding a complete ecological breakdown. Despite the gravity of the many reasons to be vegan, capitalism subsumes veganism so its radical anti-capitalist praxis is diluted into an individual alternative lifestyle choice devoid of a strong ethical framework (White, 2017). Minimizing the ideology of veganism to passive consumer choices of buying faux fur and plant-based meats is not enough as we must encompass the broader systems that maintain overlapping oppression (Nocella et al., 2014). It is imperative to reclaim veganism as a vehement stance against capitalism with the aims of environmental sustainability and inter-species justice rather than treating veganism as a single-issue effort (White, 2018).

Ecofeminists can be defined as "Women who look explicitly at the intersection of the oppression of women and other social groups with ecological" (Martusewicz et al., 2014, p. 89). Rather than a single movement or philosophy, it is a "loosely knit philosophical and practical orientation linking the concerns of women to the larger natural world" (Kheel, 2008, p. 8). Since there is a diversity of thought in this framework, it is worthwhile to distinguish between an ecofeminism that is limited to concerns for human-women and nature and the ecofeminism supported in this paper that expands to encompass non-human animals and has goals of total liberation.

Ecofeminism is the remedy for the toxic hierarchical ordering of life as it is "about the connectedness and wholeness of theory and practice. It asserts the special strength and integrity of every living thing." (Mies & Shiva, 2014, p. 14). Explicitly analyzing the connection of women and nature, specifically, can act as a rejection of the capitalist patriarchy which interweaves the devaluing of women and nature (Thompson & MacGregor, 2017). Moreover, in the capitalist marketplace, both women and nature are externalities so the social labor and reproductive labor of women and nature is not counted in the economy (Mellor, 2017). Since the oppressions are mutually reinforcing, "twentieth and twenty-first century vegan feminists and ecofeminists see their own liberation and well-being as fundamentally connected to the well-being of other animal species; in short, "we insist on moving forward together" (Harper 2010; Kemmerer 2011, as cited in Gaard, 2017, p. 116). In other words, we cannot cherry-pick issues to care about; instead, we must look at the broader picture to see the interrelatedness of oppressions and recognize that no one is free until we are all free. Ecofeminism is a guiding force to transition from the current hegemonic systems that prioritize competition and hierarchies into a paradigm focused on co-operation and mutual care of nature, human-animals, and non-human animals so we can return to valuing diversity (Mies & Shiva, 2014, p. 6).

An ecofeminist framework teaches us to reject the current dominating practices rooted in anthropocentrism, androcentrism, and rationalism. Instead we must look to co-create relations and systems that acknowledge our mutual dependency and reject any delusions that we are the center of the earth. Rather, humans are a piece of a much larger puzzle. To address anthropocentrism, an ecofeminist standpoint teaches us that we are dependent on that which we are destroying; humans rely on the health of ecosystems yet we continue business as usual in an economic system that necessitates infinite growth and poison the water and land through the destructive practices of animal agriculture. In terms of androcentrism, ecofeminism allows us to shift from viewing reproductive work as an externality to essential cycles that regenerate and sustain us all (Shiva, 2014). Anthropocentrism is crucial to the problems at hand, given the obliteration of nature translates to the destruction of the human race since humans rely on the ecosystems for survival. As Clive Hamilton argues, reconnecting human beings and nature means "recognizing that the power relation between human and the earth is the reverse of the one we have assumed for three centuries" (as cited in Adelman, 2015, p. 12).

Understanding the ecocide is mandatory to begin the healing process. To address rationalism, ecofeminism allows us to view "the world as an active subject, not merely as a resource to be manipulated and appropriated" (Shiva, 2014, p. 33). An ecofeminist lens is vital for animal liberation because the movement is primarily comprised of women, yet men have the biggest platform and, therefore, visibility (McKay, 2015, p. XIiii). When this movement is patriarchal, it fails to sufficiently address, if at all, what went wrong in the first place. By embracing an ecofeminist framework to acknowledge and deconstruct the major roots of speciesism–anthropocentrism, androcentrism, and rationalism–we can move beyond the current prevailing systems into an alternative that fights for the autonomy and respect for all human-animals, non-human animals, and ecosystems alike.

Closing Thoughts

In response to a greater awareness of anthropocentrism, androcentrism, and rationalism, and how these root causes affirm and support other ideologies, particularly speciesism and neoliberalism, we must draw upon approaches like CAS and ecofeminism. These approaches offer critical frameworks that are fully committed to overturning these ideologies and the toxic systems of deadly oppression that flow from them. For the animal liberation movement to be successful, it must find better ways to challenge the hidden beliefs that cause the problems in the first place; this certainly includes exposing the flawed logic and appeal of anthropocentrism, androcentrism, and rationalism.

Furthermore, we must also be fully aware that the power of ideologies cannot be successfully challenged or dismantled unless the individuals who believe in them are conscious of them and are able to reject them. In other words, we must be able to influence others to the extent that dominant normalization processes are recognized and unlearned. To encourage such a critical shift to take place at the individual level requires the ability to successfully create experience(s) in which a person will, "see and *hear* and *feel* another person give voice to an alternative perspective [from which that] point of view becomes something real, 'in your face,' and subjectively potent" (Maiese & Hanna, 2019, p. 278). This might be achieved through communication: hearing the voice of someone speaking candidly about the harsh reality of the animal industrial complex[1], or through other visceral sounds, such as hearing the screams of its victims. Alternatively, the process of deep re-evaluation might be prompted through visual images, for example by seeing the footage of a cow hanging upside down while her throat is slashed open. The point being made here is that bearing witness to the lived experiences of these non-human animals is pivotal to get the general public to understand how anthropocentrism, androcentrism, and rationalism manifest as life or death situations.

Any goal short of total liberation will ultimately fail to recognize the tightly interconnected ideologies that sustain a toxic hierarchy which grants some lives value and meaning, and other lives none at all (Nocella, Sorenson, Socha, & Matsuoka, 2013). To work toward a paradigm shift that breaks away from speciesism, we must commit to vocalizing the critiques and values of CAS and ecofeminism. Importantly these approaches do not shy away from the urgent task of building solidarity through identifying multifaceted oppression and engaging fearlessly with the political economy of neoliberal capitalist that must be dissembled for true liberation to be found. In short,

1 The animal industrial complex, a concept from Barbara Noske (1989), refers to the myriad of institutionalized stakeholders and systems that exploit non-human animals. Quite simply stated, Dillard (2008) notes that the "animal-industrial complex, a gigantic maze of factory farms, slaughterhouses, and packaging plants, is a heavily integrated industry in the United States that kills and processes over 9 billion animals per year" (pp. 1-2).

CAS and ecofeminism not only push us to look clearly at speciesism and other toxic ideologies, but they also equip us with the tools needed to build a liberatory framework for all.

References

Adams, C. (1991). Ecofeminism and the eating of animals. *Hypatia, 6*(1), 125.

Adams, C. J. (2010). Why feminist-vegan now? *Feminism & Psychology, 20*(3), 302–317.

Adams, C. J. (2015). *The sexual politics of meat: A feminist-vegetarian critical theory.* Bloomsbury Publishing USA.

Adelman, S. (2015). Epistemologies of mastery. In Grear, A., & Kotzé, L. J. (Eds.), *Research handbook on human rights and the environment* (pp. 9–27). Edward Elgar Publishing.

Albright, K. M. (2002). The extension of legal rights to animals under a caring ethic: An ecofeminist exploration of Steven Wise's "rattling the cage". *Natural Resources Journal, 42*(4), 915-937.

Alloun, E. (2015). Ecofeminism and animal advocacy in Australia: Productive encounters for an integrative ethics and politics. *Animal Studies Journal, 4*(1), 148-173.

Best, S., Nocella, A. J., Kahn, R., Gigliotti, C., & Kemmerer, L. (2007). Introducing critical animal studies. *Journal for Critical Animal Studies, 5*(1), 4-5.

Borras Jr, S. M., Franco, J. C., & Suárez, S. M. (2015). Land and food sovereignty. *Third World Quarterly, 36*(3), 600-617.

Compa, L. A. (2004). *Blood, sweat, and fear: Workers' rights in US meat and poultry plants.* Human Rights Watch.

Cunningham, T. (n.d.). *You are what you drink: A feminist critique of milk and its consequences for the female.* Animals and Society Institute. https://www.animalsandsociety.org/human-animal-studies/sloth/sloth-volume-i-no-1-march-2015/you-are-what-you-drink-a-feminist-critique-of-milk-and-its-consequences-for-the-female/

Davis, K. (2004). A tale of two holocausts. *Animal Liberation Philosophy and Policy Journal, 2*(2), 6–25.

Dillard, J. (2008). A slaughterhouse nightmare: Psychological harm suffered by slaughterhouse employees and the possibility of redress through legal reform. *Geo. J. on Poverty L. & Pol'y, 15*, 1-18.

Federici, S. (2008). Witch-hunting, globalization, and feminist solidarity in Africa today. *Journal of International Women's Studies, 10*(1), 21–35.

Federici, S. (2009, January 27). *The reproduction of labour-power in the global economy, Marxist theory and the unfinished feminist revolution* [UC Santa Cruz Seminar]. The Crisis of Social Reproduction and Feminist Struggle, Santa Cruz, California, U.S.

Figueroa Helland, L. E., & Lindgren, T. (2016). What goes around comes around: From the coloniality of power to the crisis of civilization. *Journal of World-Systems Research, 22*(2), 430-462.

Gaard, G. (2017). Posthumanism, ecofeminism, and inter-species. In MacGregor, S. (Ed.), *Routledge handbook of gender and environment* (pp. 115-130). Routledge.

Gills, B. (2010). Going south: Capitalist crisis, systemic crisis, civilisational crisis. *Third World Quarterly*, *31*(2), 169.

Gregory, D. (1968). *The shadow that scares me*. Doubleday and Co.

Grosfoguel, R. (2011). Decolonizing post-colonial studies and paradigms of political-economy: Transmodernity, decolonial thinking, and global coloniality. *Transmodernity: Journal of Peripheral Cultural Production of the Luso-Hispanic World*, *1*(1).

Kheel, M. (2008). *Nature Ethics: An ecofeminist perspective*. Rowman & Littlefield Publishers.

Maiese, M., & Hanna, R. (2019). *The mind-body politic*. Palgrave Macmillan.

Martusewicz, R. A., Edmundson, J., & Lupinacci, J. (2014). Learning androcentrism: An EcoJustice approach to gender and education. In Martusewicz, R. A., Edmundson, J., & Lupinacci, (Eds.), *Ecojustice education: Toward diverse, democratic, and sustainable communities* (pp. 95-133). Routledge.

Mathews, F. (2017). The dilemma of dualism. In MacGregor, S. (Ed.), *Routledge handbook of gender and environment* (pp. 54-70). Routledge.

Matsuoka, A., & Sorenson, J. (2018). Introduction. In Matsuoka, A., & Sorenson, J. (Eds.). *Critical animal studies: Towards trans-species social justice* (pp. 1-17). Rowman & Littlefield.

McKay, N. (2015). Foreword by Nellie McKay: Feminists don't have a sense of humor. In Adams, C. J. (Ed.), *The sexual politics of meat: A feminist-vegetarian critical theory* (pp. xli–xlv). Bloomsbury Publishing USA.

McMichael, P. (2017). *Development and social change*. Sage Publication.

Mellor, M. (2017). Ecofeminist political economy: A green and feminist agenda. In MacGregor, S. (Ed.), *Routledge handbook of gender and environment* (pp. 86-100). Routledge.

Mies, M. (2014). White man's dilemma: His search for what he has destroyed. In M. Mies, & V. Shiva (Eds.), *Ecofeminism* (pp. 132-163). Zed Books Ltd.

Nibert, D. (2014). Animals, immigrants, and profits: Slaughterhouses and the political economy of oppression. In Sorenson, J. (Eds.), *Critical animal studies: Thinking the unthinkable*, 1 (pp. 3–17). Canadian Scholars Press Inc.

Nocella II, A. J., Sorenson, J., Socha, K., & Matsuoka, A. (2013). *Defining critical animal studies: An intersectional social justice approach for liberation*. New York, NY: Peter Lang Publishing.

Nocella II, A. J., White, R., & Cudworth, E. (2015). Introduction: The intersections of critical animal studies and anarchist studies for total liberation. In Nocella II, A. J., White, R., & Cudworth, E. (Eds.), *Anarchism and animal liberation: Essays on complementary elements of total liberation* (pp. 7-20). McFarland and Company, Inc.

Noske, B. (1989). *Human and other animals London*. Pluto Press.

Plumwood, V. (1990). Plato and the bush: Philosophy and the environment in Australia. *Meanjin*, *49*(3), 524.

Plumwood, V. (2003). *Feminism and the mastery of nature*. Routledge.

Seager, J. (2017). Rachel Caron was right – then and now. In MacGregor, S. (Ed.), *Routledge handbook of gender and environment* (pp. 27-42). Routledge.

Shiva, V. (2014). Reductionism and regeneration: A crisis in science. In Mies, M., & Shiva, V. (Eds.), *Ecofeminism* (pp. 22-35). Zed Books Ltd.

Shiva, V., & Mies, M. (2014). Preface to the critique influence change edition. In Mies, M., & Shiva, V. (Eds.), *Ecofeminism* (pp. 1-21). Zed Books Ltd.

Stewart-Harawira, M. (2005). Cultural studies, indigenous knowledge and pedagogies of hope. *Policy Futures in Education*, *3*(2), 153–163. Routledge.

Thompson, C., & MacGregor, S. (2017). The death of nature: Foundations of ecological feminist thoughts. In S. MacGregor (Ed.), *Routledge handbook of gender and environment* (pp. 43-53). Routledge.

Weitzenfeld, A., & Joy, M. (2014). An overview of anthropocentrism, humanism, and speciesism in critical animal theory. In J. Sorenson, K. Socha, & A. Matsuoka (Eds.), *Defining critical animal studies: An intersectional social justice approach for liberation* (pp. 3-27). Peter Lang.

White, R. J. (2017). Rising to the challenge of capitalism and the commodification of nonhuman animals: Post-capitalism, anarchist economies and vegan praxis. In D. Nibert (Ed.), *Animal oppression and capitalism* (pp. 270-294). Praeger Press.

White, R. J. (2018). Looking backward/moving forward. Articulating a "Yes, BUT…!" response to lifestyle veganism, and outlining post-capitalist futures in critical veganic agriculture. *EuropeNow*, (20).

Zampa, M. (n.d.). *How many animals a year are killed for food every day?* Sentient media. https://sentientmedia.org/how-many-animals-are-killed-for-food-every-day/

6. 'Before We Talk about Freedom: Let Us Free Our Slaves': An Activist's Reflections on Anarchism, Non-human Animals and Total Liberation

CARLOS GARCIA

Introduction

I feel it is important to begin this chapter by reflecting on my positionality. I am categorized by mainstream society as being "White", "European" and "male", and therefore I have decided not to explore certain themes too deeply in this chapter, such as feminism or anti-racism. This is mainly due to the unearned privileges of being a White European male, and the fear of mis-representation other gender or ethnic claims. While taking this into account, I am hoping to write as an activist for Animal Liberation. I have no academic ties; the language I use is very much rooted in activism, which it not necessarily the language of scholars! I make no apologies for this: this is not an academic treatise. I am only trying to show you a particular point of view that I have been working on for some time, mainly presenting and justifying the reasons why those who deem themselves "anarchists" should also adopt veganism as part of the so-called fight for Total Liberation. In this way the chapter acts as a starting point of discussion for anyone who identifies with anarchism and animal liberation movement, and indeed has relevance more widely, with all those who fight oppression.

Before addressing the key arguments and relevant context, it is important to outline what I understand by the concept of "anarchism" and "Total Liberation". For me anarchism, ideologically speaking, sets a clear goal, namely: full individual freedom in every aspect of our lives, based on the mutual aid and the abolition of any institutionalized form of oppression (see

Bakunin, 1814; Kropotkin, 1842). However the assumption that anarchism should apply only to humans, and human narratives of freedom, must be radically re-evaluated. It is my contention that if we seek a radical transformation of society and interpersonal relationships, and the attainment of true freedom and liberation, we cannot leave other individuals outside of the equation just because they do not belong to our species. Here one of the most persuasive articles that argues for anarchists embracing an inter-species approach to matters of social justice is Brian Dominick's essay, "Animal Liberation and Social Revolution" (1997). This in turn has been influential in informing my support for—and engaging directly with—activism in the name of Total Liberation.

Let me be clear, I understand Total Liberation as an intersectional concept, one which aims to recognize that all social justice struggles like feminism, anarchism, anti-authoritarian, between others, have much in common. If we could only recognize this commonality, this would enable more effective forms of activism to fight oppressive systems (let us think here of the quote "union make force"). In this context we should never forget that human oppression over non-human-animals, the so-called speciesism, is part of the system which we aim to fight (see Written By A Few Wild Animals, 2013). The opportunity to justify and explain more fully why this is the case is a key aim of this this chapter.

Until now, however, many anarcho-communists organizations—within other leftist movements influenced by anarchist ideas—have been extremely slow to recognize and incorporate the struggle for earth and animal liberation into their political agendas (here I am thinking of the CNT, CGT, Solidaridad Obrera, AIT, IWA, and others). This is troubling—why do those who believe in anarchist praxis to make a better world, at the same time reject animal rights / animal liberation and veganism? Regrettably, but predictably, the most common reasons I have heard have nothing to do with anti-authoritarian or emancipatory movements (see also Anon, 2017)! Dismal excuses such as "we´ve been using non-human animals for ages", "non-human animals are ours like properties", "I like the taste of meat", all are proffered to justify (these) anarchists not wanting to question their species' privileges, or think about the violence that comes with eating the bodies of other animals. Another reasons people within the anarchist movement are resistant to adopt veganism as a part of their lives is that most of these anarchist people see veganism as something snobbish, elitist even, due to the consumption of processed foods which aren't within everyone's means. Sincerely, I disagree. A vegan does not need to consume expensive processed foods in order to live, but I empathize with that (false) vision of class and veganism since the image of veganism portrayed by some organizations is indeed just *that*: a consumer capitalist lifestyle.

I am aware that questioning and rejecting these privileges and deeply-ingrained habits can be hard; despite anarchists' excellent work in deconstructing other aspects of domination, speciesism is without a doubt exceptionally complex and difficult to understand due to the fact that we deal with individuals of other species. It´s complex because non-human animals are seen as things—as objects—not unique individuals, subjects of a valuable life, like human beings are. So this "thing" concept it´s quite hard to leave due to its normalization by the oppressive system we live in since we´re young. Other reasons are even more diverse, such as taste, tradition, normalcy (as in lifelong), etc. Yet how can we—how can anarchists—deem ourselves a revolutionary force when we place our personal interest before other individuals? Why should our interests be above theirs? Do we not seek to eliminate differences, forms of authority, hierarchies, etc.? If so, why do we keep making the same excuses not to adopt habits which are completely compatible with anarchism?

All of these excuses continue, I believe, because many anarchists have only filtered oppression, violence and subjugation only through a narrow, anthropocentric perspective. Anthropocentrism, broadly understood, is a philosophical tendency which places humans atop the most privileged and elitist vantage point. For the purposes of this chapter I will refer to "moral anthropocentrism", which defines our relationship with the rest of the animals and nature. The concept of moral anthropocentrism is based on a power and domination dynamic. Yet, this is something that we need to address if we are to achieve our hopes of perform systemic change, and revolutionize society? If we reject exploitation and oppression over humankind, should not we do the same with all animals?

As an animal liberation movement we have the same interests as anarchism to forge a new society, a new world in which the words "respect" and "freedom" may acquire a deeper and richer sense of meaning. This envisages a world where social justice is not only applicable to humans but to all individuals, independent of species, is the one we aspire for. It should not be difficult to see that the society in which we live is immersed in a great crisis: social, political, economic, and environmental. The implication of this that is that no single political tactic or approach can possibly comprehend all struggles adequately, let alone begin to address them. Understanding that each social movement is connected at some significant level will enabled us to bring forward a real Total Liberation movement with the goal to fight *all* forms of oppression wherever they may be found (e.g. Pellow, 2014; Fitzgerald &

Pellow, 2014; Pellow & Brehm, 2015). It should be easy to recognize how the dynamics of power and domination underpin seemingly different oppressed groups including, gender, sex, ethnicity, ableism, race, species and also class (see Johanna, 2008; Hribal, 2003). We must understand that each form of oppression is in turn supported by another, which is why, although oppressed groups appear to be rooted in (vastly) different contexts we understand that those who oppress, reinforce and feed these forms of oppression come from the same source(s) and thus we share the same problematic. In short, as this chapter will now argue, I think the way to make a strong movement against this oppressive system is the one that actively engages all social struggles, particularly the Animal and Earth Liberation movements, to seek better understand and resist and fight domination.

If we are willing to recognize this, then this begs the next question: where to begin? One answer is rooted *within* animal liberation activism. Animal liberation activists must actively seek to connect their struggles with other struggles like feminism, antifascism or anti-authoritarianism among others. The same works in the opposite direction. There is nothing to stop ostensibly political 'human-rights' activists—the Antifa movement for example—from embracing animal rights and a vegan praxis. The convergence between different social movements allows to build bridges of understanding between social groups which previously worked in isolation. Examples of this might include 'No New Animal Labs', an anti-speciesism collective that was fighting in defense of Standing Rock, and others including the 'Freshet Collective' (see Freshnet Collective, 2013); the 'Water Protector Legal Collective' (https://waterprotectorlegal.org/); and the 'Water Protector Anti-Repression Crew' (https://www.facebook.com/WaterProtectorAntiRepressionCrew/). It should also be acknowledged how encouraging it is to see a Total Liberation praxis beating at the heart of the critical animal studies movement, which hopefully will provide much inspiration and guidance for others (see Nocella et al., 2019). This point is critical—if we want to advance a Total Liberation approach we have to learn to build ties and seek how to work together effectively to resist and overcome the multiple dimensions of oppression wherever they occur.

Speciesism as Oppressive System

While embracing a Total Liberation Approach, it is important that activists understand more fully our violent relationships with other animals, and be particularly aware of the how speciesism informs and legitimizes this everyday violence. Speciesism, crudely put, is nothing more than an arbitrary form of discrimination in the human / non-human animals relationship (see Ryder,

2010). But within non-human animals we can still come up with classes of speciesism, due to the fact that we see certain species as individuals whom to respect, love, while turning all other species into mere objects and resources to satisfy our wishes and achieve certain objectives, like eating, dressing, experimenting, entertaining, for transportation, etc. When we deny some intrinsic rights to the rest of non-human animals, we become prejudiced and discriminatory. To me, speciesism should be discussed and taken into debate inside anti-authoritarian collectives, anarchist ones, and so on. Usually, if this comes up in conversation with others I tend to comment that speciesism is a form of racism toward non-human animals, since we classify them, and value them, only according to our own interests.

If we understand that speciesism, as a prejudice, is a form of power based on the moral anthropocentrism which places humans above the rest (environment, non-human animals), we should then understand that other forms of domination and power, such as sexism, racism, ableism, etc., share the same pattern as speciesism. As such, if those of us within the Animal Liberation movement are able to see the relationship of human supremacist power over non-human animals, it shouldn't be difficult to share this point with to the sociopolitical movements where no debates have been generated with regards to veganism.

Anarchism, we believe, must seek to transgress all forms of domination. Understanding veganism, and thus the Animal Liberation movement, as a form of dismantling the colonialism which capitalism maintains over the bodies of non-human animals, elucidates the parallel with exists in the relationship between humans and non-humans (see Spassmaschine, 2017). Every person who opposes domination, whatever kind it may be, should commit, within their means, to support the fight against speciesism. In that sense, and let me be clear, I do not seek to impose a westernized vision of veganism over other cultures! We must understand the existing cultural contexts, since generally, indigenous cultures do not see other animals as beings upon which to exert domination over, but as a symbiotic part of their own lives, they have been wise enough to stay away from the concept of objectification which the imperialist conquest has thus far imposed.

Similarly, those whose activism is rooted in the Animal Rights movement (I make the distinction between the Animal Rights and Animal Liberation movements because within the latter, we are supposed to have arrived at a point of reflection about our political ideas) should understand that speciesist oppression is analogous to all other existing forms of domination which humans exert on other humans. In this respect there are many intersections of inter-species oppression that can be identified (see Hochschartner, 2014).

One of these—namely speciesism and sexism—will be considered in more detail now.

Interconnecting Oppressions

Within the speciesist discrimination toward non-human animals we can also find certain intersectional relationships with the culture of sexist exploitation. There is an important and vibrant body of critical literature which has informed much of my understanding and interpretation of this, including: "The Sexual Politics of Meat: A Feminist-Vegetarian Critical Theory" (Adams, 2015); "Mothers with Monkey Wrenches: Feminist Imperatives and the ALF" (Jones, 2004); "Women, Destruction and the Avant-Garde: A Paradigm for Animal Liberation" (Socha, 2011) and "La Ética Animal: ¿Una Cuestión Feminista?" and (Valasco, 2017). In Angélica Velasco's book "La Ética Animal ¿Una Cuestión Feminista?" she asks the critical question: is it possible to reach equality and obtain critical thought if we cannot see the connection(s) between different ways of domination?

In our everyday lives we can see the overlapping oppressions of sexism and speciesism present in commercials, and how both human and non-human animals are used as sexualized objects. Other routine acts of violence are less seen in everyday life, but they take place in order to satisfy the societal demand to consume the milk and flesh of nonhuman animals. Focusing on "farmed" animals for example, one particularly egregious form of oppression over (their) female bodies is artificial insemination. This practice is performed mostly on equines and bovines, although it does not exempt other mammals. The process is carried out as follows: a vet introduces the arm inside the animal's rectum to position the uterus, then the vet introduces an instrument with a receptacle which holds the semen. I consider the insemination against the will of animals constitutes an act of violence and a direct violation to their autonomy as individuals. This practice is usually carried out in dairy farms and extended onto others, such as pig farms. Another clear way to illustrate the relationship between speciesism and sexism is the use of insults which make reference to non-humans in metaphor as a means to denigrate humans. This includes words such as 'bitch' (female fox in Spanish) or 'slut' (female dog in Spanish), referring to those women who men/ the patriarchal culture consider to be sexually promiscuous. Also some expressions as 'eres más puta que las gallinas' (you are bitchier tan hens), are used without acknowledging that hens are forced to breed by the meat industry. Other macho words, related to speciesism, are 'you couple like a rabbit', giving the responsibility of giving birth to only women, without taking into account that sometimes they just feel the social pressure for doing so.

Patriarchal domination, as well as speciesism which has risen from anthropocentrism, have been related many times by the feminist movement. Feminism and the Animal Liberation movement have much in common, many comparisons may be drawn from the way in which patriarchy acts and the relationship with the rest of all non-human animals. The struggle for women's liberation (and thus other gender realities) is an important part of anarchism. Does that mean that we can afford to be blind in regard to speciesist domination? If we reject the idea that forms of oppression are independent amongst themselves and that the models of oppression do not act independently from one another, we may reach the conclusion that these forms of discrimination are intermingled and become one. In this sense, we may affirm that patriarchy and the consumption of animals are linked to turn women into objects, the same way in which speciesism does with non-human animals, turning them into bodies to be consumed, one group as sexual demand while the other one as food.

The relationship between speciesism and racism, as well as other forms of oppression based on geographical origin, is completely explicit. Speciesism forces us see and value non-human animals as inferior beings. This is precisely the way racial supremacists see other ethnic groups as inferior. We possess an infinity of references in the history of colonialism and imperialism, translated in the subjugation of peoples and cultures, the genocide which has been done and that which is still being done. With regards to that, I don't mean to say that speciesist people are inherently "bad", they merely follow, uncritically, a trend of indifference towards non-human animals due to the education which is imparted and a system of values which is based on anthropocentrism. But once the veil of ignorance is removed, and the facts presented front of our eyes, how can we ever argue that it morally justified to be part of such a way of discrimination again?

The Need to Ask Critical Questions and Engage in Critical Self-reflection

All sociopolitical movements, anarchism or other, should recognize that non-human animals are not here to serve our interests, in fact, no one is here to serve the interests of another, even less so to do it from a position of privilege. I aim to say that the rest of the animals have subjective relationships with the environment, just as we do. When they feel fear, they hide or flee, when they are cold, they seek warmth, when they are wounded, they suffer and experience pain, etc. What makes the different from us? The fact that they do not develop some of the same capacities we do? But then, do we base our relationship with non-human animals on matters of prejudice? This same question could be extrapolated into the scope of existing prejudices among humans. Non-human animals aren't seeking to have civil rights, access to education, be able to pilot an aircraft, etc. Their instincts merely seek to preserve their lifecycle, unharmed and revered, same as all of us. Indeed we share more similarities than differences with them.

Speciesism, just as racism, sexism, ableism, LGBTQ-phobia, etc., are social constructs based on prejudice. No one is born with these attitudes, they are learned to make it acceptable to see that one group is born to dominate and another group to be dominated. It is the common denominator we see in all forms of oppression. The question here is, are we doing anything to stop contributing to this oppressive system? The answer is that if we keep our prejudices intact, then we are in fact doing nothing. I would like to emphasize that anarchism and the anti-speciesist struggle share more common ground than differences. Anarchism, as an antiauthoritarian ideology which is opposed to the abuse generated by the current system, should be extremely conscious of the privileged use of power which humans exert on the rest of the animals.

Total Liberation? Thinking about Inter-species Violence with Reference to Capitalism and Class

For those readers generally—and anarchists specifically—who might need further convincing that a politics of Total Liberation is necessary, I'd also encourage you to think how animal and human exploitation are connected in relation to class and capitalism (see Nibert, 2017a, 2017b). Class can be understood as another uneven relationship of power which oligarchies and bourgeoisies uphold against those that they identify as inferior. In sociopolitical terms, our non-human homologues may get to be part of that society of classes, due to what we have been discussing, the relationship which human animals maintain with non-human animals, is one of power and submission. Capitalism maintains this relationship of power through its vested economic interest: every day non-human animals are scarified in the name of profit (White, 2015a, 2017). In the meantime, most of those who consider themselves anarchists (but still buy meat) contribute to this dark truth. Why then do we accept a *modus operandi* which is profoundly authoritative and violent? As anarchists, shouldn't we fight to eliminate this speciesist relationship of forcing non-human animals, which is at least as immoral as other forms of discrimination (see Nocella et al., 2015)?

Capitalism is a key pillar for oppressing non-human animals, taking their lives to gain profit. However, it should also be acknowledged—though rarely is—that capitalist exploitation and oppression that takes place in the farming and killing of other animals *also* exploits and oppresses humans (see Torres, 2007; White, 2017). In short, capitalism survival is based on the ongoing exploitation of *all* individuals, irrespective of their species. Capitalism is based on benefits no matter their provenance. Within this economic model, non-human animals are seen as properties and never as free individuals. What does the anarchism pretend apart from the liberation from the capitalist oppression? We can also use as an example all the different ways humans take animals' lives and the benefits obtained by their slavery ('cattle' raising, circuses, zoos, fish farms, labs, fishing, etc.). Capitalism together with speciesism are convergent links of a domination system, and therefore anti-speciesism must be also an anti-capitalist struggle. I want to make clear that speciesism was not created by capitalism per se, as it has existed for millennia while capitalism is something more recent. However, it has implemented mechanic production processes for killing an unimaginable amount of innocents (see White, 2017).

The different social movements as I mentioned earlier have a common enemy (the global oppressive system we are in); in identifying these common goals present themselves which, through mutual aid, we can achieve. Just as we want all these social movements to understand and support the struggle for Animal Liberation within their own political agendas, the movement for Animal Liberation should understand and adopt other forms of social struggle against the different injustices which surround and affect us. That's a broad scope of the problem. This convergence is what we can refer to as the movement for Total Liberation or the union of all the different political perspectives of human, animal and earth liberation.

Veganism: A Critique

Many radical activists I have been talking with are of the opinion that veganism has lacked a real political radical base of action. This may be because normally the strategies within the mainstream 'Animal Rights' movements tend to echo the ones adopted by reformist, pseudo-progressive groups. These groups are willing to compromise their abolitionist position on animal-rights if this allows small changes to be made, such as 'improve' the welfare of animals during captivity.

Moreover, veganism is seen problematically as being dominated by male white elitists where personal ego is aggrandized. This happens because you can see most of the Animal Rights organizations in public places. Just look around groups like *Animal Equality, Mercy For Animals, Anonymous For The Voiceless, Libera!, Vegan Outreach, Compassion Over Killing*, for example. The (perceived) reality is that these organization are focused *only* on animal rights issues to the exclusion of other kind of oppressions; they are structured and organized by a dominant top-down hierarchy; they are classist and they don't expand the ideas of either intersectionality and/ or a Total Liberation movement. Too many times you can see them promoting welfares campaigns urging to improve better conditions for exploited and murdered non-human animals, rather than seeking to agitate for ways to abolish these conditions themselves! In this context Veganism can also be seen as an internally incoherent or fragmented 'movement' due to incorporating numerous contested ideas, many of which cause much internal debate, not least around ethics. For example should veganism be influenced by appeals to welfarism, sentiocentrism, suffercentrism, reductionism, or utilitarianism and so on?

All too often in my experiences, and in discussion with other activists, Animal Rights groups have not been willing to work with other collectives that focus their struggle around Human-Rights or social justice movements. This isolation is something which, I fear, is currently growing in certain quarters. This, arguably, is due to the increasing number of people who believe that the struggle for non-human animals should be *the* main struggle, and are intent on holding non-vegans accountable for the "genocide" visited upon non-human animals. This position, regrettably, signals a clear lack of transforming political perspective in society. There has also been a tremendous hostility across human rights/ social justice organizations on "The Left" to engage with the oppression of other species too (Crimethinc, 2000). This is another reason—or excuse—why the other social movements do not incorporate veganism as part of their struggle (see also Kidby, 2017).

Let me be clear though, the animal liberation movement has no choice but to cooperate with other sociopolitical groups if we expect them to incorporate veganism as part of their political agenda. In order to establish an alliance for cooperation we should start with those more open to understand that any form of oppression is related. It does not matter if other activist groups have not yet recognized the arguments for veganism and animal liberation: we must trust that this will change. In the here and now we can learn from and mutually enrich each other, but we must work for it, we must work with an open mind, that'll be the moment when the rest of the social movements will understand veganism as part of their struggle. As an example, I have been working—alongside with other friends in the Animal Liberation movement—to agitate for Total Liberation to be inserted into the political discussions within an anarcho syndicate (CGT). This has been met with some success, and it is pleasing to note that the number of vegans in this syndicate are rising day by day. Other promising examples of an inter-species social justice coming together can be seen in the No New Animal Lab campaign, where they also works with other individuals and groups or campaigns like supporting political prisoners like Eric King (https://supportericking.org), or Standing Rock. Elsewhere important examples of anti-speciesist collectives working together with other collectives focused on issues of gender, anti-sexism and so on exist. One excellent illustration of this is the Vegan Pays Basque collective, who uphold the concept of Total Liberation we´ve already discussed in this text (see http://www.veganpaysbasque.org/).

Anarchism: Re-connecting with Non-Human Animals

Much as these broader reflections around converging struggles toward Total Liberation, are meaningful and important, it is necessary to bring the chapter back to its intended focus on anarchism. Even though it may not have extended in any major way nor be a part of any political agenda to organizations or collectives with libertarian ideals, it is true that within anarchism there has always existed a great sensibility with regards to the human-animal relationships. This is reflected in older texts (we must remember the context within they were written since not all vegetarians from that time were strict) which reference libertarian veganism (inside the Spanish state), such as the magazine "Helios" (1916-1939), or "Acción Naturista" (1931-1936). Through resources clearly illustrate how a moral consideration toward non-humans was taken seriously, and how these led to the adoption of exclusively vegetable diets (although not everyone, we must understand the context), rejecting the use of garments made from animal materials, as well as questioning the practice of vivisection (see Roselló, 2003) The rejection of animal consumption was seen as a form of symbiosis between humans and their commitment toward nature and health, on a big scale, they were part of a framework of respect and peaceful coexistence. There is much information about that which I reference here. An example would be the work "El Vegetarianismo" (Vegetarianism), from the philosopher Carlos Brandt, where he explores the reasons why veganism came to be. One of the main reasons he cites here is a moral imperative: "when one considers killing animals in order to consume their flesh, the act is more immoral due to two main reasons: that we animals are all one family, and that destruction of life separates us from the natural world, by acting against the law of life conservancy." (Brandt, 2011, n.p.)

Some of the most influential anarchist thinkers and activists have also demonstrated a real sense of compassion and care for nonhuman animals. Take Buenaventura Durruti (Spanish anarchist militant) for one example. In an interview made to his granddaughter Marta Durruti for "La Directa" newspaper, Marta commented that "He was a vegetarian. He couldn't bear to see caged animals, so one time he let a parakeet go, which his grandfather had given as a gift to some of his cousins." (See Durruti, 2015). We can also find accounts regarding vegetarianism from the hand of anarchist geographer Élisée Reclus in the journal "A propósito del vegetarianismo" (1901), where he affirms "to wait for the day in which all earthly creatures may live in harmony among themselves, and with humanity taking its place among the rest of all beings." These are just some local examples to illustrate the relationship between and anarchism above mentioned (see also White, 2015a, b). It is also worth noting that concern for other animals was not solely focused on the question of food and the abstention of meat and dairy products. For example one of the main objectives of the Vegetarian-Society Congress in Monte Verita (Ascona, Switzerland) was to protest against vivisection (testing and experimenting on non-human animals while alive). This congress has taken place at the counter-cultural, primative socialist, community in Ascona since 1900, a place where anarchists such as Raphael Friedeberg or Otto Gross moved to live there.

If anarchists are serious about challenging forms of power and discrimination, then we *must* take that commitment beyond the human sphere (Nocella et al., 2015). Institutionalized violence has found its way into schools, from textbooks which perfectly reflect the kind of society we live in and which the system has created. They show conquerors and invaders as individuals who bring peace and "civilization" to other parts of the world, imposing their systems of belief and in turn obliterate other cultures. Such a change of attitude is not easy: we are aware that the dominant forms of education for example, teach us to be malleable and obedient according to the interests of the elites in society. When depicting other animals most school books are highly speciesist. From the earliest ages children are encouraged to think about, and treat animals differently according to their species (domestic compares to wild animals for example) and 'value' them according to human interests. Therefore we are encouraged to follow an ethics of care for 'companion' animals (dogs, cats), yet remain indifferent to the violence that 'farm' animals (sheep, pigs, cows, chickens) inevitably face. Rather than encourage critically questioning about these hierarchies and categorizations, the mainstream educational system only wants our obedience both internalizing speciesist values, and also it should be noted neoliberal capitalist values (rewarding individual success and eliminate collectiveness). Within the paradigm changes I have highlighted earlier in our relationship with animals, it is very important to promote a new form of education for the new generation to make them understanding that all animals should be respected not being used and letting them being free, and we should take care of the place we are living and the environment (see Nocella et al., 2019).

Raising consciousness about other animals through critical education has always been an important part of vegan praxis. In the Spanish State for example, important discussions around veganism were introduced in the 80s through the anarchist insurrectionist movement, especially inside "liberated" spaces (squats). This was mirrored elsewhere though anarcho-punk music and some fanzines—musical as well as political—such as "La verdad Jode", "Calimero ′zine", "The Paper", "Heartattack", "Anxiety Closet", "One Way Straight Edge", "Tilt!", "Relativ(E)", "International StraightEdge Bulletin" and "Fiera", among others. Objectively speaking, veganism is a movement of liberation which fights against the oppression upon non-human animals, but which also encompasses other struggles that fight this oppressive system. Our ability to articulate and communicate this successfully is incredibly important to successfully achieving our future goals and visions.

Our rejection of authority must be anchored in our rejection to all forms of oppression, including that which we exert over the rest of the animals (see Watkinson & O'Driscoll, 2014)! There is no reason to keep flaunting a privilege that has been acquired on the grounds of belonging to a "superior" species, is this species-based discrimination not analogous to other forms of oppression which find their origin in the privileges of gender, race, class, functionality, etc.? As I said before, we can see that as anarchists have more in common with veganism than what people usually think, as both ideologies often overlap along their paths.

Important intersectional examples of human and nonhuman oppression quickly come to mind when given critical attention. For instance, if we understand prisons to be sites for the deprivation of freedom, subjugation and repression of ideas, we can find there another similarity; putting an end to all sites for confinement (human and non-human) (see Morin, 2016). The anarchist movement has a great tradition of abolitionist work in prison, like Anarchist Black Cross for example, which is active around the world (see https://www.abcf.net). Nevertheless, we tend to forget other individuals who are dispossessed of their freedom, who live their lives incarcerated. Farms, zoos and cages all incarcerate innocent beings: they are places where these lives will be wasted away until the time they face violent and untimely death. Some will die in cages for the amusement of humans while others will be sent to the slaughterhouse, perhaps the first and last moment in which they will ever see sunlight (the vast majority of victims come from factory farms).

Anarchism has always been deeply rooted in ecology, but mostly from an anthropocentric perspective, to make a better world for humans (first) and their descendants, and then for the rest of the living beings with which we share the planet. This anthropocentric vision is centered mostly on the protection of certain species (endangered species become more important) over the individual, independently from the species to which it belongs and the environment in which we live. It is a very limited vision which does not concede the real importance which considering all individuals must have. On the other hand, apart from anthropocentric ecology there have developed more radical currents, which use direct action as a means of fighting destructive capitalism whose endgame is the usual, power and domination, in the case of environments. Radical ecologist movements strive to live and enjoy nature without hierarchies and try to minimize the damage which humans cause to the environment. However they don't usually extend those ideas to the subject matter of my argument: veganism must be a political praxis inside the frame of anarchism. Despite this, we must place hope in the fact that more and more radical movements are embracing an anarchist perspective that Earth Liberation needs vegan praxis must be a key part of their struggle (see Do or Die, 2010). No hierarchies should mean that non-human animals should be considered and be part of their liberation in every way. As we can see, the relationship of anarchist theories against any form of authority, domination, violence, human oppression, is intrinsically related to the violence exerted upon non humans.

We must also reject the excuse which many anarchists like to put on the table, namely that the production of animal byproducts be made in accordance to "ethical" treatment. Veganism is not centered upon the way non-humans animals are treated *per se*, but upon ending their captivity, freeing them from all the obligations which we humans have laid on them in order to gain benefit from them. Many support the theory of "good" treatment, but that should not serve as a reference to the whole of a struggle for liberation. Is anarchism based on the better treatment of oppressed humans? Or does it seek liberation and eradication of all forms of power and domination? I understand that the affirmative answer would be for the latter, thus, in regard to animals there should not remain a doubt about it. Veganism seeks their liberation, eliminating speciesism as a form of discrimination and stop using them as a way to gain benefits in every sphere, regardless of them being in factory farms or small farms where they are "treated ethically", who won't hesitate in sending them to the slaughterhouse when they stop being productive. "When they stop being productive", does that sound affirmative to you?

Anarchism, Veganism and Total Liberation: Final Reflections

Despite large sections within the anarchist movement appearing reluctant to adopt Animal Liberation as part of their political agenda, it's true that more have started to acknowledge its legitimacy as part of a radical theory and revolutionary practice. Similarly, many more vegans are being influenced by anarchist praxis: this gives us great cause for hope! If we are aware that there is a root from which all forms of oppression come, it should be easier to understand that all struggles are intermingled and that we all need to end this oppressive system. The same way anarchism promotes radical ideas with a clear objective, the Animal Liberation movement and thus, veganism, should adopt radical practices in its activism. One thing I would like to clarify is the definition of radical, which is usually treated as having negative connotations by the mainstream media, repressive institutions and the state itself, with politicians at the helm. Radical is described as a way to seek the root of social problems with the objective of getting a solution, radical is usually related to fanatics or extremists, when nothing could be farther from the truth. Radical activists do not limit themselves to seeking reform in the solving of problems, they make no lighthearted concessions for the different forms of oppression (see Roberts, 1986; Young, 2010). In short, vegans understand oppression which is done upon non-human animals and their way of life as well as their struggle is highly politicized.

Within this chapter I have tried to show the link between human and non-human animal exploitation, and why (anarchists) must address these by embracing an intersectional politics of Total Revolution. The society in which we live in legitimizes, enacts and excuses appalling levels of violence toward humans, nonhuman animals, and the earth. The belief that we can ignore these complex intersections is absurd, if our goal is to bring forward a fairer and respectful society. We can see and prove that institutionalized violence toward other animals (among other kinds of violence) becomes a normal part of our lives, which in turn makes us believe that their use and consumption is part of our nature and thus, consumption becomes compulsory, nothing could be farther from reality if we understand how moral anthropocentrism and speciesism are key to the relationships of power and oppression which animals endure, and as anarchists, we seek to cease being a part of that cycle of death by adopting veganism as part of our everyday lives. Importantly being vegan is achievable for many. Veganism shouldn't be based on privileged academic theories, nor promoted in the names of celebrities, as if it were elitist or classist. Moreover, veganism, from an anarchist perspective, is not about personal purity and individualism, rather it is spread among friends, family, etc., by means of a community effort which is based on mutual aid.

Finally, I would like to add that, from this text's anarchist perspective, our goal must always remain that of breaking free from that which limits us in any way. We are born, we live and we die with a series of limitations held in place by this system which, in the name of democracy, sustains all possible forms of domination and power. This power/submission relationship is where currently non-human animals find themselves, those who have no voice of their own to defend themselves from a system which oppresses them, which lest we forget oppresses us also. In this reading, it is our duty to provide them with a voice, to make visible how this system which lacks moral values has verily made their lives a living hell, and their deaths, the largest genocide ever inflicted. According to official date by the FAO (and by this I am not defending gradualism as a tendency within the Animal Liberation movement, which argues that it's better to take small steps to achieve an end), it is estimated that annually more than 60 billion terrestrial animals, and over a trillion aquatic animals are slaughtered (See Koeder, 2017; Sanders, 2018; Fish Count, 2019).

Before this, can we remain unmoved? Can we turn our heads and look the other way as if it was not our responsibility? Of course not, now it is the time to take control over our actions and be conscious about individuals who live and die due to human interests. It is wise to make decisions and veganism, as a political tool for liberation, is one. Who has given us the right to take their lives and do what we, as humans, want with them? Do we see ourselves as gods? These two questions confront anarchist ideals, we do not believe in anyone's authority, we all want to be free as individuals and collectively, is it really so hard to extend that which we want for ourselves to other individuals of different species?

Oftentimes during debates there are speciesists who declare themselves as anarchists and reject veganism. Honestly, if you deem yourself an anarchist, have access to information about veganism, anti-speciesism and the Animal Liberation movement and still continue to have speciesist habits, you run the great rick of inviting the justified accusation of rank hypocrisy, of not really being an anarchist. Understanding ourselves and the relationships that exist in the world around us is the first step toward real social revolution and that includes considering non-human animals. Our role inside said social revolution is rather simple: being an example of the kind of society you/we want to see.

We shouldn't limit our struggle, no struggle is above others, we can and must draw a line which encompasses all forms of oppression and every strategy and corrective measure to combat and eradicate them. I would like to end with a sentiment which defines everything I have written: "Before we talk about freedom, let's free our slaves" (making a clear allusion to non-human slaves and with all due respect to those who suffer and continue to suffer slavery). In this spirit, I've tried to be as truthful as possible, thank you and I hope you found this interesting reading.

Salud and Revolution.

Acknowledgements

I want to mention the persons who has helped me with the translation/grammar review of this chapter: Sal Fuentes, Lara López, Xabi Agirre, Iris Pereiro, Richard White, Anthony Nocella. All my close friends who were giving me the strength to make this happens. Thanks to all of you for the support and patience. I also want to show my gratitude to ICAS for letting me being a part of this wonderful project and all the people which are part of my life, activism, militancy and heart, love you all.

References

Adams, C. J. (2015). The sexual politics of meat: A feminist-vegetarian critical theory. Bloomsbury Publishing USA.

Anonymous. (2017) *BITING BACK: A Radical Response to Non-Vegan Anarchists.* Retrieved from https://warzonedistro.noblogs.org/files/2017/09/BITING-BACK-A-Radical-Response-to-Non-Vegan-Anarchists.pdf.

Bakunin, M. (2005). *Bakunin: Statism and anarchy.* Cambridge University Press. Retrieved from https://libcom.org/files/statismandanarchy.pdf

Brandt, C. (2011). *El Vegetarianismo.* Retrieved from http://tiempoanimal.blogspot.com/2011/03/el-vegetarianismo-por-carlos-brandt.html

CrimethInc. (2000). *Veganism.* Retrieved from https://es.crimethinc.com/2000/09/11/veganism

Do or Die. (2003). *Down with the Empire! Up with the Spring*! The Anarchist Library. Retrieved from https://theanarchistlibrary.org/library/do-or-die-down-with-the-empire-up-with-the-spring

Dominick, B. (1997). *Animal Liberation and Social Revolution. A vegan perspective on anarchism or an anarchist perspective on veganism,* with a preface by Joseph M. Smith. Retrieved from https://theanarchistlibrary.org/library/brian-a-dominick-animal-liberation-and-social-revolution

Durruti, M. (2015). "Pepe come and fix it". Retrieved from https://anarquismoenpdf1.wordpress.com/2015/10/22

Fish Count (2019). *Global fish caught from the wild each year.* Retrieved from http://fishcount.org.uk/fish-count-estimates-2/numbers-of-fish-caught-from-the-wild-each-year

Fitzgerald, A. J., & Pellow, D. (2014). Ecological defense for animal liberation: A holistic understanding of the world. *Counterpoints, 448*, 28-48.

Freshnet Collective. (2013). *The frontlines are everywhere: Protect yourself, your comrades, and the movement.* Retrieved from https://itsgoingdown.org/frontlines-everywhere-protect-comrades-movement/

Hochschartner, J. (2014). Vegan angela davis connects human and animal liberation. *Counterpunch.* Retrieved from https://www.counterpunch.org/2014/01/24/vegan-angela-davis-connects-human-and-animal-liberation/

Hribal, J. (2003). "Animals are part of the working class": A challenge to labor history. *Labor History, 44*(4), 435-453.

Johanna (2008). *Explaining racism to White Veg*Ns & speciesism to Non-Veg*N POCs.* Retrieved from https://vegansofcolor.wordpress.com/2008/07/05/explaining-racism-to-white-vegns-speciesism-to-non-vegn-pocs/

Jones, P. (2004). Mothers with monkey wrenches: Feminist imperatives and the ALF. In. S. Best, & A. J. Nocella (Eds.), *Terrorists or freedom fighters?* Reflections on the liberation of animals, 137-156.

Kidby, D. (2017). *The radical left's top 10 objections to veganism (and why they suck).* Retreived from https://medium.com/@Veganarchy/the-radical-lefts-top-10-objections-to-veganism-and-why-they-suck-5f27d19e801d

Koeder, C. (2017). *Cracking the FAOSTAT code* ("the FAO kill numbers"). Retrieved from http://www.christiankoeder.com/2017/08/cracking-faostat-code-fao-kill-numbers.html

Kropotkin, P. (1902). *Mutual Aid.* Retrieved from https://theanarchistlibrary.org/library/petr-kropotkin-mutual-aid-a-factor-of-evolution

Morin, K. M. (2016). Carceral space: Prisoners and animals. *Antipode, 48*(5), 1317-1336.

Nibert, D. (Ed.). (2017a). *Animal oppression and capitalism. Volume one: The oppression of nonhuman animals as sources of food.* Praegar Press: California.

Nibert, D. (2017b). *Animal oppression and capitalism. Volume two: The oppressive and destructive role of capitalism.* Praegar Press: California.

Nocella, A. J., Drew, C., George, A. E., Ketenci, S., Lupinacci, J. Purdy, & I. Joe Leeson-Schatz, J-L. (2019). *Education for total liberation: Critical animal pedagogy and teaching against speciesism.* New York, NY: Peter Lang.

Nocella, A. J., White R. J., & Cudworth, E. (2015). *Anarchism and animal liberation: Essays on complementary elements of total liberation.* Jefferson, MA: McFarland Press.

Pellow, D. N. (2014). *Total liberation: The power and promise of animal rights and the radical earth movement.* U of Minnesota Press.

Pellow, D. N., & Brehm, H. N. (2015). From the new ecological paradigm to total liberation: The emergence of a social movement frame. *The Sociological Quarterly, 56*(1), 185-212.

Robert, J. J. (1986). *Animal liberation 1972-1986.* ARC Print. Retrieved from http://www.thesparrowsnest.org.uk/collections/public_archive/PAR0100.pdf

Rosello, J. P. (2003). *La Vuelta a la Naturaleza. El pensamiento naturista hispano (1890–2000): Naturismo libertario, trofología, vegetarismo naturista, vegetarismo social y librecultura.* Editorial Virus, Memoria Collection, Barcelona.

Ryder, R. D. (2010). Speciesism again: The original leaflet. *Critical Society, 2*, 1–2. Retrieved from http://janegerhard.com/wp-content/uploads/2017/01/Speciesism-1970.pdf

Sanders, B. (2018). Global animal slaughter stadistics and charts. Retrieved from https://faunalytics.org/global-animal-slaughter-statistics-and-charts/

Spassmaschine (2017). *Beasts of burden – Antagonism and practical history.* Libcom.org. Retrieved from http://libcom.org/library/beasts-burden-antagonism-practical-history

Torres, B. (2007). *Making a killing: The political economy of animal rights.* AK press.

Valasco, A. (2017). *La Ética Animal¿ Una cuestión feminista?* Madrid: Cátedra.

Watkinson, K., & O'Driscoll, D. (2014). From animals to anarchism. *Dysophia.* Open Letter #3. Retrieved from http://dysophia.org.uk/wp-content/uploads/2014/10/ARzineweb.pdf

White R. J. (2015a). Critical animal geographies and anarchist praxis: Shifting perspectives from the animal 'question' to the animal 'condition. In K. Gillespie, & R.-C. Collard (Eds.), *Critical animal geographies: Power, space and violence in a multispecies world.* Routledge: London.

White, R. J. (2015b). Following in the footsteps of Élisée Reclus: disturbing places of inter-species violence that are hidden in plain sight. In A. Nocella, R. J. White, & E. Cudworth (Eds.), *Anarchism and animal liberation: Critical animal studies, intersectionality and total liberation.* McFarland Press: Jefferson.

White, R. J. (2017). Rising to the challenge of capitalism and the commodification of animals: Post-capitalism, anarchist economies and vegan praxis. In D. Nibert (Ed.), *Animal oppression and capitalism.* Praeger: Conneticut.

Written by a Few Wild Animals. (2003). *Total liberation. Freedom for both human and human animals.* Warzone Distro. Retrieved from https://archive.org/details/TotalLiberationFreedomForBothNonhumanAndHumanAnimals_20140311

Young, P. D. (2010). *Animal liberation front: Complete diary of actions, the first 30 years.* Warcry Communications.

7. *Animal Victims in the Colombian War*

TERRY HURTADO

The historical truth about war, and the victims of it, is a key element of reconciliation. Colombia has gone through a more than 50 year old political armed conflict in which humans, non-human animals, and nature have been heavily damaged. However, recognition of the status of "victim" has not yet been achieved by non-humans animals. This lack of institutional recognition, and the absence of research on the impact of armed conflict in Colombia, represents a barrier to constructing the historical truth of what happened during the unfinished war period. This chapter confronts some of the implication of Colombian warfare for non-human animals and proposes categories of violence suffered by other than human beings. I first briefly touch on the motivations and contexts that allowed the armed conflict to sprout. Secondly, I recall the various types of victimizations suffered by humans. Next, I describe the ways in which non-human animals have been victimized during the Colombian war. Finally, I attempt to apply International Humanitarian Law to non-human animals.

Colombians and Political Armed Conflict—A Long Thread

Fifty-four years ago, while the crisis of USSR missiles in Cuba was happening and the Cold War was at its peak of tension, two guerrilla movements began in Colombia: the FARC (Revolutionary Armed Forces of Colombia) and ELN (National Liberation Army). These guerrillas are heir of the so-called Period of Violence, a period in which extreme violence between the members of the two parties of that time, the Liberal Party and Conservative Party, took place. Their way out of that violence was an agreement between elites called The National Front, in which the president would switch form one party to the other in every election, but this agreement didn't take in to account how to address the basic needs of the people. This unjust pact between oligarchies was the seed from which the guerrillas would sprout.

After the FARC and the ELN were funded, other guerrillas started as well. The EPL (Army of Popular Liberation) followed the Maoist approach. The Armed Movement Quintin Lame was an indigenous guerrilla group founded in 1984. The M-19 was a more heterodox guerrilla group which had gathered members from other guerrilla forces. On one hand, FARC's starting core was basically a group of peasants coming from the Liberal guerrillas of the Period of Violence. Shortly after its foundation, it followed the USSR approach, whereas the ELN would be inspired by the Cuban revolution and the Latin-American insurrections and had university students as part of it from its beginning and playing a key role in its foundation. During 12 years of massive propaganda from the State, the Colombian army was posed as heroes, and people lost any sense of critical analysis, including human rights violations. This lack of analysis hurt non-human animal as well, for even most of the animal protection movement overlooked what was happening with animals in the Colombian police and army, including their exposure to war.

In 2012, the government and the FARC started a peace negotiation process. Since the peace process started to advance for humans, the animal rights movement began to campaign for peace for animals. In August of 2016, the government and the FARC came to a Peace Agreement, which did not meet the expectation of the animal rights movement, for no mention to non-human animals was included in to the Agreement. On 2 October, the acceptance of the Peace Agreement was taken to validation on a referendum that asked citizens if the Peace Agreement should be accepted. Voting "yes" would validate the Agreement, but the "no's," as promoted by the right wing, won.

Violence against Humans in Colombian Armed Conflict

A moral community is a set of individuals for which we acknowledge an intrinsic value. War leads to an attitude in which, most of the time, especially for troops, the others are not acknowledged as equals in value. The others are pushed out of the moral community, making for higher levels of violence and terror.

International Humanitarian Law (IHL) attempts to regulate armed conflicts and protect the lives of civilians and soldiers who are not taking part in combat to pursue respect for their physical and moral integrity (ICRC, 2014). This is, to take minimum standard of care and avoid cruelty, to guarantee that no one is, in fact, being expelled from the moral community. Nonetheless, Colombia is one of the cases in which IHL failed. Even when relying on the most moderate data, the numbers are horrifying. From 1958-2012, 218,094 people died as a consequence of the political-armed conflict in Colombia, but only 19% were combatants, either government soldiers, guerrilla, or paramilitary members, whereas 81% were civilians (GMH, 2013). The following details the diverse forms these murders have taken.

1. *Selective Murders*

The Group of Historical Memory (GMH) of The National Centre of Historical Memory found that during 1961-2012 in Colombia, there were 16,340 cases of attacks that ended with at least one person murdered, but that could in some cases go up to three murders in one attack. In all these attacks, 23,161 people were killed (GMH, 2013). As to who was responsible for these murders, paramilitary forces were the main drivers in 38.4% of cases followed by the different guerrillas (16.8%) and by government forces (10.2%). There is a high level of non-identified groups responsible for the attacks in 27.7% of the cases (GMH, 2013).

2. *Terrorist Attacks*

During the period of 1988-2012, the data shows 95 terrorist events produced 233 victim fatalities (GMH, 2013). In addition, another 1,343 people were injured during these type of attacks. Guerrilla groups were responsible for the violence 82% of the time, responsibility was not identified in 16.8% of cases, and paramilitary forces were responsible in 2.6% of the attacks (GMH, 2013).

3. *Massacres*

Murders that went above three people in a same place, whether the massacre happened in a bar, a house or a village, resulted in 11,751 victims between 1985 and 2012 (GMH, 2013). Of the 1,982 cases recorded, many left behind unbearable images of cruelty. The paramilitary groups were the main perpetrators being responsible for 58.8% of the massacres. Following the ultra-right wing forces, the guerrillas committed 17.3% of the atrocities. The government forces were directly responsible for the not inconsiderable amount of 8% of massacres. Furthermore, an extra 1% has been recognized as joint actions by the paramilitary and other forces, one of them government forces. Non-identified groups carried out 14.9% of the massacres (GMH, 2013). But death is not the only face of violence in war. Other aspects bring as much suffering.

4. Forced Disappearance

In Colombia between 1985 and 2012, 25,007 people went to work, study, visit a friend or go shopping and never came back home (GMH, 2013). Bodies found years after the forced disappearances show that torture is a common practise suffered by people taken against their will. Examples of this were found in the 300 bodies located in the "Comuna 13," a slum of Medellin. This story reached the international headlines as the "world largest urban mass grave" (Reuters, 2015). This type of violence caused relatives of victims to suffer as well. In many cases, relatives don't have a clue as to what happen to their beloved family members, or why. They hold on to the hope that their loved ones will come back one day. So, as spine-chilling as it may be, the Colombian headline of 2009 about "mass grave with 2000 bodies" (Kovalik, 2010) was actually good news for people who hadn't had any news from their relatives. Perhaps they could find peace in the results of the exhumations.

5. Sexual Violence

Between 1985 and 2012, it was recorded that 1,754 people suffered sexual attacks (GMH, 2013). This type of violence might be one of the most unbearable for victims, as it deeply undermines the self-esteem of the victim, and some express that they would preferred to have been killed rather than have gone through that experience. This type of violence is sometimes undertaken for the direct sexual pleasure of victimizers, but it is mostly to harm the victims, one of the victim's relatives, or to pursue a further goal, as in forced displacement. Sometimes, a female victim of sexual violence would be abused not only by one man, but by many. Occasionally, after the sexual assault, a victim then had to cope with a murder of a relative who was killed because they tried to prevent the abuse. These traumatic episodes were prolonged in some cases when victims caught venereal diseases or were impregnated by their attacker (Londoño, et al., 2000).

6. Kidnappings

From 1970 to 2010, 27,023 people were kidnaped (GMH, 2013); guerrillas were responsible for 90.6% of the cases followed by paramilitary forces (9.4%). Kidnappings often came with a financial aim since it was a way for guerrillas to fund their operations. Family members of kidnaped victims were indirect victims due to the level of distress they went through in a sort of "virtual captivity" of not knowing where their loved ones were or if they would ever be returned (Navia & Ossa, 2001).

7. Forced Displacement

Between 1985 and 2012, 5,712,506 people had to leave their homes and territories against their will in order to save their lives; most of this happened from 1996 to 2012 in which 4,774,046 people where forcedly displaced (GMH, 2013). This mass displacement represents 15% of the total population of Colombia, equal to the populations of Medellin and Cali combined, the second and third biggest cities of the country, or the populations of Rome and Paris. Territorial control and economic motivations are the main drivers of this type of victimization, which stripped peasants of 8.3 million hectares of land. That is the twice as big as The Netherlands or Switzerland. People forcedly migrated to save their lives after a massacre or when they had the intuition that they might be targeted. In some cases, they left their land to forget horrific experiences of sexual abuse. In fact, women in some villages were all raped in order to frighten them and make them leave their homes.

Broadening the Truth of the Colombian War

Truth is essential for reconciliation and peace building since it is the basis for developing a process of transitional justice. Many victims express relief after hearing victimizers' confessions because they get to clarify what happened to their relatives, who was responsible, and why it happened. This allows some time for forgiveness within the intimate realm of victim and victimizer (Delgado, 2011). In contrast, reconciliation refers to a social sphere where the social and political agreement is rebuilt in order to achieve reparations—both material and symbolic. It further offers a guarantee that the violence won't be repeated and institutional changes will occur, including the re-establishment of rights (Delgado, 2011; Comisión de Entrega, 2004).

But during Colombian warfare, there have been other victims not yet brought into personal or social consideration: non-human animals. The acts of violence that occurred during Colombian conflicts have been categorized for humans into 11 modalities by the National Centre of Historical Memory, of which I explored 7 types (above. Herein, I propose 7 categories of violence against animals drawing on what has been found so far in an effort to broaden and strengthen the IHL framework. Advancing in that direction seems necessary to acknowledge the victims ignored thus far and the types of violence they have suffered.

1. Animals as Weapons

Within the conceptualization of some left wing guerrillas there is the distinction between the weapons the State uses and the ones the rebels use. "People's armament" is the name given to those weapons that are easily made without a huge budget and that do not require high technological knowledge nor equipment. The most commonly used and destructive that began to be used during the 90's by the FARC were the domestic gas tanks.

But another bombing attack method, mostly used by the FARC guerrilla, were the horse bombs. Donkeys or horses were loaded with sacks that contained dynamite. They were sometimes left in front of their target, such as State military units. Others waited for their targets to pass by, at which moment the charge would be activated. These equines who lived their lives as slaves carrying heavy weights or pulling massive wagons became weapons for the last seconds of their lives. Although, horses were most frequently used in these type of attacks, dogs were made into bombs as well. It is not the first time that dogs were used as bombing devices, for during World War II, canine units were used in the same way (Sorenson, 2014).

Using animals as a bombing method was not exclusive to guerrilla groups but also used by paramilitary forces. The paramilitary AUC (United Self-defence of Colombia) used animals as direct instruments of torture and murder. Dogs were used to terrify and torture people who the paramilitary captured (Verdad Abierta, 2012). Snakes were handy weapons for the paramilitary; their bites were used as methods for murder that the paramilitary would use to undercover massacres, used to give the appearance of such deaths as isolated accidents (Llanos, 2008). Victims were also thrown to crocodiles, both alive and dead, as a way not to leave traces of the bodies and avoid getting the attack listed as a massacre by State agencies and international bodies (Infobae, 2011; Verdad Abierta, 2012). A woman tells the story about what she found out had happened with her husband: "[A]fterwards I found out he was thrown alive to the crocodiles. He had been tied and thrown to the crocodiles, as he was dressed and with his ID. Because nothing was found, not even his ID. Noting was found" (Ruta Pacífica, 2013b, p. 67).

The police used horses by the "Carabineros" and the "ESMAD, Escuadron Movil Antidisturbios" (anti-riot squad). The "Carabineros," ridden units, used horses as transport for police. Horses have also been considered by the mounted police as a weapon when used to control riots against civilians. The use of horses for this purpose has happened for many years without any training that considered the protection of the animal (Momentos, 2015). During more recent years, the anti-riot special force, ESMAD, brought in horses equipped with armour when fighting with protestors (Police, 2013).

The military have, for a long time, used dogs to track guerrilla troops and search for mines. In 1962, German shepherds were imported to the country from the Federal Republic of Germany, and training lessons were delivered by German trainers. Ninety dogs were brought to the country in order to control the liberal guerrillas of that time. Accordingly, the German shepherds received training in tracking.

Following the seek and destroy method, some dogs were trained as "commando dogs" for the army's Special Forces that were in charge of tracking down "high targets" in Colombia's armed conflict. According to the Committee of Truth and Memory of Colombian Women, 0.71% of tortures were reported in which a woman was a victim of a dog attack as overseen by humans: "There was a dog, a German Shepard, you must know, we have this dog to tear apart people. -You will be killed be this dog. They instigated the dog to bite me and it was very close" (as cited in Ruta Pacífica, 2013b, p. 107).

2. *Animals as Transport*

The use of animals as a way to transport troops, equipment, food supplies, weapons and ammunition has been present in many cultures over a long period of time (Sorenson, 2014). Colombia is not an exception. However, this essay is only looking into the current political armed conflict. Although the mounted police has its origins back in the 19th century, it was after the huge riots started on April 9, 1948 due to the murder of the liberal leader Jose Eliecer Gatian, that this police force was reinforced to "pacify" the country during a time considered to be the starting point of the current war of Colombia (Momentos Historia Policia, 2018). The carabineer police was created with the intention of being in charge of the rural security of the country. Nevertheless, it has a presence in the cities as well. The number of horses under their control is not well determined, but in 2010, 1,892 equines were imported from Argentina (Momento Historia Policia, 2018).

3. *Animals as Defence*

From the 1970s, the Colombian police received support from the USA, England, Argentina and Italy to train dogs to detect drugs and bombs. As with other military doctrines, the Colombian armed forces followed the North American approach regarding K-9 divisions as well, and Colombian police were trained by the Baton Rouge Police Department in 1987. This training was used to counter bombing attacks by the drug cartels. With US military financial support, called the Colombian Plan, dogs acquired skills as bomb detectors. In 2006, the police started Project Rattus which is the use of rats for mine detecting. The first group of rats were imported from Norway, but now they are being bred in Colombia. These rats are kept in cages of 50 cm and trained daily to find different types of explosive material (Kienyke, 2012).

4. *Animals as Tax and Loot of War*

There are many cases in which the different armed parties have taken the animals of villagers. In situations in which the armed groups were not adequately supplied with food, animals such as cows, chickens, and pigs would be taken to feed the troops. As one survivor stated, "The crime we committed was to give them food. We had to give them food otherwise they would kill us. They said 'look, kill that pig, kill that chicken,' 'look, I am going to kill that cow and will take it.' They did what they wanted with us" (as cited in Ruta Pacífica, 2013b, p. 89, para 3).

In some cases, animals were taken after killing people who owned or took care of the animals. One man explained the following upon arrival at his parents' farm: "So I looked to the barn, the first I did was to look to the barn. There were no cattle, they had took all the cattle ... there was nothing there, only the dead" (Bolivar, as cited in Ruta Pacífica, 2013b, p. 156, para 4). Animals may also be a material reward for the victorious, for they are seen as mere loot that can symbolise the power of who won, of who has the control.

Guerrilla forces would carry out financial extortion against wealthy land owners, but sometimes these people would not pay the "tax." To offset the unpaid tax, the rebels would steal cattle or horses from the landowner, or expropriate, as they would see it. On the other hand, paramilitary forces, who named themselves "self-defence forces," would also "tax" wealthy landowners in order to protect them from guerrillas. Again, the animals were then often used to feed the troops.

5. *Animals as Drivers of Damage*

When cattle farmers would not pay a tax to the guerrillas and cattle were not stolen as a way of compensation, it was most likely that the bovines would be targeted with violence as a message that the guerrilla tax must be paid. In cases such as this, animals are the drivers of economic damage. For example, a FARC front member tells of having all of the animals they owned systematically injured and killed in the area where they were camping. They did not find out who was responsible of this (Hurtado, 2017a, interview).

As a way to send the message that a territory is not safe anymore, that peasants are not the ones in control, paramilitary groups kill some of the animals of the local people. This attitude towards animals builds on fear and fortifies the idea that the armed group are the ones in charge. Even if they did not execute anyone when arriving to a village, a dog could get shot if he barked too much, sending a fearful message (Hurtado, 2017b, interview). As a peasant explains, "The Self-defence [unit] burnt our home, we couldn't take out nothing. They eat the chicken. We had some pig, they took those, killed them and eat them ... the cow they took as well. The horses we don't know ... I lost everything, everything, everything. I couldn't take nothing" (qtd. in Ruta Pacífica, 2013a, p. 334, para 3).

6. *Animals as Training*

Firearm training is a regular practise, and parties in conflict might develop unconventional training methods to train and retrain their troops. Animals are sometimes used as one of these unconventional training methods. Using animals as shooting practice is sadly not uncommon, but there are two emblematic cases from Colombia. The first case happened in 2011 in which a group of soldiers of the Battalion Ayacucho from the city of Manizales shot a leashed dog four times before he received a lethal shot (Noticias Uno, 2011). The other case is from the Battalion of Infantry Number 27 from the city of Pitalito. A soldier who was late one day to practise at the shooting range, was led by his top rank to do the training with a dog who served the troops as mine detector. The dog tied to a tree was shot by the solider (El Pais, 2012).

The use of animals for these type of trainings has an extra intention above refining one's shooting precision. This type of training also aims to desensitize the soldiers from their feelings of compassion and empathy so they can perform in a more lethal way. The intention is to harm animals as a way to detach from any feeling of empathy or regret. In the city of Buenaventura, there are houses known as "chopping houses," which are used to torture people. Some of those responsible for torturing in the "chopping house" have been trained by torturing dogs first (Servicio Jesuita, 2014).

7. *Animals as Collateral Damage*

The euphemism of "collateral damage" was coined by the US military to refer to people killed or wounded who are not combatants or their property. It is formally defined as "unintentional damage or incidental damage affecting facilities, equipment or personnel occurring as a result of military actions directed against targeted enemy forces or facilities" (FAS, 1998, p. 179). One of the most common sources of collateral damage comes from air operations. Bombing, for instance, produces much damage depending on the type of the bomb. For instance, the Colombian military industry INDUMIL currently produces a series of IMC XUE bombs that have radius of lethal action from 15 metres, by explosive wave, up to 45 meters, and a lethal radius of action by fragmentation up to 100 metres according to its characteristics (INDUMIL).

During Colombian Air Force bombing, which is developed in forest areas, a single aircraft can carry up to six of the most powerful bombs. The number of animals who have died or been injured in these attacks has not been quantified, but the number must be enormous. Collateral damages also occurs to wildlife during combat by lost bullets. However, this impact is still to be studied. Domestic animals, such as dogs that travel with the different troops, are also injured during combat. Furthermore, I recorded a case in which a dog developed what seems to be post-traumatic stress disorder syndrome after being affected during an Air Force bombing. He became scared of people wearing uniforms (Hurtado, 2017c, interview). This post-traumatic syndrome behaviour in dogs has also been recorded in Afghanistan (Dao, 2011).

Another procedure performed from the air in the context of Colombian armed conflict is the airplane fumigation of coca crops. Crops for illegal use have been interlocked with the different parties in political armed conflict in Colombia. These fumigations reach other near crops, affecting animals that feed from them, and seeds and fruits in general, affecting mostly birds. All sorts of water sources are affected. Rivers get highly polluted due to the fumigation, affecting fish and animals that drink from this water.

It is obvious that self-defence forces consider humans their enemies, in many cases, these human are civilians. As to the animals these civilians look after, were not always targeted by the paramilitaries. Therefore, the animals left behind after the mass murders often do not have anyone to take care of them. This clearly makes them collateral damage of war. A member of a family that managed to run away from his town tells of what happened the day after they left: "The next day, pitifully the village was a river of blood. Seven families were killed; there was a mass displacement of all the village. Only the dogs, the chickens and cows remained in the streets" (qtd. in CNMH, 2018, p. 163, para 2). Another survivor reports: "We took care of the farm with so much love, the dog we had, that we had raised, the chicken that we had raised with so much care, were left back, got lost, got stolen" (Ruta Pacifica, 2013b, p. 383, para 5).

Concluding Thoughts on Non-humans during Wartime

The fourth Convention of Geneva relative to the protection of civilian persons in time of war refers in Article 3 to conflicts such as the Colombian one. Since Colombia is a Contracting Party of the Convention, the conflict in Colombia should "be bound to apply, as a minimum" some humanitarian provisions (ICRC, 1949). But, due to the cruelty that unfolded during the war years, as showed before, the provisions have not been meet. Therefore, IHL has not been guaranteed in Colombians internal conflict.

Although claims have been made to legally acknowledge personhood to non-human animals (Wise 2013; Holdron, 2013), and there is an ongoing discussion about morally acknowledge animals as persons (Gruen, 2017), there has been no consensus about animal personhood. However, we should not give up on this push for International Humanitarian Law for other-than-human persons.

Acts that remain prohibited at any time and in any place whatsoever determined by point 1 of article 3 of the Convention are:

a) violence to life and person, in particular murder of all kinds, mutilation, cruel treatment and torture;
b) taking of hostages;
c) outrages upon personal dignity, in particular humiliating and degrading treatment;
d) the passing of sentences and the carrying out of executions without previous judgment pronounced by a regularly constituted court, affording all the judicial guarantees which are recognized as indispensable by civilized peoples.

These four banded acts should be applied to non-human animals as well. Particularly for those living with humans, they could be stated as:

a) violence to life and person of animals, in particular murder of all kinds;
b) mutilation, cruel treatment and torture;
c) taking animals away from their human families as an act of war, using animals to extort or as hostages;
d) outrages upon personal dignity of animals, in particular humiliating and degrading treatment as subjects of their own lives;
e) to execute animals without a humane reason, or for a public health issue, without previous concept of professionals, and performed in a humane manner.

Drawing awareness to the diverse forms of violence non-human animals have experienced during times of conflict is a step to achieving recognition that they have been also victims of the Colombian war. Such acknowledgment might be a contribution for a broader recognition of violence towards animals and a new corpus of protection to their integrity. In the meantime, we as humans hopefully will also expand our conceptions of who gets counted in the moral community.

References

CNMH, Centro Nacional de Memoria Histórica. (2018). *Bloque Calima de las AUC. Depredación paramilitar y narcotráfco en el suroccidente colombiano. Informe No. 2.* Retrieved from https://www.jep.gov.co/Sala-de-Prensa/Documents/bloque-calima-auc.pdf

Comisión Histórica del Conflicto y sus Víctimas (2015). Contribución al entendimiento del conflicto armado en Colombia. Retrieved from http://www.altocomisionadoparalapaz.gov.co/mesadeconversaciones/PDF/Informe%20Comisi_n%20Hist_rica%20del%20Conflicto%20y%20sus%20V_ctimas.%20La%20Habana%2C%20Febrero%20de%202015.pdf

Dao, J. (2011, December 1). *After duty, dogs suffer like soldiers.* Retrieved from https://www.nytimes.com/2011/12/02/us/more-military-dogs-show-signs-of-combat-stress.html

Delgado, M. (2011). *Una justicia transicional sin transición: verdad, justicia, reparación y reconciliación en medio del conflicto.* Retrieved from https://revistas.utadeo.edu.co/index.php/RAI/article/view/86/100

El Pais (2012, November 16). *Polémica por video en el que soldados del Ejército asesinan a un perro.* Retrieved from https://www.elpais.com.co/colombia/polemica-por-video-en-el-que-soldados-del-ejercito-asesinan-a-un-perro.html

Federation of American Scientist (1998, February 1). *USAF Intelligence. Targeting Guide.* Retrieved from https://fas.org/irp/doddir/usaf/afpam14-210/part20.htm#page180

Garcia, C., (2018, May 15). *Paramilitares se Benefician de Empresas Palmicultoras: Corte.* Retrieved from https://www.rcnradio.com/colombia/paramilitares-se-beneficiaron-de-empresas-palmicultoras-corte

GMH, Grupo de Memoria Histórica. (2013). ¡Basta Ya! Colombia: memorias de guerra y dignidad. Bogotá, Colombia. Imprenta Nacional.

Gruen, L. (2017, August 17). *The Moral Status of Animals.* Retrieved from https://plato.stanford.edu/entries/moral-animal/

Holdron, C. (2013). The Case for Legal Personhood for Nonhuman Animals and the Elimination of their Status as Property in Canada (Master of Law). Faculty of Law, University of Toronto.

Hurtado, T. (2016). *Building space for animals in Colombian peace process.* Presented at 15th Annual North American Conference for Critical Animal Studies, Fort Lewis Collage, Durango, 2016.

Hurtado, T. (2017). *Building space for animals in Colombian peace process version 2.* Presented at the Fifth European Conference for Critical Animal Studies, Lund University, Lund, 2017.

Hurtado, T. (2017a, December). Personal interview.

Hurtado, T. (2017b, December). Personal interview.

Hurtado, T. (2017c, December). Personal interview.

Hurtado, T. (2018). *Building space for animals in Colombian peace process version 3.* Presented at Minding Animals Conference, Universidad Autonoma de Mexico, Ciudad de Mexico, 2018.

ICRC, International Committee of the Red Cross. (2014, December 24). *What is international humanitarian law?* Retrieved from https://www.icrc.org/en/document/what-international-humanitarian-law

INDUMIL. Retrieved from. *Catalogo General, Productos Militares.* https://www.indumil.gov.co/wp-content/uploads/2016/03/Catalogo_general.pdf

Infobae (2011, November 17). *Paramilitares usaban a sus víctimas como alimento de cocodrilos en Colombia.* Retrieved from https://www.infobae.com/2011/11/17/1038206-paramilitares-usaban-sus victimas-como-alimento-cocodrilos-colombia/

International Committee of the Red Cross (ICRC), *Geneva Convention Relative to the Protection of Civilian Persons in Time of War (Fourth Geneva Convention)*, 12 August 1949. Retrieved from https://www.unscn.org/web/archives_resources/files/GenevaConventions1949.pdf

Kienyke. (2012, Marzo 7). *El escuadrón de ratas de la Policía.* Retrieved from https://www.kienyke.com/historias/el-escuadron-de-ratas-de-la-policia

Kovalik, D. (2010, January 6). U.S. and Colombia cover up atrocities through mass graves. *Huffington Post.* Retrieved from https://www.huffingtonpost.com/dan-kovalik/us-colombia-cover-up-atro_b_521402.html

Llanos, R. (2008, March 3). *'Paras' usaron serpientes venenosas para matar a sus víctimas, reveló desmovilizado a la Fiscalía.* Retrieved from https://www.eltiempo.com/archivo/documento/CMS-3984686

Londoño, M. L., Ortiz, B., Gil, A. M., Jaramillo, A. M., Castro, R., & Pineda, N. (2000). Embarazo por violación, la crisis múltiple. Cali, Colombia. Si-Mujer y ISEDER.

Mingorance, F., Minelli, F., Le Du, H., Human Rights Everywhere (HREV) and Diocesis de Quibdo (2004). EL CULTIVO DE LA PALMA AFRICANA EN EL CHOCÓ. Legalidad Ambiental, Territorial y Derechos Humanos. Retrieved from https://pacificocolombia.org/wp-content/uploads/2016/05/023633300128571 4975.pdf

Moloney, A., (2015, July17). Colombia to unearth "worlds largest urban mass grave." Retrieved from https://www.reuters.com/article/us-colombia-mass-graves/colombia-to-unearth-worlds-largest-urban-mass-grave-official-idUSKCN0PR1YT20150717

Momentos de la historia de la Policía Nacional de Colombia (2015, Noviembre 20). *Leyenda Del Caballo De Nombre "Comején".* Retrieved from https://historiapolicianacionaldecolombia.blogspot.com/2015/11/leyenda-del-caballo-de-nombre-comejen.html

Momentos de la historia de la Policía Nacional de Colombia (2018, April 3). *Génesis de los Carabineros de Colombia.* Retrieved from https://historiapolicianacionaldecolombia.blogspot.com/2018/04/genesis-de-los-carabineros-de-colombia.html

Moreno-Sánchez, R., Instituto de Investigación de Recursos Biológicos 'Alexander von Humboldt' (2000, Agosto). *Biosíntesis 21 – Incentivos económicos perversos para la conservación de la biodiversidad: el caso de la palma africana.* Retrieved from http://repository.humboldt.org.co/handle/20.500.11761/32637

Navia, C. E., & Ossa, M. (2001). El Secuestro, un trauma Psicosocial. *Revista de Estudios Sociales, 9*, 68-74.

Noticias Uno Colombia (2011, December 4). Soldados registraron como mataron un perro con sus fúsiles. Retrieved from https://youtu.be/zJpcDuQB2VE

Policia Nacional de Colombia (2013). *Tras Las Huellas De Los Guías Caninos De La Policía Nacional De Colombia. 100 Años De Historia. 1913-2013.* Retrieved from https://www.policia.gov.co/file/123753/download?token=d7I1U_CX

Reátegui, R., Ciurlizza, J., Perata, A., & Comisión de Entrega de la Comisión de la Verdad y Reconciliación (2004). Hatun Willakuy Versión abreviada del Informe Final de la Comisión de la Verdad y Reconciliación. Perú Retrieved from http://repositorio.pucp.edu.pe/index/bitstream/handle/123456789/110702/2008-Hatun%20Willakuy.%20Versi%C3%B3n%20abreviada%20del%20Informe%20Final%20de%20la%20Comisi%C3%B3n%20de%20la%20Verdad%20y%20Reconciliaci%C3%B3n%20%E2%80%93%20Per%C3%BA.pdf?sequence=1&isAllowed=y

Ruta Pacífica de las Mujeres. (2013a). La verdad de las mujeres: víctimas del conflicto armado en Colombia, Tomo I. Retrieved from http://rutapacifica.org.co/documentos/tomo-I.pdf

Ruta Pacífica de las Mujeres. (2013b). La verdad de las mujeres: víctimas del conflicto armado en Colombia, Tomo II. Retrieved from http://rutapacifica.org.co/documentos/tomo-II.pdf Servicio Jesuita a Refugiados. (2014). Caracterización de la situación de los niños, niñas y adolescentes afro descendientes e indígenas, en riesgo de reclutamiento y cualquier otra forma de uso y utilización - Buenaventura. Defensoría del Pueblo. Bogotá

Sorenson, J. (2014). Animals as vehicles of war. In C. Salter, A. Nocella II, & J. Bentley (Eds.), *Animals and war* (pp.19-35). Lanham: Lexington Books.

Verdad Abierta. (2012, May 24). *Las fórmulas de tortura del Bloque Vencedores de Arauca.* Retrieved from https://verdadabierta.com/los-genios-del-terror-y-las-torturas-en-arauca/

Wise, S. (2013). Nonhuman rights to personhood. *Peace Environmental Law Review, 30*(3).

8. *Cow Releases as Staged Liberations in Agri-Tourism*

Erica von Essen and Michael Allen

In May of each year, some 150,000 visitors gather on Swedish dairy farms to watch the exuberant if clumsy displays of joy by cows released from their indoor pens to summer pasture. Families travel to farms in their county to enjoy a day of countryside air, happy cows, milk and traditional Swedish cinnamon buns in a stylized representation of their now lost agrarian past. The popular spectacle engages several themes. Interaction with the cows reflects a growing popularity of an embodied turn in animal-based recreation (Lovelock, 2008). Specifically, such events respond to calls on both societal and individual levels for nature reconciliation, at a time when many perceive modern life as inauthentic and alienated (Franklin, 2003; MacCannell, 1976; Taylor, 2001). Cow releases also represent attempts to reconcile people with their mode of production and source of food by breaking down barriers between producers and consumers (Ateljevic & Doorne, 2003).

Consequently, cow releases purport to supply *genuine emancipatory experiences for both the cows and the tourists* observing their release. As they 'liberate' the cows from winter confinement spent in barns, the farmers simultaneously 'liberate' urban tourists from their feelings of alienation from nature and separation from the countryside. This simultaneity of purported liberations creates a profound relationship between bovines and people as both join in a shared multisensory experience of early summer. Ostensibly, then, summer cow releases represent a *total*, embodied experience of *liberation and joy* in the unity of nature across species lines. Nevertheless, we challenge this assertion through a critical examination of cow releases as liberatory. On the one hand, we argue they are not meaningfully liberatory if dairy cows continue to spend "90% of the year" in otherwise dark conditions (Djurens Rätt, 2018). In this respect, cows remain exploited and oppressed animal workers in the dairy industry. Their labor is merely temporarily redeployed from productive to performative.

Since the early 2000s, Swedes pilgrimage to so-called *kosläpp* (cow releases) also called *betessläpp* (pasture releases) on weekends in May. Arla, the biggest dairy producer in Sweden, provides the cost for arranging these events at their affiliated farms (offering free coffee). On the back of Arla's milk cartons, anticipatory countdowns to the cow releases are sometimes posted in the weeks following up to the season: *"the cows have taken their positions – have you?!"* Recently, privately coordinated cow releases turn up on the side. Cow releases may have started small and focused mainly on the principal activity: opening the doors of the barn for the cows to make their way out to pasture. Today, events usually last several hours and offer mini versions of farmers' markets at the site, selling locally produced goods like cheese to guests. It has hence become a way for farmers to showcase their livelihood more broadly to visitors and potential consumers of their products who appreciate 'farm-to-fork' or 'farm-to-table' food (Dodds & Holmes, 2017). Still, Ståhlberg (2014) notes, the profit margin at these single events is not usually significant for the farmer.

The principal commodity remains the joy of the cows, and this is ostensibly free of charge. The cows' otherwise calm and docile manner is dramatically unsettled at the sight, smell and feel of green grass after a long winter indoors. The spectacle is hosted by a *conferencier*, usually the local farmer. Parking valets in bright orange vests usher the crowds to the right place. Country music often plays in a classic Swedish style of *dansbandsmusik*. Some sites offer thoroughly embodied experiences of farm life. At Stabby Gård in Uppland, for example, one can participate in horse-riding, ranch-work, shepherding, churning butter and hand-milking dairy cows (anachronistically as much milking is now industrial and robot-based). Other places may offer 'cow safaris' where they take out urban guests on the back of a tractor and drive around the pastures to look at the cows. Families with small children constitute the perhaps main demographic, and they often bring picnic gear to enjoy the day. If the farm has sheep, children can sometimes also watch lambs at close distances. In Ståhlberg (2014), a guest enthuses about the event thus:

> "The best part for sure is the happy animals. You just get so excited by animals. They seem to have such few worries in life. They just sort of gallop out and get to eat grass. I'd like that for myself, sometimes!" (p. 274)

Consistent with the above remark 'I'd like that for myself,' we contend the primary attraction of the kosläpp is the 'liberation aspect' of releasing animals. Released cows symbolize for urban dwellers an ideal of natural freedom and simple joy. This is an experience of freedom and joy many feel they have lost but want to regain in some measure (Smith, 2012). Other contemporary kinds of agri-tourism invite visitors into the homes and everyday lives of farmers, allowing them a glimpse of their homesteads and daily routines. To this extent, it generally relies on commodifying an intimate backstage experience of agrarian life. Here, ancillary activities like cow-milking, lamb-petting, cheesemaking and milk-churning may offer more embodied and intimate relations with animals. Nevertheless, observing cow releases takes on a character of a *front stage* liberation spectacle (Daugstad & Kirchengast, 2013), even if it is in back stage to the dairy industry at large. But the farmers who host and narrate the events are mostly shepherds herding the cows out of the barn. This relegates any one-on-one interactions between farmers and visitors secondary at best, by contrast with, say, culinary tourism where there is generally more opportunity for meaningful engagement in conversation.

Nevertheless, if urban-rural and fork-to-farm connections are secondary and the liberation is the principal spectacle and commodity, questions inevitably arise concerning the authenticity of liberation. 'Oh look!' exclamations and delight at cow antics may stem in part from seeing displays of animal autonomy and spontaneity. Such displays are potent because they contrast with the expected "rules, routines, repetition, predictability and inevitability" (Marvin, 2006, p. 17) which otherwise characterizes the food industry. In response to such mundanity, the 'autonomy' of dairy cows has become a new buzzword (Millar, 2000) and animals 'breaking out' of agricultural norms is a cause for celebration. Indeed, cows' reactions to their release are valued precisely because of their unpredictability and various lively manifestations. For example, cows may initially express their autonomy by stubbornly resisting the release so that they need a push from the farmer. They may bump into each other awkwardly, go the wrong way or stumble amusingly to the pleasure of the laughing crowd.

Moreover, a range of cow interaction delight audiences, including play or hierarchical behavior in response to the situation. Often, cows are anthropomorphized in their displays of joy, given names given what Scruton (2000) terms 'honorary personalities' (p. 36). These anthropomorphisms play up their unique quirks, their bovine choices on the day and distinct behaviors vis-à-vis others. This also emphasizes the cows' animality and individual subjectivity simultaneously, a key component to animal-based tourism (Bertella, 2014). However, humans also clearly orchestrate bovine autonomy and spontaneity at such events. In the words of Driessen and Heutinck (2015), cow "agency and character are intricately connected to the material and human networks in which [they] are caught up" (p. 11). In this respect, cow releases are arranged to emphasize animal liberation—shaking the shackles of barn life—and getting back to a more 'wild' nature within their limited position as a domestic agricultural animal bred for hundreds of years (Millar, 2000).

On the ideas of Desmond (1999), the cows may be said to "perform a fiction of themselves as wild" (p. 151) before the audience. Ultimately, sensational cow behavior is effected by human negotiation of space and time (Daugstad & Kirchengast, 2013; Lynch, 2005). Humans control the physical confinement of cows (securing them in a barn and then releasing them) and the duration spent in this facility (controlling time/season). Indeed, their stumbling is a result of their muscles having atrophied in sedentary winter conditions, as animal rights activists are quick to point out. Their excitement, according to the latter, is above all a contrasting expression to the malaise and monotony of the barn they endure for the rest of the year. Indirectly and directly, farmers thus provide the physical and temporal, and hence the emotional and behavioral context, for cow reactions to their release. Conceptually, this is not dissimilar to circus directors having performing animals on a stage to the bemusement of the crowd.

Nevertheless, in their commentary on cow releases for the crowd, farmers describe the cows in empathetic and amusing human terms, downplaying their control over these animals. Such attributions of humor to animals that do not have a sense of humor, however, is problematic according to some scholars (Scruton, 2000) because it binds animals into schemes of obligations, rationality and responsibility that they cannot comprehend. In this instance, it is the performative labor of the cow as an entertainer that is sought. Additionally, Scruton maintains that we are deluding ourselves if we believe that animals can ever be as happy as we are—and hence deserving of these terms—as they are merely pleased, comfortable and well. This is not necessarily a problem in terms of dishonesty, or inauthenticity, insofar as many spectators of cow releases acknowledge the staged or orchestrated character of the events. However, it may be a problem if it leads visitors to believe that cows are always truly this happy and continue to consume dairy irresponsibly in ways that reflects this mistaken belief.

We contend the *kosläpp* spectacle redeploys the productive labor of cow to provide a spectacle for tourists. The cows enter a different relationship with humans, not just as units of milk and cheese production, but also as marketable exemplars of summer joy and a world of agrarian bliss lost to them as urban dwellers. As for the tourists, they are released from uncomfortable feelings of alienation or separation from nature. The latter has been conceptualized elsewhere as the 'extinction of experience' (Pyle, 1993); a 'nature deficit' disorder (Louv, 2005); ecological boredom (Monbiot, 2013) leading to a loss in public health (Soga & Gaston, 2016) and in self-reliance (Morris, 2013) and to psychological shame (Jordan III, 2003; Swan, 1995). Estrangement from the natural world is a root cause of environmental degradation because it cycles unsustainable production and consumption patterns (Kareiva, 2008; Miller, 2006). Tourists are thus released from uncomfortable feelings of 'consumer guilt' concerning the exploitation of dairy cows. Such feelings may result from campaigns by environmental and animal rights activists to increase public awareness of the conditions endured animal laborers in industrial scale food production (Ellis et al., 2009).

Environmentally-minded dairy consumers might worry the cows themselves—as morphologically altered units of dairy production—are increasingly alienated from nature, herded into anonymous metal pens to have electronic suction tubes attached to their teats (Smith, 2012). To the extent, releasing cows into summer pastures releases tourists from these anxieties. Tourists are liberated to feel the fulfilment of being connected again to nature and to the cows themselves as inter-corporeally experiencing the same summer joys. To be sure, such feelings not entirely the same for the cows as it is for the tourists. Sensory *intercorporeal experiences*—breathing, smelling, etc.—may well be the same. Nevertheless, these experiences will have *meanings and resonances* for the tourists they cannot have for the cows. Indeed, they may evoke for the tourists nostalgic ideals and assumptions about lost continuity with an imagined agrarian past beyond the cognitive capacities of bovines (see e.g. Schucksmith & Brown, 2016; Wenz, 1986). However, guilt over the loss of such an ideal of unity is 'exploited' by agri-tourism *as a source of profit.*

Nevertheless, we do not suggest agri-tourism is devoid of all green sensibilities or animal welfare convictions. After all, as we said above, it might redeploy the labor of dairy cows to provide tourists with an experience of authenticity. In the familiar language of negative and positive freedom (Berlin, 1969), cow liberation is *authentic* because they are:

1) liberated *from* conditions of confinement restricting their freedom of movement during the winter months, and
2) liberated *to* graze summer pastures, joyfully fulfilling their natural inclinations and desires.

Second, urban tourist liberation is authentic because they are:

1) liberated *from* discomforting feelings of alienation from nature as urban dwellers (and perhaps also guilt as environmentally minded

consumers aware of dark conditions endured by dairy cows most of the year) and

2) liberated *to* reconnect with nature and agrarian life by sharing basic intercorporeal and sensory experiences with animals from whom they feel separated as urban dwellers (and they worry they might simply exploit as consumers).

Nevertheless, a skeptic might contest the above descriptions of cow and tourist liberations as authentic and *total* (Best, 2014; Pellow, 2014) by providing counter-descriptions of them as staged and inauthentic. On this argument, they are inauthentic to the extent they cannot deliver on the promises they make of 'freedom from' or 'freedom to,' instead supplying only the false *perception* of a total interspecies liberation of cows and tourists alike.

Hence, from the standpoint of the cows, 'liberations' are staged in the sense that cows remain:

1) oppressed workers morphologically bred to fulfill exclusively human purposes of production and consumption (who are never 'freed from' exploitation and use by humans for their own purposes, and
2) whose labor is only temporarily redeployed to fulfill a human consumer demand for 'authenticity' (such that they are not genuinely 'free to' fulfill their natural desires and inclination but rather satisfy and new consumer demand of humans).

Further, from the standpoint of the tourists, their 'liberations' are staged in the sense that they are fundamentally:

1) oppressed consumers in a stage-managed spectacle exploiting their feelings of alienation (and possibly also guilt) that necessarily fails deliver what it promises (genuine 'freedom from' such feelings and anxieties) and
2) whose consumer demand is never the basis for any genuine interspecies community based on equal belonging or partnership with animals (such that there is no genuine 'freedom to' reconcile with bovines as partners in production and cooperation).

Indeed, on this skeptical view, the *kosläpp* signals a novel *intersection of oppressions* for cows and humans rather than any total interspecies liberation (Mohai et al., 2009). Cows are exploited and oppressed to the extent their labor is redeployed to service alienated but environmentally minded human consumers. However, the latter are equally exploited and oppressed through their wanting to feel disalienated and connected to the cows, sharing with them multisensory, intercorporeal experiences of early summer in the countryside. Consequently, embodied agri-tourism may not be benignly green, combing commercial profit with environmental concern by reconciling cows and tourists. Instead, it might be a cynical attempt to maximize profit by exploiting a novel consumer demand for such reconciliation in modernity by making undeliverable and misleading promises of liberation.

The above alternate descriptions of the potentials for liberation and oppression concerning both cows and tourists in the *kosläpp* now help us to refocus our original research question. To what the extent do these spectacles establish total relations of authentic co-liberation for cows and tourists and to what extent does it instead establish intersecting relations of interspecies oppression? Here, we appeal to the categories of total liberation and intersecting oppression often employed in critical animal studies. In this approach, the basic idea is that liberations and oppressions are always linked in some significant respect. If cows are liberated in the *kosläpp*, then tourists will likely experience some intersecting liberation, and vice versa. If cows are oppressed in the spectacle, then tourists will likely experience some intersecting oppression, and vice versa. To be sure, some criticize this analytical assumption of intersecting liberations and oppressions by claiming liberations and oppressions do not always intersect (Cochrane, 2010).

For example, a female executive who breaks the glass ceiling at McDonalds will remain an oppressor of cows efficiently processed into hamburgers: she may be 'liberated' from a sexist oppression, but the cows are not. Nevertheless, we do not find this fully convincing as a purported counterexample to the intersectionality of liberations and oppressions. After all, the capitalist system may still oppress the 'liberated' female CEO by requiring her to exploit her minimum-wage workforce economically in the interest of corporate profits. This perhaps establishes a triple intersectionality of oppressions intersecting CEO, workers and cows. Of course, this does not immediately bear upon our analysis of cows and tourists, in the *kosläpp*, as liberated under one description but oppressed under another. Nevertheless, we believe the example of the female executive helps inform this analysis. It does so by shedding light on the notion of liberations *as staged* and authenticity as merely *felt* or perceived. The female CEO may feel *negatively freed* from the constraints of a sexist corporate culture. Moreover, she may use her newfound position of influence within the corporation to lobby for improved conditions and remuneration for her human workforce.

Perhaps she even lobbies the cattle industry to improve the living conditions of the cow workforce prior to its slaughter. In these respects, she feels she *positively frees* her human and animal workers to experience more fulfilling lives, reconciling them with the profit driven system that depends on their labor. Our point is that capitalism *stages* various nodes of liberation and reconciliation for its various participants from within its system of *total* exploitation. Moreover, the participants may feel or perceive such liberations and reconciliations as authentic. With better conditions and remuneration, the human workforce may feel more truly who they are—not just cogs in the corporate machine—reconciled with the corporation exploiting their labor for private profit. As for the cows, any improvements in their living conditions, like greater freedom of movement, may facilitate their fulfilment as the kinds of beings they are before industrial processing as hamburgers. To this extent, McDonalds executives, workforce, and consumers may *all* feel connected to the cows and their welfare.

What does this now tell us about cows and tourists in the *kosläpp*? We claim that the *kosläpp*'s function in essentially the same way, by staging intersecting nodes of liberation and reconciliation in a system of total oppression. In contrast with the above example, however, the *kosläpp* stages its various liberations and reconciliations for cows and tourists in a quite explicitly theatrical manner. That is, it stages them not just as intersecting points or nodes in a system, but as spectacular tourist events. As we put it in the section before last, the *kosläpp* presents a 'front stage' spectacle of liberating cows promising to liberate and reconcile alienated urban tourists. Nevertheless, this double staged liberation of cows and tourists neither releases cows from industrialized dairy production nor alienated urban dwellers from hyper-rationalized modernity. Morphologically bred for human exploitation and use, the cows cannot be totally liberated from the system exploiting their labor as much as they can be given a temporary respite from their otherwise dark year-round conditions.

However, this temporary respite from suffering simultaneously redeploys their labor to turn an additional profit through tourism. This is not to deny the cows may experience joy and fulfilment in their release from their winter quarters. Nevertheless, it is to say that the *kosläpp* effectively *commodifies* 'disalienated bovines' in a novel extension to the total system of exploitation for profit. As for the tourists, the *kosläpp* commodifies their feelings of alienation from agrarian life and perhaps, for some of them, feelings of consumer guilt over the exploitation of animal labor. Can it, though, do any better delivering on its promise of 'release' and liberation for tourists as opposed to cows? We see this as unlikely. Clearly, the tourists experience some joy and fulfilment observing the summer antics of the cows. After all, as an agri-tourism event, the spectacle succeeds only because it meets a green consumer demand by environmentally minded tourists for such an experience.

Nevertheless, most of them are aware that the event is partly staged and that the cows will remain units of industrial dairy production. Ultimately, they may be "...aware of the artificiality and inauthenticity of postmodern touristic spaces yet seem content to gaze nostalgically and playfully upon the lives of others" (Everett, 2008, p. 342). In this respect, urban tourists are not simply gullible fools deceived into thinking the event is somehow real. Instead, grasping its staged character, they knowingly participate in it because it provides them with experiences that feel 'real enough.' It is thus sufficient for visitor satisfaction (Chhabra, Healy, & Sills, 2003) that the event delivers *only the perception* of authenticity (Everett, 2008; Urry, 1990).

That said, however, this notion of the *kosläpp* delivering a perception of authenticity complicates our analysis from the previous section of it as exploiting and oppressing tourists by failing to deliver *genuine* dis-alienation and reconciliation. It complicates this analysis in two ways. On the one hand, it potentially implicates the tourists as not victims but rather perpetrators—indeed *willing participants*—in extending the total system of exploitation and oppression. On the other hand, it raises the objection that the tourists are *not actually exploited and oppressed at all* because they get what they want and know what they are getting: a spectacle and perception, nothing more. Concerning the first complicating factor, we might try to address this by claiming their 'willing participation' is an expression of enlightened false consciousness (Fleming & Spicer, 2003).

To this extent, they perform acts resistance as cynical or ironical distance through their bemusement with staged cow antics. Nevertheless, even granting they might internalize their own exploitation and oppression in their enjoyment of the spectacle, their willingness to go along with the charade remains problematic. Indeed, some externalization of disbelief is required for resistance (Fleming & Spicer, 2003). In other words, for it to have any *genuine liberatory consequences*, resistance entails acting for change, contesting the total system of exploitation and oppression, not just tacit awareness of the oppression "on the inside."

Consequently, our response to the first complicating factors is to say:

(1) tourists are exploited and oppressed (as we claimed in the previous section),
(2) they may be conscious of their own exploitation and oppression, and
(3) they may respond to (1) and (2) with cynical or ironical distance, but
(4) that has no genuine liberatory consequences (either for the cows or for themselves).

As for the second complicating factor, we can now say that the tourists are indeed exploited and oppressed. That is, they are exploited and oppressed despite their getting what they want and knowing what they get: a mere perception of total liberation—dis-alienation and reconciliation—for cows and humans in which neither are released or liberated *from* the total system of exploitation for profit *to* enter any genuine relations of interspecies equality and belonging. This is not to say that genuinely dis-alienated and reconciled relations with the cows is an impossibility. After all, we might radically reconceive dairy production to reduce the suffering and exploitation of cows year-round, recognizing them as equally belonging to the system of social cooperation and economic production.

For example, Gandhi spent most of his life trying to devise national policies in India for recognizing sacred bovines as equally belonging to the expanding circle of social interdependencies as valued partners in shared economic production (Burgat, 2004), that is clearly *not* the purpose of the Swedish *kosläpp*. Indeed, on our present analysis, its purpose is *not* to reconcile environmentally minded urban tourists to dairy cows as partner in any non-exploitative relations of production and cooperation. On the contrary, its purpose is to reconcile them to the existing system of *total* exploitation and commodification, as willing if cynically or ironically distant participants settling for a mere perception of dis-alienation and reconciliation.

Our verdict for cow releases as liberatory events is thus grim. Animal rights activists join in this critique. The latter's increased presence at these events, however, may be a way forward in triggering sustained or critical engagement on the part of visitors with the injustices of the dairy cow industry. Farmers in their role as event conferenciers have adapted their commentary on cows in light of increased animal rights critique to include cow welfare discussions. Their speeches on cow antics thus connect also to broader issues of animal rights. However, this may be further staging, damage control or neutralization of harms, as it is on farmers' terms and at their discretion. Nevertheless, the increased demand by the visiting public for longer discussions on cows at least point to a basic awareness of potential welfare issues. It is not implausible to think that such an interest may evolve into Q&A sessions with the farmer, holding them accountable for more than a mere commentary on cow antics.

At the same time, new developments in society, including technology, also make the future scope of spectacles like cow releases more unpredictable. Covid-19 lockdown saw a profound increase both in nature and animal recreation of the kind that *kosläpp* represent, and in digital encounters with animals (Turnbull et al., 2020; von Essen et al., 2021). Since 2021, kosläpp have gone digital: streamed live by municipalities or Arla on their facebook pages. Insofar as the sensory, intercorporeal and immersive qualities of attending a cow release in the field are concerned, then, digitization means a reduced and flattened experience for visitors. The implications of this need to be researched. Finally, it appears as though not only tourists will have to make do with truncated digital encounters in the future; investments into virtual reality goggles for cows that simulate green pastures the year-around, are increasing.

In conclusion, we have critically examined the prospects of cow releases, as a new form of agri-based tourism involving embodied connections with animals, as liberatory events for cow and human participants. We have conceded the role of an ephemeral kind of authenticity and guilt alleviation that is generated among human visitors upon observing the spectacle. For cows, similarly, we have conceded a physical release. However, our examination of this event has revealed serious shortcomings in promoting an actual, total, interspecies liberation for cows and human visitors alike. This is insofar as the cow release event merely temporarily redeploys the labor of cows from units of agricultural production to performers and mascots to affirm a total system of oppression and commodification.

Consequently, visitors are sufficiently liberated from guilt in consuming dairy, but this alleviation outlet also means they remain loyal consumers in the industry for the rest of the year. We have hence argued that capitalism *stages* various nodes of liberation and reconciliation for its various participants from within its system of *total* exploitation. Cow releases are on this interpretation not dissimilar to a letter of indulgences offered by the Catholic Church: they sell a commodity that neutralizes anxieties and guilt in order to have its subjects remain loyal, but oppressed, in the long term.

References

Ateljevic, I., & Doorne, S. (2003). Culture, Economy and Tourism Commodities: Social Relations of Production and Consumption. *Tourist Studies*, *3*(2), 123-141. https://doi.org/10.1177/1468797603041629

Bertella, G. (2014). The Co-creation of Animal-based Tourism Experience. *Tourism Recreation Research*, *39*(1), 115-125. https://doi.org/10.1080/02508281.2014.11081330

Best, S. (2014). *The Politics of Total Liberation: Revolution for the 21st Century.* Palgrave Macmillan.

Burgat, F. (2004). Non-Violence towards Animals in the Thinking of Gandhi: The Problem of Animal Husbandry. *Journal of Agricultural and Environmental Ethics*, *17*(3), 223-248. https://doi.org/10.1023/B:JAGE.0000033082.58743.5b

Cochrane, A. (2010). *An Introduction to Animals and Political Theory.* Palgrave Macmillan.

Daugstad, K., & Kirchengast, C. (2013). Authenticity and the Pseudo-Backstage of Agri-Tourism. *Annals of Tourism Research, 43,* 170-191. https://doi.org/10.1016/j.annals.2013.04.004

Desmond, J. (1999). *Staging Tourism: Bodies on Display from Waikiki to Sea World.* University of Chicago Press.

Dodds, R., & Holmes, M. R. (2017). Local Versus Visitor Perceptions of Farmers' Markets. *Journal of Food Products Marketing, 23*(2), 167-185. https://doi.org/10.1080/10454446.2017.1244785

Driessen, C., & Heutinck, L. F. M. (2015). Cows Desiring to be Milked? Milking Robots and the Co-evolution of Ethics and Technology on Dutch Dairy Farms. *Agriculture and Human Values, 32*(1), 3-20. https://doi.org/10.1007/s10460-014-9515-5

Ellis, K. A., Billington, K., McNeil, B., & McKeegan, D. E. F. (2009). Public Opinion on UK Milk Marketing and Dairy Cow Welfare. *Animal Welfare, 18*(3), 267-282. https://www.ingentaconnect.com/content/ufaw/aw/2009/00000018/00000003/art00007

Fleming, P., & Spicer, A. (2003). Working at a Cynical Distance: Implications for Power, Subjectivity and Resistance. *Organization, 10*(1), 157-179. https://doi.org/10.1177/1350508403010001376

Franklin, A. (2003). *Tourism: An Introduction.* Sage.

Jordan III, W. R. (2003). *The Sunflower Forest: Ecological Restoration adn the New Communion with Nature.* University of California Press.

Kareiva, P. (2008). Ominous Trends in Nature Recreation. *Proceedings of the National Academy of Sciences, 105*(8), 2757-2758. https://doi.org/10.1073/pnas.0800474105

Louv, R. (2005). *Last Child in the Woods: Saving our Children from Nature-Deficit Disorder.* Algonquin.

Lovelock, B. A. (2008). An introduction to consumptive wildlife tourism. In B. A. Lovelock (Ed.), *Tourism and the consumption of wildlife: Hunting, shooting and sport fishing* (pp. 3-30). Routledge.

Lynch, P. A. (2005). The Commercial Home Enterprise and Host: A United Kingdom Perspective. *International Journal of Hospitality Management, 24*(4), 533-553. https://doi.org/10.1016/j.ijhm.2004.11.001

MacCannell, D. (1976). *The visitor: A New Thory of the Leisure Class.* Schoken Books.

Marvin, G. (2006). Wild Killing: Contesting the Animal in Hunting. In *The Animal Studies Group* (pp. 10-29): University of Illinois Press.

Millar, K. M. (2000). Respect for Animal Autonomy in Bioethical Analysis: The Case of Automatic Milking Systems (AMS). *Journal of Agricultural and Environmental Ethics, 12*(1), 41-50. https://doi.org/10.1023/A:1009548025408

Miller, J. R. (2006). Restoration, Reconciliation, and Reconnecting with Nature Nearby. *Biological Conservation*, *127*(3), 356-361. https://doi.org/http://dx.doi.org/10.1016/j.biocon.2005.07.021

Mohai, P., Pellow, D., & Roberts, J. T. (2009). Environmental Justice. *Annual Review of Environment and Resources*, *34*(1), 405-430. https://doi.org/10.1146/annurev-environ-082508-094348

Monbiot, G. (2013). *Feral: Searching for Enchantment on the Frontiers of Rewilding*. Allen Lane.

Morris, S. P. (2013). Challenging the Values of Hunting: Fair Chase, Game Playing and Intrinsic Value. *Environmental Ethics*, *35*(3), 295-311. https://doi.org/10.5840/enviroethics201335327

Pellow, D. N. (2014). *Total Liberation the Power and Promise of Animal Rights and the Radical Earth Movement*. University of Minnesota Press.

Pyle, R. M. (1993). *The Thunder Tree: Lessons from an Urban Wildland*. Houghton Mifflin.

Schucksmith, M., & Brown, D. L. (2016). *Routledge International Handbook of Rural Studies*. Routledge.

Scruton, R. (2000). *Animal Rights and Wrongs*. Claridge Press.

Smith, K. (2012). *Governing Animals: Animal Welfare and the Liberal State*. Oxford University Press.

Soga, M., & Gaston, K. J. (2016). Extinction of Experience: The Loss of Human–Nature Interactions. *Frontiers in Ecology and the Environment*, *14*(2), 94-101. https://doi.org/10.1002/fee.1225

Ståhlberg, J. (2014). Kosläpp: den urbana människans folknöje. In K. Ek-Nilsson, L. Midholm, A. Nordström, K. Saltzman, & G. Sjögård (Eds.), *Naturen för mig: Nutida röster och kulturella perspektiv*. Göteborg: Institutet för språk och folkminnen.

Swan, J. (1995). *In Defense of Hunting*. Harper Collins.

Taylor, J. P. (2001). Authenticity and sincerity in tourism. *Annals of Tourism Research*, *28*(1), 7-26. https://doi.org/https://doi.org/10.1016/S0160-7383(00)00004-9

Turnbull, J., Searle, A., & Adams, W. (2020). Quarantine Encounters with Digital Animals: More-than-Human Geographies of Lockdown Life. *Journal of Environmental Media*, *1*, 6.1-6.10. https://doi.org/10.1386/jem_00027_1

von Essen, E., Turnbull, J., Searle, A., Hofmeester, T., Jorgensen, F. A., & Van der Wal, R. (2021). Wildlife in the Digital Anthropocene: Examining Human-Animal Relations through Surveillance Technologies. *Environment and Planning E: Nature and Space*. https://doi.org/10.1177/25148486211061704

Wenz, P. S. (1986). Conservatism and Conservation. *Philosophy*, *61*(238), 503–512.

Afterword

Tony Quintana

Conversations about critical animal studies, total liberation, and intersectionality within animal rights movements continue to be imperative, perhaps now more than ever, as we face potential irreversible damage to our planet and the COVID-19 pandemic exacerbated and revealed inequities and unethical exploitations of both human and non-human animals. I began my journey into activism 13 years ago, focusing on health disparities and seeking to understand the ways in which I can work to address health inequity among humans. Throughout the course of my studies, career, and activism, I inevitably became an advocate for animal liberation. Some may question how I jumped from human health equity to animal liberation, while those with a genuine understanding of intersectionality might think that the reason for that jump is apparent.

I started out being interested in health inequity based on my personal experiences and those of my family and community being impacted by diet-related diseases, food-insecurities, and mental health concerns. As I went deeper, I began to understand how additional factors relate to poor health outcomes, such as systemic racism and white supremacy, capitalism, police brutality, and the school-to-prison pipeline, to name a few. I began to realize how I have been impacted by all of these systems throughout my life, and how these have contributed to my own health outcomes. I eventually decided to focus my efforts on food justice, thinking that ensuring that everyone has equitable access to healthy food and water is one of the best ways that I can personally work towards health equity. Alas, my understanding of how our access to healthy food and water (or lack thereof) is tied to our coexistence with non-human animals began to take form, and my inner animal rights activist was released.

It is important to understand that we as humans cannot separate ourselves from the rest of the Earth's inhabitants, and anthropocentric and speciesist viewpoints are not conducive to humans' thriving. A simple example is the fact that the exploitation of animals for human benefit is creating an environment that we biologically cannot inhabit, not to mention creating zoonotic diseases and antibiotic superbugs that threaten our very existence. Personal health is tied to public health, public health is tied to environmental health, and all three are inextricably linked to our coexistence with non-human animals. Many humans seem to have some grasp of this concept; for example, many claim that having a companion animal in their life (such as a cat or dog) enriches their emotional, physical, and/or spiritual wellbeing.

As we navigate animal rights activism today, it is critical that our actions and movements adapt, and that animal rights activists re-think their activism to ensure inclusivity and intersectionality and do away with the misanthropic approach once and for all. In order to grow the animal rights movement, it must integrate other movements in genuine ways that are more than just "supportive" or "in solidarity." We must continually examine how our animal rights activism can be more anti-racist, anti-ableist, anti-homophobic, anti-transphobic, anti-xenophobic, anti-misogynist, anti-ageist, and so forth. We must do the deep work it takes to understand the true meaning of intersectionality and put the theory into practice. Historically and in the present, conversations of intersectionality have caused divisiveness within animal rights groups, as some argue that we must put animals first and foremost, and/or that supporting other movements takes away from advocating for animals. When considering inclusivity and intersectionality, it becomes apparent that the opposite is true—*not* supporting other movements takes away from advocating for animals. If a person is actively concerned for their safety since they might be shot by a police officer because of the color of their skin, or jumped and beaten because of their gender expression, they may not feel compelled to focus on the rights of non-human animals, particularly alongside a group of individuals holding privilege who refuse to actively support their struggles. Considering the opposite, if the animal rights group recognizes the need to be actively anti-racist and actively support movements supporting BIPOC and LGBTQ+ folks, more individuals may be interested in topics of animal liberation.

Still, many single-issue animal rights activists claim that if all humans learned compassion for animals then all other oppressions and injustices would cease to exist. While this might be rooted in truth, how can someone exhibit true compassion for animals while not exhibiting the same compassion for humans? By the definition of compassion—concern for the sufferings or misfortunes of others—the stance of single-issue animal rights advocates is illogical, contradictory, and thus takes away from the movement. The only way to be effective as an activist is to be truly intersectional. This book is a tremendous resource in unpacking what it means to be intersectional, to work towards animal liberation, and how to effectively grow and adapt the movement, all of which encompass the very foundation of critical animal studies.

My journey in activism has taught me to be an advocate for animal liberation while also actively advocating for the environment, BIPOC, LGBTQ+ folks, women, people with disabilities, people who are shelter less, and any groups working against systems of oppression and exploitation, as all of these movements are tied together and benefit greatly from intersectional activism. We must continuously dive deeper into total liberation, activism, transformative justice, scholarship, critical thinking, and intersectionality, until all are free…

Contributors' Biographies

Michael Allen is a professor of social, political, and legal philosophy at East Tennessee State University. He has published extensively on crimes of dissent and the political status of nonhuman animals.

Maria Marta Andreatta has a B.Sc. in Nutrition and a Ph.D. in Health Sciences, and conducted postdoctoral studies on performance ethnography under the direction of Professor Norman Denzin at the University of Illinois at Urbana-Champaign. She is a member of the Editorial Board of the *Latin American Journal for Critical Animal Studies*, and a researcher at the National Council of Research in Science and Technique in Cordoba, Argentina, where she does research on the field of food and eating, focusing on veganism.

Kiana Avlon is a current graduate student at Westminster College in the Master of Arts in Community Leadership program. She has presented research on the rhetoric surrounding houselessness in Salt Lake City this year at the Western Social Science Association conference and continues to study rhetoric as it pertains to speciesism. With a focus on the root causes of speciesism, Kiana grounds her research in ecofeminism, critical animal studies, and anarchism with the goal of total liberation. She dedicates time to participate in vegan street outreach and to work at local animal sanctuaries.

Erica von Essen is an associate professor working at the Department of Social Anthropology with Stockholm University, where she conducts research on human-wildlife relations, including conservation, hunting, commodification and surveillance of wild animals.

Carlos Garcia is an activist with a long animal liberation history. His first contact with animal liberation was through hardcore-punk music and since almost 30 years right now he has been involved in autonomous collectives with an anarchist point of view. Carlos organizes meetings about animal liberation issues, the connection between patriarchy and speciesism, the link between hardcore-punk music and veganism/animal liberation and the Animal Liberation Front (ALF), the different activist strategies and tactics, and the lack of politics within veganism.

Nathan Grande holds a Master of Fine Arts degree from The University of Texas at Dallas. Currently, he is a philosophy doctoral student at the University of North Texas.

Alex Hinchcliffe is a recent graduate in Geography from Sheffield Hallam University, and is interested in animal rights, total liberation, environmentalism and intersectionality. As an activist, Alex is involved in a variety of issues, from animal rights struggles, climate crisis campaigning to tackling food poverty and homelessness.

Terry Hurtado is an activist and independent researcher based in Cali, Colombia. Holds an MSc in Holistic Science. Is board member of the Federación de Liberación Animal, from which runs the Animal Liberation School. ICAS board member, and is part of the redaction committee of the Latin-American Journal for Critical Animal Studies. Is also a long term peace activist, and conscience objector to compulsory military service. Currently is part of the city of Cali Human Rights and IHL committee, and the state peace committee.

Aljaž Krivec is a Slovenian literary critic and editor. He is the co-founder and co-editor of a Slovenian CAS website Animot (https://www.animot-vegan.com/). He's been writing on animal issues for five years now; he is particularly interested in non-human animals in literature and in animal rights topics.

Danni McGhee, founder of DAM Good Vegan, is a Plant-Based Nutrition Coach dedicated to inspiring and encouraging individuals to choose healthy vegan options to improve their health and overall well-being. She provides guidance on the principles of plant-based nutrition while introducing fun and easy ways to incorporate healthier options into their already busy lifestyle. When you work with her, you will be empowered and equipped with all the knowledge and tools you need to make healthier choices every day. DAM Good Vegan promotes eating a plant-based diet as the best way to optimal health and wellness. We offer online courses to help our students become empowered to navigate in a world that doesn't always make healthy, nutritious options convenient and accessible, and support you through our membership site that gives you access to 100+ plant-based recipes PLUS grocery & shopping lists, instructional cooking videos, education on detoxing, and weekly live Q&A calls. For more information, visit her website at DAMGoodVegan.com.

S. Marek Muller is an Assistant Professor of Rhetorical Studies at Florida Atlantic University. Dr. Muller holds a PhD in Communication from the University of Utah. They research and write on anti-speciesism and total liberation. In particular, Dr. Muller focuses on the intersections between communication, critical animal studies, and animal law. They have published numerous articles in communication journals, held leadership position in environmental communication for the Western States Communication Association, and reviewed articles for international journals in environmental communication and animal studies. Their seminal book *Impersonating Animals: Rhetoric, Ecofeminism, and Animal Rights Law* was published by the Michigan State University Press in 2020.

Anthony J. Nocella II, Ph.D., scholar-activist, is an Associate Professor in the Department of Criminal Justice in the Institute of Public Safety at Salt Lake Community College. He received his masters and doctorate from Syracuse University and another masters from Fresno Pacific University. He is co-founder of the fields of critical animal studies, Hip Hop criminology, disability pedagogy, lowrider studies, and revolutionary environmentalism. He is the editor of the *Peace Studies Journal*, managing editor of the *Transformative Justice Journal* and *Green Theory and Praxis Journal*, and co-editor of five book series including *Critical Animal Studies and Theory* with Lexington Books and *Hip Hop Studies and Activism* with Peter Lang Publishing. He is the Executive Director of the Institute for Critical Animal Studies, Director of the Academy for Peace Education, National Coordinator of Save the Kids, and acquisitions editor for Arissa Media Group. He has published over 100 book chapters and articles combined and 40 books. His website is www.anthonynocella.org

Tony Quintana, also known by his stage name I.Q. the Professor, is an activist, educator, and emcee from Albuquerque, NM. He has worked in the field of Health Education for over 10 years and has managed health promotion programs focusing on a wide variety of topics including nutrition, fitness, diabetes, obesity, and HIV. He is also an experienced fitness instructor and has led fitness programs in a variety of settings. Tony has been vegetarian since 2007, vegan since 2016, and enjoys sharing information on the many benefits of a plant-based diet through his music, education, and activism.

Anja Radaljac is a Slovenian literary and theatre critic. She is the co-founder and co-editor of a Slovenian critical animal studies website Animot (https://www.animot-vegan.com/). She's been writing about animal rights for six years now and had publish a book of essays titled *Puščava, klet, katakombe* (The Desert, The Basement, The Catatombs) addressing this issue in 2016.

Richard J. White, Ph.D is Reader/Associate Professor in Human Geography at Sheffield Hallam University, UK. Greatly influenced by anarchist praxis Richard's main research agenda explores a range of ethical and economic landscapes rooted in the intersectional contexts of social justice and total liberation movements. He has co-edited *Vegan Geographies* (2022); *The Radicalization of Pedagogy, Theories of Resistance, The Practice of Freedom* (all 2016, Rowman & Littlefield); and *Anarchism and Animal Liberation* (2015, McFarland Press).

Index

A

B

C

RADICAL ANIMAL STUDIES
AND TOTAL LIBERATION

Anthony J. Nocella II, SERIES EDITOR

The **Radical Animal Studies and Total Liberation** book series branches out of Critical Animal Studies (a field co-founded by Anthony J. Nocella II) with the argument that criticism is not enough. Action must follow theory. This series demands that scholars are engaged with their subjects both theoretically and actively via radical, revolutionary, intersectional action for total liberation. Founded in anarchism, the series provides space for scholar-activists who challenge authoritarianism and oppression in their many daily forms. **Radical Animal Studies and Total Liberation** promotes accessible and inclusive scholarship that is based on personal narrative as well as traditional research, and is especially interested in the advancement of interwoven voices and perspectives from multiple radical, revolutionary social justice groups and movements such as Black Lives Matter, Idle No More, Earth First!, the Zapatistas, ADAPT, prison abolition, LGBTTQQIA rights, disability liberation, Earth Liberation Front, Animal Liberation Front, political prisoners, radical transnational feminism, environmental justice, food justice, youth justice, and Hip Hop activism.

To order other books in this series please contact our Customer Service Department:

PETERLANG@PRESSWAREHOUSE.COM (WITHIN THE U.S.)
ORDERS@PETERLANG.COM (OUTSIDE THE U.S.)

To find out more about the series or browse a full list of titles, please visit our website:

WWW.PETERLANG.COM

www.ingramcontent.com/pod-product-compliance
Lightning Source LLC
Chambersburg PA
CBHW050653280326
41932CB00015B/2889